ELECTRONIC QUILLS

A Situated Evaluation of Using Computers for Writing in Classrooms

TECHNOLOGY IN EDUCATION SERIES

Edited by
Raymond S. Nickerson

ELECTRONIC QUILLS

A Situated Evaluation of Using Computers for Writing in Classrooms

Bertram C. Bruce
*University of Illinois
at Urbana-Champaign*

Andee Rubin
*Technical Education Research Center
Cambridge, MA*

with contributions from
Carol Barnhardt
and
Teachers using QUILL in Alaska

 LAWRENCE ERLBAUM ASSOCIATES, PUBLISHERS
1993   Hillsdale, New Jersey   Hove and London

Lawrence Erlbaum Associates, Inc., Publishers
365 Broadway
Hillsdale, New Jersey 07642

Library of Congress Cataloging-in-Publication Data

Bruce, Bertram C.
    Electronic quills : a situated evaluation of using computers for
writing in classrooms / Bertram C. Bruce, Andee Rubin.
        p.   cm. – (Technology in education series)
    Includes bibliographical references (p.) and indexes.
    ISBN 0-8058-0985-6. – ISBN 0-8058-1168-0 (pbk.)
    1. English language–Composition and exercises–Study and teaching
(Elementary)–Alaska–Computer-assisted instruction. 2. English
language–Alaska–Computer-assisted instruction. 3. Word processing
in education–Alaska. I. Rubin, Andee. II. Title. III. Series.
    LB1576.7.B78 1992
    808 '.042 '078–dc20   OCLC: 24845683   91-38520
                                                       CIP

Printed in the United States of America
10 9 8 7 6 5 4 3 2 1

We dedicate this book to all teachers working to create writing environments in their classrooms.

Contents

Preface

We began to design QUILL in the Spring of 1981, while responding to a request from the U.S. Department of Education for proposals on the use of technology for basic skills instruction. Our idea was to build on existing computers and writing research (e.g., Levin, 1982; Rubin, 1980, 1982; Sharples, 1985) and present QUILL as a classroom version of the powerful writing environments we used for our own writing.

The QUILL project was funded for a 3-year period. During the first year, we discovered the power of even the most rudimentary electronic mail system to engage students in writing (Rubin & Bruce, 1985). As we worked with teachers and students using QUILL in the classroom, we gained ideas for QUILL activities, many of which were incorporated into the *QUILL Teacher's Guide*. Students and teachers offered many ideas for improving the software. As a result, many of the software features and activities in the *Teacher's Guide* were essentially created or designed by teachers and students in field-test classrooms. During this early phase, we also worked out many of the ideas for teacher preparation and support. With The NETWORK of Andover, Massachusetts, we developed plans for field testing, teacher preparation, and dissemination.

During the second year of the project, we conducted a formal field test of the software. In general, we found improvement in writing among students who used QUILL. This improvement was statistically significant, both in terms of growth from pretest to posttest and in comparison with students who did not use QUILL. We also found that many changes were taking place in the classrooms that could not be captured by formal field testing measures. These changes are the substance of chapters 5, 6, and 7, which examine the characteristics of various realizations of QUILL.

Based on field-test results, QUILL was approved for use in Grades 3–5 by the Joint Dissemination Review Panel of the U.S. Department of Education. This approval led to its inclusion in the 1985 catalog of the National Diffusion Network (National Dissemination Study Group, 1985), which in turn led to its wider use in schools. Early in 1983, D. C. Heath & Co. agreed to produce a commercial version of QUILL, which appeared in 1984. During this period, The NETWORK refined its approach to workshops and began offering them to school districts throughout the United States. They established the QUILL Training and Assistance Center to give teachers the support they needed to use QUILL effectively and a hot line for teachers to call when they encountered problems.

During the third year of the project, we worked with QUILL in schools throughout the country, including Alaska. The Alaskan context was a fertile one for the introduction of QUILL, with many teachers having had experience with process writing through the Alaska Writing Project or with computer technology in their classrooms.

The QUILL Alaska project had actually begun in March 1982, when Ron Scollon, a professor at the University of Alaska, invited us to give a series of talks on QUILL in Fairbanks. Several of the attendees at the talks, especially Carol Barnhardt (who worked at the University of Alaska) and Bonnie Bless-Boenish (who taught in Shungnak), were determined to start a QUILL project in Alaska. By September 1983, five school districts (Fairbanks North Star Borough, Iditarod Area, Juneau Borough, Kashunamiut, and Northwest Arctic) and the University of Alaska had agreed to support the project.

We conducted a 3-day QUILL workshop in Fairbanks in October, 1983. Participants included classroom teachers, three school district administrators, one professor from the University of Alaska at Fairbanks (in addition to Carol Barnhardt), and two University professors who worked in X-CED, an off-campus program for cross-cultural teacher education in rural areas. Following the workshop, we traveled to each of the participating schools, helping teachers cope with hardware and software, integrate QUILL with other classroom activities, and reorganize their classrooms, as necessary, to take advantage of the computer. During the year we stayed in contact with the participating teachers through a monthly mailing of QUILL writing samples, new teaching ideas, reports of classroom experiences, and a long-distance electronic network.

In March and April, 1984, we returned to Alaska to visit each of the classrooms again and to attend the annual Alaska Association for Computers in Education (AACED) conference in Anchorage, along with most of the participants in the QUILL Alaska project. The group held a day-long meeting to discuss their classroom experiences, share classroom videotapes, and plan a presentation for the conference on their use of QUILL.

The participating teachers were eager to expand the QUILL project, even though initial funding had ended. They saw a need for two different university courses to support QUILL's continuation: a course similar to that offered in October 1983 for teachers who wanted to use QUILL, and an advanced course that would prepare experienced QUILL teachers to teach courses to others interested in QUILL. During the summer of 1984, these two courses were taught at the University of Alaska. Participants in the advanced course helped teach the beginning course as practice for conducting courses on their own during the next year.

Electronic Quills centers on the words and experiences of the teachers and students who used QUILL. We look in detail at their stories and consider questions relevant for other teachers, students, researchers, and developers of educational innovations: What does it mean to develop an environment for literacy in a real classroom? How can a teacher create an environment in which students work together towards meaningful goals? How can a teacher promote the rich communication so necessary for developing language? What is the role of technology in the practice and development of literacy?

Our examination of the QUILL experiences provides a fuller and more revealing account of what it meant to use QUILL than would have been possible through standard evaluation techniques. At the same time, the focus on the particulars of QUILL finds analogues in analyses of similar pieces of open-ended software or of educational innovations in general. Chapter 1 introduces general issues on which our analysis of QUILL sheds some light: What happens as people try to implement their vision of change? What are the problems and contradictions that arise? How can new approaches to teaching and literacy development be evaluated?

In chapter 2, we discuss literacy development in relation to society, culture, learning, and social contexts. We consider the characteristics of an environment conducive to literacy development, such as collaborative work, meaningful goals, and real audiences. We also look at the contribution of computers, communication networks, and other new technologies to teaching reading and writing. These ideas comprised the theory underlying QUILL.

In chapter 3, we focus on QUILL as an innovation. We describe it first as a software system, then consider the activities that accompanied the software and the support system for its use. Thus, we characterize the *idealization* of QUILL. In chapter 4, we describe the social context in which our study took place: the classrooms in Alaskan cities, towns, and villages; classrooms with new and experienced teachers; classrooms with students from diverse ethnic backgrounds; and classrooms with widely varying resources and needs.

In the next three chapters, we look at *realizations* of QUILL in Alaskan classrooms. The stories from these classrooms are told in part by the teachers themselves.[1] In chapter 5, we discuss the complex and important idea of "purpose" in learning and describe alternate realizations of QUILL with

---

[1] In general, we use the teachers' real names and pseudonyms for the students.

respect to purpose. In chapter 6, we describe how QUILL's approach to fostering revision was realized, or, how new properties of the innovation emerged in a variety of settings. In chapter 7, we present the evolution of a community of teachers, one linked by an electronic communication network. We discuss the role of the network in fostering this community and its characteristics that contributed to the community's evolution.

In chapter 8, we present a theoretical framework for studying innovations and change and the implications of that framework for evaluation. We first describe the evaluation of QUILL as an example of the standard paradigm for evaluation, which conceives of an innovation as a fixed and well-defined entity, which may cause change within a social system, such as a classroom. We found that this paradigm was an unproductive starting point for a deeper understanding of the realities of QUILL classrooms. In order to account for the varied interpretations and implementations of QUILL we developed an alternative paradigm, which we call *situated evaluation*. Among the differences between the standard paradigm and situated evaluation are (a) an emphasis on patterns of *realization* of the innovation, (b) an added focus on how the social context changes the innovation, and (c) a consideration of differences among realizations as well as similarities. The implications of these distinctions are explored in detail in chapter 8.

An innovation in education represents a challenge to traditional beliefs, values, and practices. This challenge implies a tension between old and new practices that can be resolved in various ways. For some, the answer is to reject the new technology. For others, it is to abandon old practices. But more generally, people create new practices that reflect complex and situation-specific compromises between the old and the new. Because the new practices were not even envisioned in the original conception of the technology's use, their very existence raises serious questions for traditional views about educational change, evaluation of innovations, the role of teachers in implementing innovations, and even the basic notion of what an innovation is.

ACKNOWLEDGMENTS

In a process that has extended over nearly a decade, it is difficult to acknowledge everyone who has made important contributions. Still, we would like to thank a few of the people who have made this book possible.

First, we would like to thank the many people at Bolt Beranek and Newman (where we both worked until 1990) who contributed to QUILL's development.[2]

---

[2]The development of QUILL was supported by the Center for Libraries and Education Improvement within the United States Department of Education under contract number 300-81-00314. Frank Withrow and Sheldon Fisher gave us important support and guidance in the early stages of QUILL development. Later work on the book was supported in part by the U.S. Office of Educational Research and Improvement (OERI) through the Center for the Study of Reading at the

Allan Collins played a major role in the early stages. Kathleen Starr and Cindy Steinberg made special contributions to making it work in classrooms. The QUILL software incorporated Writer's Assistant, which was developed by Jim Levin at Interlearn. Programming of QUILL itself was done by Adam Malamy, Andy Fox, Maureen Saffi, Rinsland Outland, and the authors. Bill Woods and Ray Nickerson provided additional support within Bolt Beranek and Newman.

Staff at The NETWORK in Andover, Massachusetts, including Susan Loucks-Horsley, Denise Blumenthal, David Zacchei, and Annmarie Lenson were major participants in the development of materials, in work with teachers and in classrooms, and in the dissemination of QUILL. Joyce Bauchner made a major contribution through her role in charge of the field test evaluation. At D. C. Heath & Co., Karen Goldstein was a strong supporter of QUILL and was instrumental in developing and promoting it as a commercial product.

The Advisory Board for the QUILL project played an active role in the design of QUILL and in its evaluation. The Board included Rexford Brown, Colette Daiute, Susan Florio, Linda Flower, Judith Langer, Gene Mulcahy, Marlene Scardamalia, Rudine Sims, and Robert Tierney. While Donald Graves was not on the Advisory Board, his work was a source of inspiration for QUILL, and we benefitted from many discussions with him.

Hundreds of QUILL teachers deserve thanks for their coinvention of QUILL. We can't list them all here, but it seems most appropriate to thank those who participated in the original QUILL field trials: Carolyn Miller in Brookline, Massachusetts, Jim Aldridge, Gertrude Avery, and Gene Mulcahy in Hartford, Connecticut, Freda Helmsteder, Evelyn Balunis, and Maxine Pearce in Bridgewater, New Jersey, and Marie Coleman, and Peggy Dean in Easton, Massachusetts.

Without the invitation from Ron and Suzanne Scollon to visit the University of Alaska at Fairbanks, QUILL might never have gone to Alaska. The Scollons saw the value of electronic networking and open-ended writing software for the Alaska classrooms. Several of the QUILL teachers in Alaska had studied networking or interethnic communication with Ron or Suzanne. Jim Levin's networking work in Alaska provided a fertile ground for QUILL and the Alaska QUILL teachers' network.

We would like to give special thanks to Carol Barnhardt, who has been a constant source of encouragement and guidance. Early on she recognized the potential for open-ended software for supporting writing and followed up that recognition by playing a central role in bringing QUILL to Alaska. As the

University of Illinois at Urbana-Champaign under Contract number 400-81-0030 and Cooperative Agreement No. OEG 0087-C1001, by OERI through the Center for Technology in Education at Bank Street College of Education under Grant No. 1-135562167-A1, and by Bolt Beranek and Newman, Inc. through the Science Development Program. We are grateful for this support. Of course, the book does not necessarily reflect the views of any of the institutions supporting the research.

coordinator of QUILL in Alaska, she was essential to its success there. More than anyone else, she worked to make the Alaska QUILL project, not just a project, but a community of teachers, administrators, researchers, and students. She also served as a "human gateway" between two electronic networks, thereby humanizing them so that more teachers found ways to use them. Her son, John Barnhardt, also filled this role, and in addition, provided important technical assistance in the Alaska QUILL workshop. Ray Barnhardt was also important in supporting the Alaska QUILL project and in helping us understand the cultures of Alaska.

Carol's papers about QUILL in Alaska (Barnhardt, 1984, 1985a), numerous letters, electronic mail exchanges, and discussions informed our understandings of schools in Alaska and the meaning of QUILL there. Her perceptive comments on this book were invaluable. She wrote an early version of chapter 4 based on her own experiences and writing about education in Alaska (Barnhardt, 1985b, 1991). We hope that in condensing and revising the text to fit the book we've retained her original insights.

We would especially like to thank all the teachers and administrators in Alaska who worked to make QUILL successful there. These include Bonnie and Hans Bless-Boenish in Shungnak, Helen Frost-Thompson in Telida, Mary Goniewiecha, Alexander McFarlane, Marcia Romick, Lynn Weldon, Linda Riddle, and Dick Riedl in Fairbanks, Syd Hole in Juneau, Ernie Manzie and Lena Ulroan in Chevak, Wilma Payne, Deane O'Dell, Malcolm Fleming, and Mike Baumgartner in McGrath, Don Stand in Nikolai, and Judy Tralnes and Joe Davis in Holy Cross. We are especially grateful to Helen Frost-Thompson, Bonnie Bless-Boenish, Alexander McFarlane, Syd Hole, Ernie Manzie, and Wilma Payne, for allowing us to quote from their own writing about QUILL in their classrooms.

Many people read and commented on the text and the situated evaluation ideas. Among these were Richard C. Anderson, Carol Barnhardt, Susan Bernstein, Laura Breeden, Susan Bruce, Courtney Cazden, Lizanne Destefano, Catherine Emihovich, Cristina Gillanders, Colleen Gilrane, Sarah Michaels, Denis Newman, Rebecca Oxford, Joy Peyton, Taffy Raphael, and Mitch Resnick. Julia Hough, our original editor at Lawrence Erlbaum Associates, and Hollis Heimbouch, our final editor, both provided useful comments and patient support.

Anyone who has written a lengthy document knows the value of having people who can help with typing, drawing figures, making tables, keeping track of data, and numerous other tasks only partially captured by the phrase "manuscript preparation." We were fortunate in having a number of people who helped us out over a period of many years, including Valerie Smith, Cindy Hunt, Vicki Morse, Tricia Neth, Marcia Mobilia, Barbara Trachtenberg, Jill O'Brien, Cheryl Przekwas, and Abiola Backus. Colleen Gilrane provided invaluable help in compiling the subject and author indexes. Mark Zahniser was an adventurous and steady companion for our trips to Alaska and for the first years of book rumblings.

The time spent writing the book was also the time in which Emily and Stephen Bruce appeared and grew to school age. They were patient companions during many hours of writing and eager recyclers of discarded drafts. Susan Bruce was a source of loving support throughout this period. In the final stages of writing Pauline Whorf was gracious enough to allow her 150-year-old home on Cape Cod to become a temporary writing center for the QUILL book. Although we cannot say that the setting was without distractions, it was definitely a conducive writing environment.

—*Bertram C. Bruce*
—*Andee Rubin*

Chapter 1

Introduction

About 10 years ago, we began to develop QUILL, a computer program whose purpose was to help upper elementary school students develop as writers. Our vision of QUILL was not one of a program that taught writing skills directly, but rather of one containing tools with which students and teachers could create a literacy environment in the classroom. By this we meant that QUILL would support collaboration; it would encourage writing for real audiences, with writing goals that came from the students; it would integrate reading and writing activities; it would foster a process for writing that included planning, critical thinking, and revising; and it would empower students so that they would understand the reasons for their learning and become actively engaged in furthering it.

Today, the growing use of electronic mail, bulletin boards, teleconferences, and computer-supported collaborative work systems has made increasingly apparent the intrinsic links among computers, communication, and community that QUILL exemplified (Handa, 1990; Hawisher & Selfe, 1989). Electronic systems are now used to shape, facilitate, control, or even establish communities and social relations. But in 1981 these ideas were relatively new, especially in school settings. QUILL thus represented a significant innovation in both the teaching of writing and in the use of computers in education.

We believe that the ideas in QUILL are still valid for teaching reading and writing. But our purpose is not to praise QUILL, nor to find fault with its vision of educational change. Instead it is to show that a detailed, self-critical appraisal of the evidence yields surprises and reveals a richness in what students and teachers do that belies both optimistic and pessimistic visions of technology in relation to educational change.

In order to be open to these surprises, we must make an important distinction between what an innovation purports to be and how it is used in real classroom settings. We conceptualize this distinction by contrasting the *idealization* of an innovation with its *realizations*. This book proceeds by examining how the idealization of QUILL was realized as many different QUILL*s* in diverse classroom situations. A better understanding of this realization process has important implications for curriculum development, teacher education, and evaluation of educational innovations.

INNOVATIONS IN EDUCATION

The linking of a new technology to a vision of a transformed pedagogy is a distinguishing feature in many proposed innovations in education. It is rare that the developer of an innovation would adopt the goal of simply facilitating current practices with a new technology. Instead, the argument is made that the expense of adopting new methods and tools is justified because major transformations, that is, improvements, will occur in current practices. Conversely, proposals to transform teaching practices often incorporate new technologies, broadly interpreted to include the use of new media, computers, new curricula, kits of "manipulables," or catchy multi-step procedures for teaching or learning. These reifications are viewed as essential to achieving the developers' pedagogical goals.

That new technologies are linked to visions of major educational change is not surprising. What is curious is that the new technology is often viewed as sufficient by itself to effect the desired changes. The assumption seems to be that if only teachers and students had access to the power of the new technology, then all aspects of the wonderful vision would be realized. Little thought is given to the possibility that traditional practices may be integral elements within a functioning social system and that they are unlikely to change simply because new practices are technically possible. In fact, those who do adopt innovations are typically faced with the challenging task of resolving conflicts between old practices that derive from powerful situational constraints and imperatives of the new technology.

Nevertheless, since the publication of *R. U. R.* (Rossum's Universal Robots) in 1923, one of the first fictional fantasies about computers, "thinking machines" have been seen as potentially "revolutionary" and in recent years, the word "revolution" has often been heard with respect to computers in schools. For example, in a Congressional testimony hearing shortly before work on QUILL began, one researcher declared that a revolution was possible over the next decade that would transform learning in our society, altering both the methods and the content of education. Another compared the computer technology revolution to the literacy revolution, noting that in both cases the long-term effects were unknown, but that in the current case, they were sure to occur more swiftly. In extrapolating further from the parallels between the two developments, he pointed out that in the same way that the advent of writing made possible a different definition of history, led to the growth of formal education, and eventually resulted in the equation of education with literacy, fundamental changes in the fabric of society may occur as computers and their capabilities become more integrated into our lives and educational systems. Computers could affect the way we educate ourselves, communicate with one another, and even the way we think of ourselves.

This visionary view of technology pervades much of the work that has been done on designing software and technology-based curricula for classrooms, including our own. People have been drawn to the use of the computer for learning because they see it as a source of leverage in the educational system. Its introduction will, they hope, go beyond specific pedagogical goals to catalyze fundamental educational changes, including new roles for teachers and students, as well as new views of how learning takes place.

For example, the computer is seen as enabling new forms of teaching in which students assume control for their own learning. In an early study of different types of educational software (Olds, Schwartz, & Willie, 1980), teachers looked at both narrowly directed drill-and-practice software and at software that purports to open up opportunities for students to ask their own questions. They found not only that different approaches to software design implied radically different models of learning and teaching, but also that in the process of examining software critically the teachers became more aware of their own values. The report had stated that, "teachers saw the enormous pedagogical difference between solving problems and formulating them, between answering someone else's question and generating your own" (p. 40).

Papert (1980) adopted a similar position in his description of the ideal use of the programming language LOGO:

> In many schools today, the phrase "computer-aided instruction" means making the computer teach the child. One might say the *computer is being used to program* the child. In my vision, the *child programs the computer* and in doing so, both acquires a sense of mastery over a piece of the most modern and powerful technology and establishes an intimate contact with some of the deepest ideas from science, from mathematics, and from the art of intellectual model building. (p. 5)

Papert likened the classroom environment in which he envisioned LOGO being used to the Brazilian samba schools. These are social clubs in which children and adults learn together to dance in an atmosphere both serious and fun. Describing LOGO environments for learning mathematics in relation to the samba schools, he pointed out that in both environments novices and experts are engaged in real activity: "The activity is so varied, so discovery-rich, that even in the first day of programming, the student may do something that is new and exciting to the teacher" (ibid, p. 179). Later, in discussing the way LOGO may facilitate the process of talking about thinking, he says, "in this way the LOGO culture enriches and facilitates the interaction between all participants and offers opportunities for more articulate, effective, and honest teaching relationships" (ibid, p. 180).

In the area of writing, the view of computers as an empowering force has been especially strong. Since computers can be used to foster collaboration and a process approach to teaching and learning, they seem especially well suited to the current emphasis on writing as a process. For example, several projects have explored the use of local area networks to create a new type of writing environment. Many people who have been involved in such projects see the new technology as offering not just better ways to carry out traditional teaching functions, but entirely new forms of teaching and learning. Batson (1988) stated:

> Networks create an unusual opportunity for writing teachers to shift away from the traditional writing classroom because they create entirely new pedagogical dynamics. One of the most important is the creation of a written social context, an online discourse community, which presents totally new opportunities for effective instruction in writing. . . ." (p. 32)

Writing about computers as tools to support response to student writing, Sirc (1989) described programs that facilitate interaction among students about the texts they are writing. These programs are designed to empower students by enhancing their control over their own writing and response processes: "The programs . . . allow students' work to be treated as serious writing, worthy of response. Computer response programs are best when they liberate students to write and talk about their writing" (p. 203). This idea of empowerment or liberation is one element in these new types of learning environments in which the teacher's role changes from lecturer to coach or facilitator, and the computer becomes a tool that students control, rather than the other way around.

REALIZATIONS IN THE CLASSROOM

Powerful themes run through these visions of computers in education: environments for learning, sensitivity to the social context of learning, collaboration, liberation, taking students seriously, and putting the student in control. Themes such as these play an important role in the development of innovative educational methods. They shape the design of software and activities; they provide reference points during the early stages of development when the innovation is not fully formed; and they are necessary in communicating with others. But for these reasons, the vision is often oversimplified, and as a result, rarely achieved in full, although some classrooms do fulfill many aspects of the ideal.

Regardless of one's vision, or of one's claims about how technology might change learning, a crucial question is this: What really happens when an innovation gets used? A serious examination of the ways in which an innovation becomes a functioning part of the classroom is essential to gaining a deep understanding of an innovation in use. It is also a prerequisite to seeing how changes in the innovation or the classroom setting might promote greater learning. Ultimately, it may lead to a rethinking of the original vision, to accord more with the realities of classrooms.

There has now been substantial experience with computers in schools. It is clear that one thing that has not happened is a straightforward, broad-based realization of any single vision. Instead, the diverse visions of ideal computer use have been multiplied by diverse forms of actual use in classrooms.

In many cases, computer-based innovations are reshaped to fit constraints of the existing curriculum or limited classroom resources. In fact, it is precisely those aspects of the innovation that do not challenge established methods of teaching that are incorporated most readily into school practices (Cohen, 1988; Cuban, 1986). In other cases, teachers do adopt the innovation as originally conceived, but then extend it with their own creative ideas or add elements that take advantage of particular local opportunities. Many innovations are designed with such extensions in mind; thus "using the computer as intended" means "using it in ways that cannot be specified in advance." The answer to the "What really happens. . .?" question is thus likely to be neither that the vision is realized as originally conceived, nor that institutional realities always engulf innovations.

Any study of the use of technology in schools must attend to the social, cultural, economic, and political environments for that use. In the individual classroom, these realities manifest themselves in details of classroom organization, availability of resources, mandated curricula, teacher preparation, the testing system, the ways teachers are evaluated, and so on. These factors shape the possibilities for change in the classroom, even for such a potentially "revolutionary" force as the computer. The impact of an innovation derives from the interaction of the idealized innovation with the real setting. In short, what we must analyze is not the computer as idealized innovation, but the innovation in use in real settings.

THE INNOVATION-IN-USE

This book is a study of the use of QUILL. To a large extent, the study focuses on the use of QUILL by teachers in Alaska. Although the examples we present are quite specific, including accounts of classroom interactions and of writing by teachers and students, the meaning of the examples extends beyond understanding the use of a single piece of software in a particular time and place. The Alaska setting is fascinating in its own right, but it also mirrors the diversity of American public schools in general. The classrooms we studied covered the range from multigrade classrooms in small, village schools to classrooms in urban centers. The students belonged to a variety of ethnic and language groups, and their grade levels ranged from second to eighth grade.

The stories we report show how teachers and students using QUILL and computer networks worked towards developing environments for literacy that involved collaboration, real purposes, and real audiences. In many cases, the teachers found that computer technology afforded special opportunities for enriching the literacy environments of their classrooms. These experiences corroborated our view that the development of facility with written language requires a particular kind of educational environment: one in which people use language to work together toward meaningful goals and where reading and writing served a purpose.

As we observed QUILL in use, we found that parts of our vision were fulfilled, but that other parts were not. For example, students in many classrooms wrote more often and shared their writing with others more than they had before. On the other hand, meaning-centered revision did not occur to the extent we had hoped. We also found that the actual use of QUILL expanded upon ideas that existed in a primitive form in our original vision. For example, collaborative learning among teachers developed in ways we had not anticipated, and the specific varieties of goal-directed writing that emerged were not predictable in the beginning.

While the teachers found that technology was a benefit in their teaching, they also found that it posed new problems. In their attempts to integrate technology into their classrooms, teachers had to recreate the innovation, viewing it as but one element in a complex social setting. Choosing parts that made sense, adapting others, and organizing their use in ways that accorded with their own beliefs and values about teaching, they invented something new. Their creations, the *realizations* of QUILL, were thus very different from QUILL, the idealization.

Understanding this process of second-order creation of the technology—this re-creation—is essential if we are to have sensible discourse about QUILL, but more generally about technological or, indeed, any innovations in education. The variations in use, or what we would prefer to call the unique realizations, led us to see that "QUILL" had different meanings in different settings; that we were studying the "QUILLs" that were being created in various classrooms, rather than the fixed entity "QUILL" and its effects on learning. The different ways that QUILL was used in different classrooms led us to adopt the construct of *alternate realizations*, as a way of focussing initially on differences in use rather than on similarities. Thus, this book is about the many "Electronic QUILLs."

INNOVATION AND CHANGE

To understand the recreation process we can no longer conceive of an innovation as hard and fixed, with well-defined boundaries specified in terms of hardware and software parameters, but rather as a system representing the intersection of diverse and changing interests, values, social practices, and economic forces. We need to avoid the technocentric fallacy (Papert, 1987b) of seeing technology as a single powerful object, with *its* effects, *its* use, and *its* meaning. Instead, we should realize that the "same technology" or the "same innovation" has different meanings in different settings.

We are interested in questions such as these: How does an innovation, especially one tied to the introduction of new technologies, bring about changes in a social system? How do social systems constrain and direct the uses of innovations? What kinds of control do those affected by an innovation have, could they have, or should they have, over the processes of change?

We are especially concerned with educational innovations, because the educational arena affords a rich context for studying change in both social systems and in the technology per se. It allows us to look at change initiated by the users (teachers and students) of innovations as well as those initiated by the developers. It also allows us to examine in detail the process of change that occurs when an innovation becomes part of a social system. It raises new questions about the role and responsibility of teachers in managing change in their classrooms. These questions are complex; our experience with the use of QUILL in schools provides data only for some preliminary answers.

We came to see that the realization of an innovation could not be predicted from a consideration of its properties outside of the contexts of use. For example, in some classrooms, the computer station became a social meeting ground for groups of students. The existence and nature of these groups in turn influenced what audiences, genres, and amounts of writing were done using QUILL. Thus, the implications of QUILL for learning writing in those classrooms depended on the social structure of classroom groups, which were independent of any specification of QUILL as an innovation per se. These very real and significant properties of some of the realizations of QUILL were in some sense latent in the innovation, but they emerged only through use, and, in fact, did not emerge in some classrooms.

The emergence of classroom social groups was only one example of how the uses of QUILL brought out properties latent in the idealization. We saw that modes of use were often mediated by social interactions and that the most useful description of changes that occurred as QUILL was used was indexed to changes in group or even community practices. What started as a study of a particular technology eventually included a study of evolving social practices and the larger concept of *evolving communities*.

Soon the question, "What is the effect of using QUILL?" had to be transformed into the more basic ontological question, "What is QUILL?" or even better, "What are the various forms of QUILL in use?" An answer to that question could not come from the standard paradigms for evaluation, which tend to focus on commonalities of use rather than on differences. To address questions of this type we propose a new approach, *situated evaluation*, which focuses on understanding differences in realizations. This book can thus be read as a presentation of situated evaluation and its application to QUILL.

Chapter 2

Contexts for Literacy Development

Our purpose in designing QUILL was to help students learn to write by creating environments in which they would see writing as a natural way to satisfy their need to communicate. As they wrote, we hoped they would create a writing community within the classroom, and writing and reading skills would develop within the context of meaningful communication. Thus, learning by doing was at the heart of our design for QUILL.

Although we used computers to support this pedagogy, technology was not the source of this vision, nor was technology essential to its realization. To the contrary, QUILL represented an application of ideas elaborated on in several diverse traditions including recent research on the writing process and on innovative uses of computers, as well as earlier work from Soviet psychology and American pragmatism.

In this chapter, we discuss briefly the theoretical background for the development of QUILL, focusing on relations among literacy, society, culture, and learning. We then consider how these general principles led to the design of QUILL. We discuss first the implications of this view of literacy development for the design of school environments in which students use reading and writing in meaningful ways. We then discuss the role of computers in supporting literacy development. In chapter 3, we follow this general characterization with a description of the details of QUILL and how it embodied these design principles.

Because the ideas we present here have evolved in productive and important ways since we designed QUILL, we have not restricted our discussion to the pre-QUILL period. Still, we have emphasized those ideas that most influenced us in designing the program in the early 1980's.

LITERACY DEVELOPMENT

"Literacy" is a term with many meanings. Across historical, institutional, cultural, social, and political contexts it has meant, at various times, the ability to sign one's name, knowledge of the alphabetic principle, completion of a specified number of years of schooling, passing a multiple-choice test, the use of reading and writing in daily life, or the ability to function in a modern, technological society. In the view of some researchers and practitioners, every child acquires a home-based literacy, which must then be extended by schooling; for others, literacy development has little to do with formal education[1]; and for still others, literacy is precisely what schools are about.

We will not attempt to resolve these issues here. Instead, we want to touch on some of the antecedents to the development of QUILL and to raise some additional issues that became salient for us as we examined what happened in classrooms using QUILL.

Literacy and Society

One of Dewey's major contributions to educational theory lay in articulating the intimate and complex connections among community, communication, and education. There are more than verbal ties, he argued, among words like "common," "community," and "communication," for people "live in a community by virtue of the things which they have in common; and communication is the way they come to possess things in common" (Dewey, 1966, p. 4). Furthermore, these links extend across generations:

> Society exists through a process of transmission quite as much as biological life. This transmission occurs by means of communication of habits of doing, thinking, and feeling from the older to the younger. Without this communication of ideals, hopes, expectations, standards and opinions from those members of society who are passing out of the group life to those who are coming into it, social life could not survive. [*ibid*]

Thus, social life is maintained through communication, and its survival depends on communication across generations. Not only does society "exist *by* transmission, *by* communication, but it may fairly be said to exist *in* transmission, *in* communication" (*ibid*). For Dewey, since all communication is "educative," social life is virtually equated with education.

Society exists *in* communication, but just as surely, education exists only in a communicative society. Much of what students learn, whether in formal

---

[1]For example, Taylor and Dorsey-Gaines (1988) described how families they worked with developed a facility with written language independently of schooling.

or informal settings, is how to communicate and to understand the communication of others. This applies to both appropriating new ideas and to becoming more articulate in discussing the already known. In that sense,
communication is both the means of learning, and the substance of what is
learned. It is also intimately bound up with the concept of a community—
developing what Dewey (1966) called "participation in a common understanding" (p. 4).

From these considerations, it is clear that knowing how to read and write
a language at a minimal level is of little value if that ability cannot be applied
in accord with society's culturally defined ways of thinking, interpreting, and
using language across a variety of activities and settings. Most people in Western
industrialized nations can read and write a few words and phrases, but many
cannot use written language effectively or appropriately enough to meet the
demands of the workplace, and many who can read and write do not do so
in their daily lives. Thus, to equate literacy with basic proficiency in reading
and writing obscures important aspects of literacy, in particular, its relationship to work, social practices, community, society, and citizenship.

In his definition of literacy, Gee (1990) included the ability to adopt a
Discourse[2] appropriate to a given social setting. This Discourse allows one to
be identified as part of the group:

> A *Discourse* is a socially accepted association among ways of using language, of
> thinking, feeling, believing, valuing, and of acting that can be used to identify
> oneself as a member of a socially meaningful group or "social network", or to
> signal (that one is playing) a socially meaningful "role". (p. 143)

In addition to the *primary Discourse* of the home or family, there are many *secondary Discourses* employed in institutions such as schools, courts, workplaces,
churches, and so forth. Gee defined *literacy* as control over uses of language
in these secondary Discourses.[3] Since there are many social groups, institutional settings, and domains for Discourses, there can be no single literacy that
applies universally. Literacies are thus ways of using and interpreting oral and
written language in various social settings and of integrating language use into
action. A person who possesses a literacy is seen as a proper member of the
corresponding social group or institution. Thus, according to Gee (1990), a
"Discourse is a sort of 'identity kit' which comes complete with the appropriate costume and instructions on how to act and talk, and often write, so as
to take on a particular social role that others will recognize" (p. 142).

Accordingly, literacies define communities. Speaking about writers, but making a point with implications for all language use, Bruffee (1986, p. 784) said

---

[2]This use of "Discourse" is capitalized to distinguish it from "discourse" as a segment of text.

[3]Postman and Weingartner (1969) used the term "languaging" to describe this process of using language in a new intellectual sphere. They argued that this is the essence of learning.

"A writer's language originates with the community to which he or she belongs. We use language primarily to join communities we do not yet belong to and to cement our membership in communities we already belong to." This community-membership function of language is an essential element in the maintenance and perpetuation of institutions. It is one reason for the close link between literacy and culture (see also Scribner & Cole, 1981).

Every child learns ways of using both oral and written language, which are derived from home-based values, attitudes, and ways of interacting with others. As Heath (1989) pointed out, these ways of using language are acquired through a complex process of enculturation:

> When children learn language, they take in more than forms of grammar: They learn to make sense of the social world in which they live and how to adapt to its dynamic social interactions and role relations. Through the reciprocal processes of family and community life that flow through communication, children develop a system of cognitive structures as interpretive frameworks and come to share to greater or lesser degrees the common value system and sets of behavioral norms of their sociocultural group. (p. 367)

Starting from many different home cultures, children come to a school culture with its own distinctive values and norms. The school culture defines a set of literacy practices—ways of taking meaning from and assigning meaning to language. Success in school means adopting these practices in various tasks and across disciplines in accordance with the norms, values, and expectations of the school culture.

Children from some sociocultural groups bring to school ways of interacting and using language that are denied or ignored by school-based literacy practices, while other children bring ways that match well to the school practices. Thus, school-based literacies are more closely related to the literacy practices of some homes than others. The difficulty some children encounter in school is traceable in part to this mismatch of literacy practices. Yet the school-based literacies cannot simply be discarded in favor of more culturally appropriate practices, for they exemplify the needs and values of the society-at-large, which in turn set the criteria for full acceptance and participation in that society. Even when school activities fail to address all the mainstream societal needs, they do reflect the mainstream values and practices to the detriment of those whose cultures differ. Delpit (1988), Heath (1983) and others have emphasized how important it is for students to examine both the Discourses they are familiar with and the new Discourses they are expected to master.

The cultural diversity of American society and American schools thus presents a dilemma for those who seek ways to promote universal literacy without demanding cultural uniformity. A challenge for schools is to foster literacy skills in all students, building on, rather than attempting to eliminate, their cultural values and practices. Although it presents a significant challenge, the cultural diversity of the school population is also a source of educational opportunity that teachers can build on to help students form new cognitive and social skills. Different cultural and linguistic backgrounds directly enrich the educational environment for all students. Moreover, they can support the development of a critical awareness of language function and use, if students are encouraged to think about different ways of making meaning.

Designing an educational system that provides students with ways to maintain and transmit their existing culture while still succeeding in the mainstream world requires serious consideration of the role of literacy across cultures. The intrinsic connection between literacy and culture was one of the reasons we have drawn most of the examples in this book from schools in Alaska, where students bring a wide range of linguistic and cultural backgrounds to school. These examples present in high relief the issues of cultural diversity in the context of literacy education.

Literacy and Learning

Although some children experience home-based Discourses that match relatively well with those of the school, every child must learn new ways of using language that go beyond those of the home. The ever-changing demands of modern society require students to acquire new language skills, knowledge, and the ability to reason critically about what they know. Moreover, students need to learn how to learn in new and changing environments.

In order to foster the acquisition of higher order thinking and learning skills, the school must to some extent embody the secondary Discourses students are expected to master. But a school is a culture unto itself that has yet other secondary Discourses. Just as there are multiple literacies in society-at-large, there are multiple school-based literacies corresponding to school subject areas, such as mathematics, science, social studies, or language arts. These literacies vary across tasks, such as giving an oral book report, doing a science experiment, or having a writing conference with the teacher.

A literacy entails a unique way of interacting with texts, objects, and other people, in short, successful participation in different cultures. For this reason, acquisition of a literacy is an enculturation process, one that involves initially peripheral, and later, full participation in a new culture. In our society we expect students to become enculturated into school-based literacies, and later into potentially different literacies in society-at-large. This process resembles the enculturation through apprenticeship that occurs in work settings (Lave & Wenger, 1991). It is also much like the process a person goes through in learning a new language when moving to a new country. By participating in a culture in which the language is used, one acquires facility with the language, at least as it is used in that culture.

Research on the institutional, sociocultural, and interactive factors that shape literacy development in and out of school has developed this view of literacy acquisition as enculturation (Cazden, 1988; Cook-Gumperz, 1986; Heath, 1983; Lave & Wenger, 1991; Scollon & Scollon, 1981; Taylor & Dorsey-Gaines, 1988). This work emphasizes the social settings in which people learn through processes of modeling, coaching, and collaborative problem-solving, according well with Dewey's notion that community and communication are inseparable from education. Studies of learning from sociocultural perspectives (e.g., Edwards & Mercer, 1987; Moll, 1990; D. Newman, Griffin, & Cole, 1989; Vygotsky, 1978, 1986) show that social interaction makes internal cognitive development possible.

An implication of this work is that schools should emphasize teacher support of learning and collaboration among students rather than either learning in isolation or learning under teacher control, both prevalent practices in American education. Thus, the familiar IRE sequence: <Teacher _I_nitiation> <Student _R_eply> <Teacher _E_valuation> (Mehan, 1979) is replaced by forms of apprenticeship in which students master new literacies through observing and sharing in the literacies of teachers, parents, and peers (Collins, Brown, & Newman, 1989). The apprenticeship process emphasizes the value of what both master and apprentice bring to the literacy activities. It includes direct language interactions between teacher and students, as well as meaning-centered communication among students, or between students and those in the larger community.

Apprenticeship and other forms of collaboration in learning are important because they motivate students and provide support to the learning process. But beyond these considerations they are important because they are the means by which knowledge is shared and constructed. Each participant plays an active role in creating meaning. A reader may construct ''meaning'' from a text in a way the writer never intended (Adams & Bruce, 1982). Thus, writers must be concerned with how a text will be read, not just how it is written. This is another reason why community is important in the development of literacy.

One consequence of the existence of multiple literacies is that students need opportunities to participate in diverse communities of literacy practices. A recent study conducted by the National Assessment of Educational Progress showed that these opportunities may be missing for many students. The NAEP study defined literacy as ''using printed and written information to function in society to achieve one's goals and develop one's knowledge and potential'' in its assessment of young adults (ages 21 to 25) (Kirsch & Jungeblut, 1986, p. 3). The study included tasks such as stating in writing the argument made in a lengthy newspaper column, using a bus schedule to select the appropriate bus for given departure and arrival times, and totaling the costs for items in a catalogue. Nearly all of the young adults in the study could accomplish the simplest of these tasks, thus demonstrating minimal literary skills. But only a small percentage could carry out moderately complex tasks, because they were not enculturated into the forms of literacy the tasks demanded. The failure of the schools to support this enculturation disproportionately affects low-income and minority students.

One cause for this failure may be that classroom learning environments tend not to manifest collaboration in solving problems, meaningful goals, or access to real audiences. Students typically work in isolation, and seldom see their teacher as a collaborator toward a common end. Group learning is sometimes little more than a teacher delivering a lecture to a classroom of students. Most students have a notion of "school tasks" that does not intersect with activities they consider meaningful on an everyday basis; school tasks are done for the teacher, while life tasks are done for one's own purposes. Finally, the prevalence of multiple choice tests, workbooks, and lecture format teaching does little to provide the rich communication opportunities essential to the development of literacy; students usually see their teacher as the sole audience for their writing. A central aim of QUILL was to modify these practices, through creative use of technology and new curriculum activities.

DESIGNING QUILL AND ENVIRONMENTS
FOR LITERACY DEVELOPMENT

Considering the relationships among community, communication, and education raises important questions: How do people use language, especially written language, to create, maintain, and perpetuate communities? How do they develop the ability to share, as Dewey (1966, p. 3) said, their "ideals, hopes, expectations, standards and opinions" with one another? How do people develop literacy skills that enable them to participate significantly in the society in which they live? How can such environments be created in a classroom? What role do new technologies for communication have in creating such environments? These were some of the design issues we had to consider in creating QUILL. We organized our design around the idea of *functional learning environments* (FLEs), an approach to fostering literacy development that matched well with our notions of how computers could best be used in classrooms for teaching reading and writing.

Functional Learning Environments

Ideas about "community" and "apprenticeship" provided a foundation for our design; but we needed to be more specific about when and how students and teachers could work together, what tasks they were engaged in, what role the computer should play in learning, and how the environment would shape the processes of reading and writing. There were several key elements in formulating a design responsive to these concerns.

We began with the idea that the development of a facility with written language requires an environment in which people use language to work towards meaningful goals. Literacy development is a natural product of the need and the opportunity to communicate; it flourishes in environments where reading and writing serve a purpose. Consistent with these tenets, we emphasized the use of whole language, as opposed to language components such as punctuation, spelling, and grammar. Harman and Edelsky (1989) argued that the whole language approach to teaching and learning, with its focus on meaning and use, fosters higher order language and literacy development. Moreover, it is more accepting of nonmainstream cultures and language use:

> The whole language approach is geared to the creation of texts for real use; it encourages multiple interpretations of existing texts-in-the-world; it honors and uses the language norms students arrive with; . . . it focuses on the ideas students have rather than the ones they lack; it assumes the expansion of roles so that students teach and teachers learn; it sets high but flexible standards; it emphasizes language repertoires rather than right answers; and it fosters questioning, analyzing, speaking up, and writing down. (p. 396)

Ideas about working together, meaningful goals, opportunities for communication, real language use, whole language, and acceptance of students' norms and values were all important parts of the theory underlying QUILL. To the extent that these diverse notions could be encapsulated in one concept, it was in terms of *functional learning environments* (D. Newman, 1987; D. Newman, Goldman, Brienne, Jackson, & Magzamen, 1989; Riel, 1985).[4] An FLE is one in which learning activities seen from the learner's point of view lead to goals beyond learning for its own sake.

There are many ways that FLEs can be generated. One is from the ideas of students themselves. In addition, teachers can make classroom tasks more functional by showing students the uses of what they are learning in other contexts. The critical point is that the activity must have meaning within the child's own experiences.

School activities often have one *stated purpose*, a separate *school purpose*, and yet other purposes from the students' perspectives. Usually the school purpose dominates, and students quickly come to see through the stated purpose. For example, a typical school writing activity, such as "Writing a prospectus for a TV show," has a stated purpose that is unrealizable, because no real television network is an audience for the prospectus. The school purpose, however,

---

[4]These ideas are developed further in chapter 5, which examines the role of purpose in classroom writing.

may be to develop students' grammar, spelling, and punctuation skills. For students, the same activity may serve as a way to develop social ties within the classroom, as well as to get a good grade.

In a functional learning environment, the stated purpose for a learning activity is taken seriously. Rather than being a sugar-coating for the school purpose, it is a true organizing principle for the work. Students work towards a goal that makes sense to them and is important in and of itself. They read texts relevant to a goal, not because the text is the next one in the curriculum, but because seeing what the author has to say may help in learning how to build a rabbit hutch, in deciding how to carry out an experiment on taste preferences, in understanding another culture in preparation for a trip, in forming an opinion before writing an essay to be published in a community newspaper, or in selecting texts for an anthology. Similarly, they write for audiences they know or want to know. They write to share ideas, to persuade others of what they believe, to entertain, to further their own thinking on a topic, or to stretch their own language capabilities. The important point is that these goals have meaning within the students' interests and experiences and are not simply tasks imposed from outside.

The defining characteristic of writing as a communicative act is the connection of the writer to an audience. An environment in which texts clearly are meant to communicate to a specific audience provides motivation for writing that is difficult to duplicate in contrived tasks. When students write to entertain, influence, inform, or persuade other members of their class, their teachers, parents, or the community, their creations take on a unique importance and purpose.

Once students are permitted to write for their own purposes, communication becomes paramount and a writing community can begin to develop. This can change the relationships among students and between students and teachers. It can also change the conception of the writing task from text production to "talking." This can be seen in Miceli's (1969) description of a classroom in which he shifted the emphasis from composition to communication:

> During the next month or so, letters were exchanged frequently. That is, ideas and feelings were exchanged, and never once was the word "composition" mentioned. Teachers should give that some thought. When was the last time *you* wrote a "composition"? Outside of the separate life of a school, when does anyone put pen to paper to write a composition? And if compositions bear no relationship to reality, why continue to assign them? Why not letters as a way of getting students to talk? Of course, we would have to answer the letters, to *talk back*, to respond not only to the mechanical quality of the student's writing, but also to what he has to say to us. (p. 174)

Even if one were to assume that an important purpose of schooling was to help students learn to write compositions (or what Scollon & Scollon, 1981, called "essayist literacy"), writing to real audiences with a real purpose could be the best way to achieve that.

Pedagogical Goals for QUILL

Our adoption of functional learning environments led to our identifying six pedagogical goals—characteristics of the literacy environments we wanted to foster (Rubin & Bruce, 1985). These goals essentially summarized our views of literacy development and the design of school environments to foster it. Articulating them was important for us as a guide to designing QUILL and also as a capsule summary for communicating our intentions to teachers, students, and other researchers. They serve as a concise description of our views about literacy environments at the time of QUILL's development, and thus specify part of the *idealization* of QUILL. In chapters 5, 6, and 7, our examination of the uses of QUILL reveals the ways in which these goals were realized in a variety of classrooms.

1. PG 1. Planning. QUILL's first pedagogical goal was to help children develop the skills of planning and critical thinking (Flower, 1981; Scardamalia, 1981). Planning includes generating ideas, organizing them, relating ideas to possible text organizations, and rethinking one's goals in writing (Elbow, 1973; Kaufer, Geisler, & Neuwirth, 1989). A common view of planning is that it occurs before composing. However, the generation and organization of ideas occurs throughout the writing process. Critical thinking in writing involves reflecting on one's product—on the ideas, their structure, and their expression. Writers need to think critically about both the ideas in their heads and those they have put into words as they create a text. Some writers, for instance, write down as many ideas as possible in no particular order, under the assumption that relations between ideas will emerge. Others define groupings of ideas first in order to facilitate the production of new ones. In either case, the processes are interweaved, each providing material for the other to work on.

2. PG 2. Integration of Reading and Writing. Our second goal was to integrate reading and writing (Rubin & Hansen, 1983; Tierney & Pearson, 1983). A literacy environment should facilitate processes that relate reading and writing, such as reading for information to use in writing, reading one's own text with a critical eye, and writing with the understanding that the text will be read by others. Students should view themselves as both writers and readers and feel confident in either use of written language.

3. PG 3. Publishing. The third pedagogical goal was to make writing public. Writing needs to be read by peers, by people who know what its purpose is and are expected to be affected by it. Too often students write for their teacher, but for no one else. Making writing public implies adult notions of publishing

and of presenting texts in formats meant to be read by others (Graves, 1982; Graves & Hansen, 1983). An environment for literacy should provide publishing opportunities with genuine audiences for students who are learning about the uses of written communication. This requires channels for communication that are diverse, flexible, and open, so that students have access to a variety of co-communicators.

4. PG 4. Meaningful communication. QUILL's fourth goal was to support meaningful communication with real audiences. A literacy environment should support students working toward communication goals that they consider meaningful. Students can then develop literacy skills in the context of audiences and purposes that matter to them and can judge their progress in terms of these self-defined goals. This calls for activities in which students think about who will read their texts, why they want to communicate with that audience, and why the audience might want to read what they have to say. Students should write for one another and for audiences outside the classroom. Thus, there should be a shift away from the teacher as the sole audience for student writing, with a corresponding shift in topics and purposes of writing.

5. PG 5. Collaboration. The fifth pedagogical goal was to encourage writing with others, to make apprenticeship and collaboration become classroom realities. Within such an environment, students are seen as potential teachers for one another, and students can work with teachers in the pursuit of common goals. Students can read what others have written while it is being composed as well as after it is complete; they can comment on, contribute to, learn from, and share texts as they work together. In addition, teachers may collaborate with one another, and people within the school work closely with people in the larger community.

6. PG 6. Revision. Our final goal was to facilitate revision and, in particular, to encourage students to carry out more sophisticated kinds of revision, not only to fix spelling errors marked by the teacher, but to make major changes to the text based on considerations of audience and purpose. Even young children are able to carry out such revisions (Graves, 1982), but many have the intuition that once a text is generated, it is finished. Moreover, within the typical school culture finishing writing quickly and simply is valued more than producing writing that has real effects on a real audience. As H. S. Becker (1986) said, "[students] learn that a really smart student does a paper once, making it as good as possible in one pass" (p. 44).

Contrasts Between QUILL and Restricted Writing Environments

A classroom in which QUILL's pedagogical goals were achieved would look very different from a classroom with a more restricted writing environment. For example, students in a QUILL classroom were expected to collaborate often

TABLE 2.1
Writing Practices

QUILL PG Environment	QUILL Environment	Restricted Writing
1. Planning	Brainstorming Writing as thinking	No discussion; sit and write Writing as text production
2. Integration	Multiple genres Writing across curriculum	Mostly narrative Writing only in English class
3. Publishing	Multiple real audiences Wide variety of forms	Teacher as audience One or two text types
4. Meaningful Communication	Real purposes Topic choice	Writing for a grade Designated topic
5. Collaboration	Working together Sharing writing	Hidden papers Isolated writers
6. Revision	Meaning-centered revision Conferencing	Copy-editing Red marks as response

(PG5); in a restricted writing environment, students are expected to work independently at all times—and even to keep their papers hidden from other students. Table 2.1 lists some of these differences between the pattern of the ideal QUILL classroom and that of the classroom with a restricted writing environment. For each pedagogical goal the table shows two contrasts in writing practices.

The first two columns in the table represent part of what we are calling the *idealization* of QUILL. Some *realizations* of QUILL in fact embodied these practices. But there were a variety of ways in which QUILL was realized. Some classrooms looked much like the second column in the beginning, while others looked more like the third. Some changed from the third column to the second while others did not change much at all. But most could not be so simply categorized, either before or after the introduction of QUILL. The change process is far more complex. Reaching a better understanding of it is one reason we chose to view these changes through the *situated evaluation* that follows in the rest of this book.

Computers as Literacy Environments

In designing QUILL, we were faced with deciding how to view the computer's contribution to literacy development. As uses of computers outside of school expanded to include support for communication among people, the models of using computers in literacy education expanded as well. We saw parallels between the ideas of community, communication, and functional learning environments discussed in the previous section and the possibilities for new classroom practices enabled by computers (Collins, 1983; Collins, Bruce, & Rubin, 1982; Rubin, 1983).

Not all of the ways that computers could be used were relevant to our pedagogical goals. In deciding how to make best use of the computer we considered first the role it could play in instruction. The following four perspectives informed our thinking. Each of them implies not simply a view of the technology, but assumptions about the enterprise of schooling. Thus, depending on one's assumptions about literacy education, the computer could do the following:

1. Individualize instruction, provide learning material at a controlled pace, and record student progress.
2. Make the regularities, the beauties, and the difficulties of language something that students could examine and interact with in new ways.
3. Aid in reading; allow students to produce and format texts easily; facilitate revision of texts; check for spelling errors; and store in a compact and easily accessible form all sorts of information that learners need, from style sheets to encyclopedic data.
4. Permit new forms of meaningful communication in a new social realm and reconfigure the relationships among students and teachers; make possible new modes of communication, and ''hypertexts,'' or ''hypermedia,'' which allow the intermixing of tables, charts, graphs, pictures, sounds, video, and text.

We discuss below each of these roles; the last two turned out to be most productive for the design of QUILL.

Computers as Tutors.   An early vision of the use of computers in education has students working alone at individual terminals, receiving much of their evaluation and feedback from the computer, while working on a series of tasks determined by the machine. A common implementation of this format was programmed instruction, in which students' answers to questions determined which branch in a tree of predetermined frames they would follow next. Such instruction was considered ''individualized'' because different students read different sequences of text and questions. Hundreds of such programs, which drill students on basic skills, existed when we began to develop QUILL. In general, they focused on low-level skills: spelling, grammar, and word meanings. In fact, our analysis of language arts programs as we began developing QUILL (Rubin & Bruce, 1985), revealed that 90% dealt with language at the level of letters or words. Only 7% considered any text larger than a sentence.

Moreover, regardless of language level, few of the programs called for anything more than a quick response to a computer-initiated problem.

More recently, software designers have attempted to implement an extension of traditional computer aided instruction (CAI): *intelligent tutoring systems,* in which a program can monitor a student's understanding of the domain, present appropriate examples and problems, and apply appropriate pedagogical procedures. Systems in domains such as geometry, algebra, arithmetic, programming, medicine, and electronics have been moderately successful in helping students master the subject area using this approach.

But despite interesting research efforts (Neuwirth, 1989), there are severe technical limitations to the computer tutoring approach in writing. While a computer can be programmed to produce texts within a limited domain, no program can respond to the variety of writing tasks students face. Nor can the computer effectively evaluate and respond to writing. Although some programs can evaluate grammar and usage, research in artificial intelligence is still far from constructing an adequate language understander. This means that the sort of informed diagnosis and subsequent assistance central to the notion of intelligent tutoring systems is not possible in teaching reading and writing.

These technical limitations become pedagogical limitations as well because they place limits on what can be taught and on the form of learning interactions. As Sirc (1989) said:

> . . . whenever we have our machines talking directly to students (through preprogrammed words or phrases activated by some means of textual input) in the hope of providing useful writing instruction, we limit our pedagogy. The computer, I suggest, so far can only serve effectively, in terms of a general pedagogical tool, as a medium for response rather than as a respondent. (p. 187)

Computers can directly teach only narrow aspects of language use, primarily those involving formal properties of language or those that can be expressed in short answer replies to specific questions. An emphasis on these aspects could negate efforts to foster literacy in a larger sense. Given our focus on communication with real audiences, other roles for the computer in teaching writing seemed more promising. As a result, we decided not to incorporate explicit tutoring components into the QUILL software.

Computers as Ways to Explore Language Structure. Computer-based microworlds have been developed in various areas of science and mathematics to allow students to explore new domains, test hypotheses, construct models, and discover new phenomena (Papert, 1980). The same technology can be used to create microworlds for language. Investigations within these microworlds can be highly motivating for students; moreover, they lead students to think deeply about language patterns, conceptual relationships, and the structure of ideas.

An example is having students construct programs that "talk" (Goldenberg & Feurzeig, 1987; Sharples, 1985). A gossip program, for example, can be written to produce descriptions of actions that someone else has allegedly taken, actions that are noteworthy because they involve surprising revelations about the other's character. In the programming language, LOGO, this might be expressed by the following procedure:

```
TO GOSSIP
      OUTPUT (SENTENCE PERSON DOESWHAT)
END
```

This procedure is a small computer program that, when executed, produces a sentence composed of a first part, which is the name of a person, and a second part, which is a description of some action that person did. Now, this only works if the procedures, PERSON and DOESWHAT, are appropriately defined. For example:

```
TO PERSON
      OUTPUT PICK [SANDY DALE DANA CHRIS]
END

TO DOESWHAT
      OUTPUT PICK [CHEATS.[LOVES TO WALK.]
            [TALKS A MILE A MINUTE.] YELLS.]
END
```

The first procedure, PERSON, selects one person from a list. The second procedure, DOESWHAT, selects a predicate to apply to that person. With these procedures, a student can then ask the computer to print out any number of gossip statements such as "Dale yells," "Chris loves to walk," and so on. These procedures can be revised and others added to produce arbitrarily complex gossip statements. At first, the interest for students comes from the fact that they can be playful, making the computer print out funny, and sometimes surprising statements, even though they provided it with all its data. As they continue to explore the gossip domain, though, this interest can progress to something deeper, a developing appreciation of the complexities, beauties, and regularities of language.

This perspective on the use of computers in literacy development fulfills several of the pedagogical goals identified above, and is consistent with the approach we eventually took. For a while, we included in QUILL a story-construction microworld called Story Maker (Rubin, 1980; Zacchei, 1982). Although the final version of QUILL did not include Story Maker, some classrooms used it and other language microworlds in conjunction with QUILL.

Computers as Tools.   Viewing computers as educational tools recognizes their power and flexibility. Computer tools—such as word processors, spread sheets, and graphics programs—can be used across the curriculum, in several grade levels, and throughout the year. In contrast to single-purpose programs, flexible tools can fit into the curriculum in many places. Students can approach them at varying levels of sophistication, beginning by using only a simple core of capabilities and progressing to more expert use. Teachers can select those functions that are appropriate for the students' developmental level and the role the tool is playing in the classroom.

Word processing, the most obvious language-oriented computer tool (see Cochran-Smith, 1991; Collins & Sommers, 1985), has become such a commonplace fixture within English and language arts classrooms that some people now take it for granted, saying, "We only do word processing; when will we start real computer use?" Of course, word processing is real computer use and serves an important function, even if it only helps with the practical details of creating and sharing texts within a classroom. Moreover, there is evidence that in making it easier to compose and revise, to see problems with a text, and to share texts, students become better writers and readers (Bridwell, Sirc, & Brooke, 1985; Michaels & Bruce, 1989; Collins & Sommers, 1985; Daiute, 1985; Frase, 1987; Levin, Boruta, & Vasconcellos, 1983; Rubin & Bruce, 1985, 1986; Wresch, 1984).

There are hundreds of word processing programs that allow writers to enter and revise text. But word processing is only one of the ways computers can serve as tools for writing and reading (see Britton & Glynn, 1989; Wresch, 1988). Programs with speech synthesizers, or stored speech, now assist readers who encounter unfamiliar words (McConkie & Zola, 1985; Rosegrant & Cooper, 1983). Data bases of information make it possible for students to browse text as a method of stimulating their reading and writing. There are now dictionaries, encyclopedias, and thesauruses available on compact disks.

Other programs have been designed to help with the tasks of planning and generating ideas. Pea and Kurland (1986) provided an extensive discussion of such programs. Some of these ask the writer questions to help in starting a text; some provide writing prompts; some help in outlining a text; some help organize ideas in formation. More recently, the idea of organizing ideas has blossomed into the concept of hypertext (Beeman, 1988; Bolter, 1991; Nelson, 1987), a structure in which individual notes are thought of as cards that can be connected to reflect the semantic links among them. Creating such a hypertext amounts to putting together a nonlinear document about a set of related topics. A reader of a hypertext chooses which links to follow, exploring a topic to any desired depth. Note cards can contain not only text, but video, audio, graphics, spreadsheets, and other visual images. A linked structure incorporating all of these media is called, naturally, hypermedia. These systems provide a new metaphor for communication.

With text being produced and stored on the computer, there arise new possibilities for examining the writing process. Some text editors offer a "replay" facility, which re-enacts an entire editing session, allowing student and teacher to see the process of text creation. Sirc (1989), for example, described how he uses this approach to model revision. He records every keystroke he makes during his revision of a student paper. Then he replays the revision session discussing the reasons for each step in the process. This approach allows students to peer inside the expert writer's process of revision. Computer-based tools can support many aspects of the writing process.

Computers as Communication Environments. Computers can be used to foster social interaction and thereby contribute to language development and learning. It is through feedback from others, peer tutoring, and sharing ideas, that reading and writing skills develop. Today, conferencing systems, electronic mail, and environments for collaboration on single computers are being used to facilitate these sorts of social interaction.

Electronic networks are being used increasingly for communication among students and teachers. Although electronic message technology was originally designed for government and business, it is playing an increasingly important role in classrooms. Electronic mail was possibly the most successful component of a CAI system installed at a school for deaf children (Goldenberg, Carter, Russell, Stokes, & Sylvester, 1983). Today, we see deliberate construction of electronic mail systems for learning, such as the Computer Chronicles News Network, which allows children around the world to share news items; Earth-Lab (Brienne & Goldman, 1989; Goldman & D. Newman, in press; D. Newman, Goldman, Brienne, Jackson, & Magzamen, 1989), which promotes science learning through shared data and electronic mail within a school; and the National Geographic Kids Network (Lenk, 1989; Foster, Julyan, & Mokros, 1988), in which students collect and share data on topics such as acid rain, water quality, weather, trash, health, and energy.

Teachers are also beginning to use electronic networks for communicating. In chapter 7 we describe how teachers developed a community through the use of electronic mail. Their shared need to learn better ways of teaching was partially met through the exchange of classroom ideas and mutual encouragement over an electronic network. The network made exchange of messages much faster than ordinary mail and eased the task of sending the same message to many people at once. Moreover, other writing already in electronic form, such as students' texts or a teacher's text written for a university course, could be easily transmitted and shared with other teachers. There is now, for example, a *Computers and Composition Digest* distributed electronically. Teachers, researchers, and software developers interact through issues of the digest, which are constructed out of electronic mail messages and sent via networks to over 600 sites.

Research on using real-time communication networks to teach English language skills or composition is also underway (Batson, 1988; Bruce & Peyton,

1990; Sirc, 1988; Thompson, 1987). In these systems, students engage in a written form of conversation. Their typed messages are transmitted immediately to others in the group. Such an environment requires students to formulate their ideas as written text but allows faster response than traditional writing or even electronic mail. Users of these systems have claimed that entirely new classroom dynamics are created in which students participate more and begin for the first time to see writing and reading as means for communicating and learning.

Computer-based communication environments connect people together in new ways; they also entail new ways of connecting and presenting texts (see Bruce, 1987). Explicit links between texts allow readers to travel from one document to another, or from one place within a document to another. The computer can help a reader follow trails of cross-reference without losing the original context. Electronic document systems also facilitate co-authoring of texts. A group of children, for example, can create a common electronic notebook, by making their own contributions, viewing and editing one another's items, then linking the items together. Both authors and readers can now use the same integrated tools to create, browse, and develop text. They can move through material created by other people, add their own links and annotations, and merge the material with their own writings. In consequence, the boundaries between author and reader are being reshaped.

Roles for the Computer in QUILL.   We included both computer tools and computer environments in QUILL. The tools facilitated composing, revising, planning, sharing, and publishing aspects of writing. Writer's Assistant was a text editor with all of the standard word processing functions, as well as several special-purpose tools to help beginning writers. PLANNER was a tool to help students generate ideas for writing and organize them with respect to questions or categories. LIBRARY included tools with which students could locate other students' texts using keywords and author/title lists, then read those texts using the text editor or print them out.

The role of the computer as communication environment was the most central one for QUILL (Liebling, 1984). Because students could create their own "programs" within PLANNER and share both these programs and the generated ideas, PLANNER functioned as a communication environment. LIBRARY was also an environment for communication, not just a set of tools, because within a classroom, a shared LIBRARY disk was a new way for readers and writers to interact. The prototypical communication environment, though, was MAILBAG, a simple in-class electronic mail system, with which students could write to each other, to the teacher, to a group, or to a bulletin board. Moreover, if the class had access to a telephone line, a modem, and an electronic network, they could send messages to audiences beyond their classroom. In the next chapter we describe the QUILL software in more detail and, in addition, the writing activities and teacher support that were integral to its use.

CONCLUSION

The increasing demands for literacy in a postindustrial society coupled with the movement from isolated cultures to a world culture have heightened concerns for literacy development. This concern should be addressed with an awareness of the capabilities of new technologies, for they have on the one hand caused us to rethink the very definition of literacy, and on the other provided us with new ways to address literacy needs. In classrooms of today we can see teachers searching for ways to enhance literacy development given the demands of a changing society and the potential of new technologies.

Accordingly, when we began to design QUILL, we acted on the principle that the most productive development efforts would emerge from considering our goals for literacy development in concert with what we saw as the most appropriate uses of the technology. This meant looking for those activities that fit with our pedagogical goals for teaching writing and simultaneously took the greatest advantage of microcomputer technology (Fig. 2.1).

Identifying this intersection required careful study of the writing process, the teaching and learning of writing, and the characteristics of the then-current technology. In the next chapter we describe how QUILL evolved as an innovation that attempted to make the best possible use of the available technology to foster literacy development.

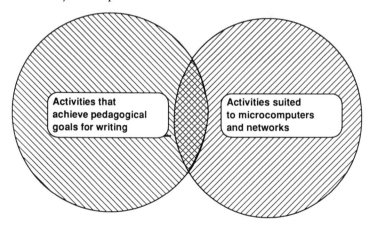

Activities that achieve pedagogical goals for writing

Activities suited to microcomputers and networks

FIG. 2.1. Intersection of activities that meet pedagogical goals with those suitable for microcomputers.

Chapter 3

QUILL: A System to
Support Literacy Development

In order to promote functional learning environments for literacy development, QUILL provided a system containing both computer-based tools and environments for writing. The previous chapter identifies six pedagogical goals that served as intermediate concepts between the broad theory underlying QUILL and the details of its component parts. In this chapter, we fill in the details of the idealization of QUILL and how that idealization was communicated to teachers.

Such an analysis of an innovation's idealization is a critical element in a situated evaluation. In later chapters, we look at different realizations that emerged as teachers and students re-created the innovation. In order to make sense of the various realizations of QUILL in classrooms, it is necessary to explicate the idealization in detail. This includes more than the hardware and software, since the QUILL system, as presented to teachers, included writing activities, materials for teachers, teacher workshops, and other manifestations of our pedagogical philosophy.

By the standards of the 1990s, the QUILL software is slow and limited in what it can do. But at the time of its development, QUILL was relatively advanced, pushing the limits of the technology. Even today, while features from QUILL can be found in various other programs, few, if any, of these programs contain as coherent a package of tools and writing environments as did QUILL, and there is nothing comparable we know of for elementary school students. In any case, the point here is neither to praise nor to criticize QUILL, but rather to use its implementation as a vehicle for studying educational innovation and change.

It is convenient to think of the whole QUILL system as a three-part innovation. First, there was software to support a new approach to using computers for teaching writing. Second, there was a new method of writing instruction that extended the writing process approach to take advantage of new technologies. And third, there was a call for a new style of classroom management, partly as a prerequisite for the successful use of the software and writing activities, but also as a desirable goal in itself, as in the case of peer collaboration in writing.

As with any innovation, there were tangible manifestations of the different aspects of QUILL. First, there was a software package that ran on the Apple II+ or IIe computer. The software provided writing tools that were embodied in the Writer's Assistant text-editing program, and writing environments (PLANNER for generating and organizing ideas for writing, LIBRARY for storing and sharing texts, and MAILBAG for exchanging messages). Each program had specific capabilities designed to assist student writers. The programs could be used individually or in conjunction with each other during a larger writing task. Second, there were activities for using the software, presented in written form in the *QUILL Teacher's Guide* (Bruce, Rubin, & Loucks, 1984). Third, there were various mechanisms for supporting teachers and helping them manage the use of QUILL in the classroom. These included a workshop for preparing teachers to use QUILL, classroom support by the QUILL developers, a hotline for help with computer questions, and local facilitators, people in a school or school district who developed special expertise to help QUILL teachers. The *QUILL Teacher's Guide* also contained the "Cookbook," a series of suggested lessons for introducing QUILL and the writing process to a classroom.

In this chapter, we present these components of the QUILL system as much as possible as the teachers perceived them. We have included descriptions from the *QUILL Teacher's Guide*, to give an accurate rendition of what the teachers actually saw as the idealization of QUILL.

QUILL SOFTWARE

The QUILL software was designed to help in the creation of functional learning environments that involved extensive writing and reading. It had many features that addressed one or more of our six pedagogical goals (PGs). It ran on an Apple II+ or Apple IIe computer with 64K bytes of memory and required two floppy disk drives, a monochrome monitor, an 80-character, upper and lower case card, and a printer. Students used the printer to obtain copies of the texts they wrote to take home, to show their teachers and friends, or to do projects such as a class newspaper. At the time of QUILL's development, even this use of a printer was an innovation, as connecting a computer

to a printer was not universally considered necessary, even for writing activities. The version of QUILL presented to teachers in Alaska included activities
in which their students could send electronic messages to students in other
schools both inside and outside of Alaska. For these, teachers needed a modem to connect the computer to a telephone line, a way to pay telephone
charges, and access to a computer network.

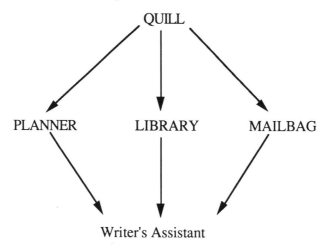

FIG. 3.1.   The QUILL software.

QUILL comprised four interrelated programs (see Fig. 3.1). Writer's Assistant was a general word processing program that was never invoked by name
but was accessed indirectly by any function in PLANNER, LIBRARY, or
MAILBAG, such as ''seeing'' someone else's text in the LIBRARY. PLAN-
NER was a tool that helped students organize ideas for writing, then share their
newly created organizing tools. LIBRARY was a writing environment in which
students could make their writing accessible to others by storing it with the
full authors' names, the full title, and keywords indicating topic, genre, or other
characteristics of the piece. MAILBAG was an in-class message system in which
students could send messages to other students, the teacher, small groups, or
a bulletin board. Students decided which program to use according to their
purpose for writing and chose it from the following computer menu (Fig. 3.2).

   In what follows we describe each program and its suggested uses, beginning with the most general and most widely used program, LIBRARY.

LIBRARY

LIBRARY created an environment that enabled students and teachers to share
their writing. Students and teachers could write about any topic they chose
and store their writing in LIBRARY so that it was available to others. In a

```
                        QUILL

     1) PLANNER       Helps you to think of ideas for
                      writing. You can take notes and
                      get a list of your notes when
                      you are finished.
     2) LIBRARY       Stores your writing so you can
                      change or add to it later and
                      others can read it.
     3) MAILBAG       Allows you to send messages
                      to your teachers and your
                      classmates or read the messages
                      they have sent to you.
```

FIG. 3.2.   The QUILL main menu.

typical word processing program, at the time of QUILL's development, texts were stored and accessed with short, often obscure file names. In contrast, pieces of writing in LIBRARY were stored and accessed by the author's full name, the co-author's name, the full title, and up to five keywords. This piece of QUILL was actually an electronic model of the familiar card catalog system in a library.

LIBRARY provided a social environment for students' writing in which sharing, evaluating, reading, and editing one's own and other people's writing were united in a communicative framework. It promoted sharing because each composition was indexed in ways that invited access. Student writers needed to think about their audience since they had to choose keywords by which other students would choose to read their pieces. Students using QUILL often responded to this need by designating one of their five allowed keywords to ''advertise'' their piece, using eye-catching words such as ''loony'' along with more straightforward informative keywords.

When a student chose the LIBRARY option, the options in Fig. 3.3 would appear:

```
                        LIBRARY

     1) SEE           Read LIBRARY entries by
                      choosing keywords or titles
     2) ADD           Put a new entry into the LIBRARY
     3) CHANGE        Change an old LIBRARY entry
     4) QUIT USING LIBRARY
```

FIG. 3.3.   The LIBRARY main menu.

A student who wanted to SEE an existing entry could select it using three separate indices. As in a card catalogue in a library, entries were indexed by *title and author*, and by subject, or *keyword*. Alternatively, they could be accessed by specifying their *entry number*. Thus, after selecting the SEE option from the screen above, the student would see the following (Fig. 3.4):

Do you want to choose an entry by using:

1. Keywords
2. Title and author
3. Entry number

FIG. 3.4.   Three methods for accessing LIBRARY entries.

If the student decided to choose an entry by *keyword*, a screen something like Fig. 3.5 would appear:

There are entries for these keywords:

1.	Review	6.	Entertainment
2.	Food	7.	Delicious
3.	Pizza	8.	Italian
4.	Animals	9.	Games
5.	Restaurant	10.	Movies

FIG. 3.5.   Choosing entries by keyword.

Following the selection of a *keyword*, the student would see a list of all entries with that *keyword* (Fig. 3.6):

Choosing the *title and author* option would produce a list of all the entries on the disk from which a student could choose a single piece of writing; choosing by *entry number* would call up a single entry.

In any case, students could choose to print out the entry selected or view it on the screen using Writer's Assistant. A sample restaurant review from the *QUILL Teacher's Guide*, is shown in Fig. 3.7.

Students could also ADD to a LIBRARY disk. After choosing option 2 on the first menu they would be placed in the Writer's Assistant program and could write any text. When the draft was done, the writer could add *keywords* (using a procedure that was also used for planners). First, a list of previously used *keywords* was presented (Fig. 3.8):

```
Keyword: Pizza
There are 3 entries with this keyword.

    TITLE               AUTHOR #1          AUTHOR #2
 1. Rita's Pizza         Steve
    Keywords: Pizza/Review/Italian

 2. Gigliotti's          Joan               Vinnie
    Keywords: Pizza/Restaurant

 3. House of Pizza       Ed
    Keywords: Review/Pizza/Delicious
```

FIG. 3.6.   Selecting a LIBRARY entry.

Pizza lovers, stay away from Rita's Pizza! I'm sorry to say that
poor Rita hasn't the knack for making pizza. When I ate there,
I had to wait 25 minutes for my pizza. The crust was mushy and
the sauce tasted like tomato juice. The center of the pizza had too
much oil on it and it dripped all over my hands and the table
when I picked it up. Maybe I went there on a bad day. It just
seemed like everything was lousy. The only good thing about
Rita's Pizza was that it had a room with video games.

FIG. 3.7.   A sample LIBRARY entry.

```
You may choose one of these words to add
to your list of keywords.

 1.  Story            7.  Visitor
 2.  Zoo              8.  Friend
 3.  Review           9.  Food
 4.  Animal          10.  Cold
 5.  Practice        11.  Shower
 6.  Revision
```

FIG. 3.8.   Choosing keywords to attach to a LIBRARY entry.

The writer could select up to five *keywords*. Following the selection of previously used *keywords* a screen for entering novel ones would appear (Fig. 3.9):

```
Keywords: /Review/Practice/
You can add your own keyword. If you don't
want to add a word, press the <ESC> key and
then press <RETURN>. Type your word and
press <RETURN>.


Games

You gave "Games." Is that okay?
Type YES or NO and press <RETURN>.
```

FIG. 3.9.   Adding a new keyword to a LIBRARY entry.

In this example, the writer has already chosen "review" and "practice" as keywords and is about to add the keyword, "games." This third keyword will be attached to the writer's entry, and will also be added to the master list for possible use by other writers. Keywords were one way to address PG2 (integration of reading and writing). Students saw that their own writing could be accessed and read by others, just as they could find and read what their classmates had written.

Each entry could have one or two authors. (Additional authors could be added by using groups or conjoining names.) The explicit request for a second author was a way the software addressed PG5 (collaboration).

Finally, the student could CHANGE previous entries in LIBRARY. He or she would select an entry to revise and then follow the same procedure used for ADDing. CHANGE was delineated as a separate menu item in order to highlight for teachers and students both the possibility and desirability of revision, thus reifying PG6 (revision).

LIBRARY encouraged writing with an awareness of audience, facilitated sharing, and eased the teacher's record-keeping burden by providing an easy way to assemble a student's portfolio. The fact that a single composition may have been written by more than one student presented no problem with QUILL's LIBRARY. The *QUILL Teacher's Guide* presented the following vision of its use:

A teacher wants to help students develop skills in giving instructions. She decides that the students will each contribute an article to a class "How To Do It Manual." Leah wants to write some instructions for building a bird feeder and add it to LIBRARY. She uses the QUILL Library disk that contains other "How To Do It" articles. She adds an entry to this disk, which already contains five articles by other students in the class. When she finishes her article, Leah types her title, "How to Build a Bird Feeder to Attract Birds," and then her name. The program then asks for one or more keywords—words that will give others a good idea of what her article is about. Leah looks at the list of existing keywords, generated by students who have already entered their pieces. She selects "outdoor" from the list as one of her keywords. She also wants to add another, more specific keyword to the existing list. She types in the word "carpentry." The program automatically updates the keyword list, and "carpentry" will appear the next time anyone uses this disk, either to add their own article or read those other students have written. Her article thus becomes part of the "How To Do It Manual," automatically indexed for quick referral.

Later, Arnold tells Leah he has read her article and couldn't follow one piece of the instructions. After she explains it to him, he suggests a way she might make her piece more understandable. Together, they rework the offending paragraph and save the new version. Arnold then has the opportunity to add his name as a second author of the piece and, with Leah's permission, he does. Other students will now see both authors' names when they list all the articles on this disk.

Leah used LIBRARY to add information; Jeff wants to use it to find information. He needs some information about sharks for an adventure story he is writing. He chooses the LIBRARY disk containing an *Animal Encyclopedia* his class has put together and looks through the keywords. The list is long and starts out: arctic, cats, fish, horses, whales . . . Sharks do not appear on the list, so Jeff decides to look at all entries with the keyword "fish." After he chooses this keyword, the titles of four articles about fish are shown on the screen, one of which is called "Denizens of the Deep." He suspects the article might be about sharks, so he decides to read it. The article gives him some new information about sharks, but it is not as focused as the article he is writing. He decides to add his article to the *Animal Encyclopedia* when it is finished, and to add the keyword, "sharks" that will make it easier for fellow students to find his article. Easy access to LIBRARY provides important information for Jeff's writing, as well as motivation for him to contribute his own piece to fill in a gap in the *Animal Encyclopedia*.

PLANNER

PLANNER was designed to help students generate and organize ideas and reflect on their writing as it took shape. It was a specific way that the software was designed to help achieve PG1: to help children develop skills for planning and critical thinking. It could also be used to help achieve PG6: to encourage students to do more sophisticated kinds of revision.

A planner[1] consisted of a series of questions or prompts that encouraged students to brainstorm, organize, or revise their piece. In addition, because

---

[1]"PLANNER" refers to the QUILL program, which operated upon a list of questions generated by the teacher or a student.

students could create and modify planners as well as use them, planners could be shared and edited, just like any other piece of writing. The process of constructing a planner was, then, a metacognitive process: one in which students had to think about the process of writing.

When a student chose the PLANNER option, the menu in Fig. 3.10 would appear:

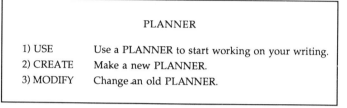

FIG. 3.10.   The PLANNER main menu.

The USE, CREATE, and MODIFY options were analogous to those for LIBRARY (SEE, ADD, CHANGE), the essential difference being that the text within a planner was interpreted to produce a question–response interaction with a student. Planners were selected by exactly the same procedure as for LIBRARY, by *keywords, title and author*, or *entry number*. Thus, after selecting the USE option, the student would see the menu in Fig. 3.11.

```
Do you want to choose a PLANNER by using:

   1. Keywords
   2. Title and author
   3. Entry number
```

FIG. 3.11.   Three methods for accessing planners.

If the student decided to choose a planner by *title and author*, something like Fig. 3.12 would appear.

In this example, there are three planners on the disk. They are listed in order of creation, with *title, authors*, and *keywords*. If the student decided to choose a planner by selecting a *keyword* first, a screen with all the *keywords* on that disk would appear first (Fig. 3.13), just as in the LIBRARY program.

Following the selection of a *keyword*, the student would then choose a planner from a list of all the planners with that *keyword*. Once a planner was selected, the student would see an introductory message (written by the creator of the planner), such as the one in Fig. 3.14.

After seeing the introductory text, the student would see a list of topics, ideas, or questions posed by the planner. The idea was to select from this list

There are 3 PLANNERS on this disk.

	TITLE	AUTHOR #1	AUTHOR#2
1.	Lab Report	Susan	Zack
	Keywords: /Report/Science/		
2.	Book Review	Jenne	Steve
	Keywords:	/Report/Review/	
3.	Mystery Story	Jonathan	
	Keywords:	/Story/	

FIG. 3.12.   Selecting a planner.

There are PLANNERS for these keywords:

1. Story   5. Newspaper
2. Report   6. Entertainment
3. Science   7. Review
4. Food

FIG. 3.13.   Choosing a planner by keywords.

This planner suggests topics for you to include
in a review of a restaurant. Choose those that are
appropriate for your review.

FIG. 3.14.   An introductory message for a planner.

and respond with anything from short answers to extended text. In the case of the restaurant review, the student might see the list in Fig. 3.15.

After selecting an item from the list, the student could then write any amount of text on that topic. In the example here, most of the questions suggest short replies, but students could write as much as they wished. Other planners contained more open-ended questions. The notes created in this way could be used as a starting point for a later writing task.

Students or teachers could also create and revise their own planners. They used Writer's Assistant to produce a text file with the introductory message followed by the list of topics or questions, which were later presented in an appropriate format to the user of the planner.

Planners could have a variety of purposes. They were often used to support brainstorming. They could be used to remind the writer of items to include

---

1)   What is the name of the restaurant?
2)   Where is it located?
3)   On a scale of 1 to 10, how would you rate the
     restaurant?
4)   Would you go back again?
5)   Who owns it?
6)   What kinds of foods are served there?
7)   What is their specialty?
8)   How is the service?

FIG. 3.15.   Questions from a planner.

in a text within a conventionalized genre, as in the restaurant review example. They could be used as aids to revision (PG6), by suggesting questions to consider in evaluating a first draft. They were also used to structure data collection that led to expository writing. Students in one class created interview forms; in another they used planners for recording laboratory data.

The *QUILL Teacher's Guide* presented the following vision of the use of PLANNER:

> To use planners as an idea generating device, a teacher might involve students in a brainstorming session to generate a list of questions or topics to consider for an assignment. If they are writing movie reviews, the students might consider acting quality, photography, intended audience and subject, to name a few. The teacher can make this list into a planner on the computer, so that when students begin composing their movie review, they can use it to help them start generating ideas. Later in the writing process, PLANNER can help students revise their work. It might ask students to identify a possible weak point in their piece or think of another example they might include. Using a revision Planner students can rework a written draft.
>
> For example, Steve and Karen are going to write a review of their favorite restaurant, Chich's Parlor. Using their class-generated Planner for restaurant reviews, they type in responses to most of the topic questions (overall assessment, best food, price, atmosphere, location, hours, needed improvements, appropriate patrons). They print their notes on the printer and can then decide how to organize what they want to say, composing sentences and paragraphs from their notes.
>
> Once Steve and Karen have finished the review, they can use a revision Planner to help them refine their work. This Planner might ask them if they were persuasive enough when they described Chich's as the best restaurant, or what changes could be made to the end or the beginning of the review that would make the piece more persuasive, so that a reader might decide to visit that ice cream parlor.

Across the room, Melinda and Jose are working on a review of a movie. They decide to modify Steve and Karen's restaurant review planner since they feel some of it is relevant to their piece. They keep the questions on overall assessment, appropriate patrons, and needed improvements and substitute for the other questions some that are more useful for their purpose. They then post a note on the electronic bulletin board using MAILBAG (see later) telling everyone that they have constructed a movie review Planner, in case someone else would like to use it.

MAILBAG

MAILBAG supported direct communication among individual students, groups of students, and teachers. It combined features of the post office, the telephone, and a bulletin board; written messages could be sent between individuals, or a message could be posted to provide information to a group.

MAILBAG made concrete the ideas of audience and purpose that are so central to effective writing. Students could not use MAILBAG without specifying an audience, as that was as much a part of using the environment as addressing a letter is in the postal system. Moreover, their audiences were real (fellow classmates and teacher) and were likely to respond. In several classrooms, teachers found that students communicated with them in ways they had not in the past, making suggestions about scheduling (one student said he liked having the week's schedule on the blackboard) and subject matter (another student requested more time for art instruction), or discussing personal problems. Some of the most interesting MAILBAG entries are probably those no one will ever read. In several classrooms, teachers told students that MAILBAG was ''private'' and that no adult would ever eavesdrop on their electronic conversations. Not surprisingly, those disks filled rapidly—but the teachers have yet to see what is on them.

When a student chose the MAILBAG option, the following screen would appear (Fig. 3.16):

```
                          MAILBAG

        1)   READ      Read messages to you, a group,
                       or the Bulletin Board.
        2)   SEND      Write messages to other people, groups or the
                       Bulletin Board.
        3)   QUIT USING MAILBAG
```

FIG. 3.16.   The MAILBAG main menu.

Note that there was no modify or change option as with PLANNER and LIBRARY. Although in software terms MAILBAG was simply a program that provided an alternate method for accessing files, we intended it to be interpreted by students and teachers as an electronic mail system. Thus, as with ordinary postal mail or other electronic mail systems, once mail was "sent," it could not be changed. We expected that this limitation would foster a different type of writing—more informal, more conversational, less "perfect." The contrast between LIBRARY and MAILBAG was intended to stress the different purposes writing can serve in a variety of functional learning environments. In general, MAILBAG was a reification in software of PG4 (meaningful communication with real audiences).

If the student wanted to READ mail, the screen in Fig. 3.17 would appear:

Which would you like to do?
    1. See YOUR OWN mail.
    2. See the mail of a GROUP.
    3. Look at the BULLETIN BOARD.

FIG. 3.17.   Choosing among mailboxes.

Mail could be sent to a student's or teacher's real name or to an agreed-on pseudonym. To use option 2, mail to a GROUP, several students would have to decide on a group name (which they sometimes kept secret) to use on MAILBAG. In contrast, the BULLETIN BOARD was essentially open mail for all to read. Following the entry of the person's or the group's name, a list of messages would appear. From this list the reader would select which messages to read and/or print out.

The writer of a MAILBAG message used Writer's Assistant, just as for PLANNER and LIBRARY. Once the message was complete, the following screen (Fig. 3.18) would appear:

Type subject and press <RETURN>.

Type sender #1 and press <RETURN>.

Type sender #2 and press <RETURN>.
(If there isn't another sender press
the <ESC> key and then press <RETURN>.)

FIG. 3.18.   Providing header information for a MAILBAG message.

Note that QUILL provided for two "senders." In LIBRARY and PLANNER, there was also space for two co-authors. The software was designed this way to encourage collaboration (PG5) and because having a limited number of computers inclined most teachers to have students work in pairs or small groups. If more than two students worked together, they could use group names or compounds, such as "Ralph S & Maria J" for the authors.

After author(s) were specified, the next screen (Fig. 3.19) asked for recipients.

You can send your message to up to five
addresses. If you don't want to send your
message anywhere else, choose #4.
    1. Send this message to a PERSON.
    2. Send it to a GROUP.
    3. Post it on the BULLETIN BOARD.
    4. None of the above.
Type a number and press <RETURN>.

FIG. 3.19.   Choosing recipients for a MAILBAG message.

The teacher's guide presented the following vision of MAILBAG's use:

MAILBAG has two complementary functions. First, students can send messages. In a classroom with an active MAILBAG, Jacqueline sends a message to Marilyn about a very embarrassing experience at the movies on Saturday. Matt sends a message to the Animal Club, asking for good sources of information about sharks. The teacher sends a message to all the boys telling them that a new Boy Scout troop is being formed and giving them information about joining. Jon uses the Bulletin Board part of MAILBAG to ask the class if any of their grandparents were born in this town. He has an oral history assignment and wants to interview some old timers about their school days in the one room school. In each of these cases, MAILBAG is an efficient vehicle for sharing and seeking information, and at the same time providing opportunities for written expression that are not often present in school.

MAILBAG's second function is to receive messages. In that same classroom, each student "checks his or her mail." First, students look at their personal mail by typing their name and receiving a list of their messages, selecting those they wish to read. They can then request mail for specific groups to which they belong. Finally, they can view the Bulletin Board and read messages that have been posted for everyone. For example, Maria consults MAILBAG by typing her name. She has two messages, one titled "Urgent" and the other "Secret Letter." She reads both and learns that her mother has left her lunch money for her at the office (a message conveniently left for her by the teacher), and that her ardent (but as yet unidentified) admirer wants to meet her after school. When she asks for messages for the Soccer club, she finds out there is a practice on Thursday after school. Consulting the Bulletin Board, she learns that Wallie is looking for recommendations for a new adventure book to read and is soliciting opinions for and against each book suggested.

Writer's Assistant

Writer's Assistant (Levin, Boruta, & Vasconcellos, 1983) was a general word processor that students used for any writing. It contained all the standard word processing capabilities, such as insert text, delete, replace, and find. By making textual changes easier, we hoped Writer's Assistant would make revision more frequent and more comprehensive, in pursuit of PG6, facilitating revision.

To encourage revision, the QUILL curriculum and workshop followed many of the suggestions developed by other research on the writing process (Graves, 1978, 1982; Newkirk & Atwell, 1988). We recommended the use of writing conferences—meetings between the teacher and individual student writers, or small group meetings—in which students would discuss problems they were having with their writing. The writing conference was a setting in which the focus was to be on meaning, not simply on formal details, and where the reasons for changes could be discussed in terms of the audience and purpose for the text.

In the Alaska QUILL workshops, we used examples from other QUILL classrooms to illustrate meaning-centered revisions. The effects of one teacher's comments can be seen in changes across two drafts (Figs. 3.20 & 3.21) of a "New Jersey resolution" written by two fourth-grade boys. The assignment was to develop a resolution that the legislature could pass to help improve New Jersey.

                    Drugs are Dumb
Benjamin M.   Darren S.

What is bothering us the most in New Jersey is underaged kids
are taking drugs. their not getting enough education. Some kids
even get killed! Adults should educate their children not to take
drugs. It would take a few months or weeks to get over this problem.
It is important to solve this problem because sometimes people get
killed.

Keywords: /psychiatrist/drugs/children/killed/education/

FIG. 3.20.   First draft of "Improving New Jersey" composition.

Their discussion with their teacher about this piece focused on the need for snappy conclusions and on how long it would really take to kick a drug habit. The emphasis was on the content of the resolution, not simply on grammatical features. Benjamin and Darren then produced the final draft (Fig. 3.21; changes in boldface).

To accomplish these structural changes with a typewriter or paper and pencil the writer would be forced to recopy the whole piece. A text editor can make revision easier to accomplish. It can change a student's concept of changing a text from "erasing something until there is a hole in the paper" to "pressing a few keys on the computer."

Dangerous Damaging Drugs
Benjamin M.   Darren S.

What is bothering us the most in New Jersey is underaged kids are
taking drugs. **They're** not getting enough education. Some kids even
get killed! Adults should educate **their children not to take drugs or
not to get involved with drugs. To get help you should go to a
psychiatrist. Try not to take drugs.** If you take drugs, go for help! It
would take **an unlimited amount of time** to get over this problem. It is
important to solve this problem because sometimes people get killed.
So be smart, make sure you don't take drugs!

Keywords: /psychiatrist/drugs/children/killed/education/

FIG. 3.21.   Final draft of "Improving New Jersey" composition.

Despite QUILL's focus on meaning-centered revision, we also promoted
the idea that computers could help with low-level formal corrections of things
such as spelling, punctuation, and subject–verb agreement. There was, for example, a command called MIX, which displayed all the sentences in a student's text (defined as a set of words followed by a period) starting at the left
margin (Fig. 3.22).

A student could quickly scan the list of sentences and see if any first letters
of sentences were not capitalized, if end punctuation were missing, if there

---

We'll tell you some things about Shungnak.
In the winter it is very cold.
In the summer it is very warm.
A lot of people in Shungnak like to go hunting and go get wood.
They shoot a lot of animals and bring them home and share.
A lot of people go camping in the summer.
If they seine they will get a lot of fish.
They smoke salmon fish for the long winter.
Some people make dried fish for fish for the winter.
In the winter we have dog races.
Sometimes we need water.
We just get ice.
Next we put hot water so it could melt.
We go ice fishing in the winter.
It is fun playing slide in the winter on top of steep hills.

FIG. 3.22.   A MIXed text in sentence format.

> We'll tell you some things about Shungnak. In the winter it is very cold. In the summer it is very warm. A lot of people in Shungnak like to go hunting and go get wood. They shoot a lot of animals and bring them home and share. A lot of people go camping in the summer. If they seine they will get a lot of fish. They smoke salmon fish for the long winter. Some people make dried fish for fish for the winter. In the winter we have dog races. Sometimes we need water. We just get ice. Next we put hot water so it could melt. We go ice fishing in the winter. It is fun playing slide in the winter on top of steep hills.

FIG. 3.23.   A MIXed text in paragraph format.

were any run-on sentences, if the sentence length or structure was repetitious, or if there were any sentence fragments. The computer would not identify any of these problems; it just made it easier for students to see and repair problems. The sentences could then be reformatted into a paragraph (Fig. 3.23).

QUILL also included a feature (WORD) that could be used for limited checking of spelling and word choice. It used a dictionary that students and teachers themselves compiled. If a word was in the dictionary, the writer could highlight it, for example, "deer," and the computer would present choices of similarly spelled (e.g., "dear") words with their definitions.

The *QUILL Teacher's Guide* gave the following description of the use of Writer's Assistant:

> The Writer's Assistant helps students enter and revise written text quickly, easily, and clearly. Using this program, students can write their pieces, then correct spelling, spacing, and punctuation; remove, add or rearrange words, sentences, or paragraphs; try out new ways of expressing the same ideas. Editing can be done while entering text onto the computer, or it can take place after the student works on a printed-out version of the original text either alone, with other students, or after conferencing with the teacher. Revisions are easy, and they eliminate the frustration of "spoiling" a piece of work by erasing, crossing out, or having to start over. Help commands are included as part of the Writer's Assistant, to offer on-screen assistance when using the Writer's Assistant commands.
>
> The Writer's Assistant can be used with the MAILBAG, LIBRARY, and PLANNER. When students store a piece of writing in the LIBRARY or write a message using the MAILBAG, they can edit what they are writing. QUILL's Writer's Assistant is a valuable tool for facilitating writing for all students, although it is especially helpful for those who are easily discouraged or mistake-prone, or for students who are "messy" writers.

Summary

The QUILL software provided tools to facilitate writing by students and teachers, and environments to foster real communication. In addition to these

TABLE 3.1
QUILL Software

Pedagogical Goal	Software Features
PG1. Planning	PLANNER: Creating and using planners
	Reading others' entries in LIBRARY
PG2. Integration of reading and writing	LIBRARY as a shared text environment
	SEE in LIBRARY = > texts will be read by others
PG3. Publishing	Writer's Assistant formatting features
PG4. Meaningful communication	MAILBAG: Messages to individuals, groups,
	Bulletin Board
	Keywords as way to facilitate access to one's text
PG5. Collaboration	Slots for two authors
	Bulletin Board and group mail
	Keywords as shared indexing scheme
PG6. Revision	MIX and WORD in Writer's Assistant
	CHANGE as separate option
	Revision planners

broad purposes, the software embodied specific features designed to satisfy our six pedagogical goals. Some of these are summarized in Table 3.1.

QUILL ACTIVITIES

The QUILL software had many features to support our six pedagogical goals. But the technology alone could not change classroom writing practices. Doing so required the adoption of new writing activities and, for some teachers, a new approach to teaching writing.

We hoped that individual teachers would create most of the QUILL activities for their own classrooms out of setting-specific interests and needs, as that sensitivity to local audience and purpose was central to the QUILL philosophy. But we realized that teachers needed support in getting to the point where they could develop their own activities. The *QUILL Teacher's Guide* (Bruce, Rubin, & Loucks, 1984) described suggested QUILL activities in a written form. It also contained a general description of QUILL and software documentation, but its primary purpose was to support teachers in developing effective writing activities that addressed one or more of our pedagogical goals.

For example, the teacher's guide described the process of producing a class newspaper on the computer, and this became a popular activity in QUILL classrooms. Assembling a newspaper addressed several pedagogical goals. Students could identify a real audience for their articles—other class members, other students in the school and parents—thus supporting PG4 (meaningful communication with real audiences). Writing jointly authored articles encouraged focused social interaction among the students, thus supporting PG5 (collaboration). The computer made writing and editing articles simpler, thus supporting both PG6 (revision) and PG3 (publishing). The *QUILL Teacher's Guide* contained suggestions about how to manage a class newspaper for those teachers who needed help in getting started. Below is an extract from the guide for a class newspaper activity (from p. 85):

Modern Times: A Class Newspaper

Programs: PLANNER/LIBRARY

Materials:

Samples of the various types of newspaper articles
PLANNER and LIBRARY disks

Purpose:

- To write in different formats: news items, book and TV reviews, sports stories, want ads
- To edit and revise for appearance and clarity
- To encourage students to evaluate and make judgements about the interest value of different articles

Preparation:

1. Choose a managing editor and an editor for each section of the newspaper.
2. Decide what sections should appear in the newspaper: for example, class, school, or town news section; sports section; book, movie and TV review section; poetry section; classified ads; biographies; notices of coming events; joke section; opinion section; and so on.
3. Prepare models and/or explanations of news items not familiar to the students.
4. Create a publishing schedule. Decide when the newspaper will come out.
5. CREATE Planners for news articles, sports articles, and so on.

Procedure:

1. Have students write one or more news articles either individually or collaboratively in LIBRARY.
2. Students should use keywords to classify articles: ad, news item, recipe, review.
3. Section editors should use keywords to find their articles and discuss revisions to make the articles clearer or more interesting.
4. Each section editor uses Writer's Assistant to make revisions. The revised article is then submitted to the managing editor for approval.
5. Managing editor will use Writer's Assistant to prepare a masthead. A table of contents might also be made. These can be prepared as LIBRARY entries.
6. Add LIBRARY title and author listing as a headline and byline for each article.

7. The managing editor is responsible for the overall layout of the mast-head, sections, and so on. Each section editor is responsible for the lay-out of his or her section.

8. The newspaper can be produced by the printer in 80-column format. Make enough copies for everyone in the class plus extras. Alternatively, the class can produce 40 column versions of each article and paste together a master copy for distribution.

Here are some of the other activities described in the guide.

"Where I'd Like to Live": Students do research on different places they would like to live, using encyclopedias, travel brochures, maps, and magazines. They use PLANNER to record what they learn and LIBRARY to store descriptions of their fantasy choices. *Comment:* This activity involved a use of PLANNER as an information recording and organizing device, thus emphasizing a different aspect of planning (PG1). It also highlighted a way of integrating reading and writing (PG2), as students explored various sources in order to gather information for their choice locales.

"Animal Encyclopedia": Rather than simply using reference books written by others, students can create their own. One idea is an encyclopedia for animals built around a classification system the students themselves devise. *Comment:* This activity was intended to foster collaboration (PG5) and the integration of writing and reading (PG2) as students read each other's encyclopedia entries and added their own contributions to the class text.

"Disease Digest": Students do research on the symptoms and the treatments for diseases they have had. They use magazines, brochures from hospitals or clinics and books such as *Baby and Child Care*, by Benjamin Spock (1985). They create and publish (PG3) their own digest of childhood diseases indexed with *keywords* such as "contagious," "headache," and "spots." *Comment:* Similar to the animal encyclopedia, this activity fosters integration of reading and writing (PG2) and collaboration (PG5).

"Classified Ads": Students work in groups to study the classified section from a newspaper. They create their own classified ads for things they want to sell or exchange, announcements they want to make, or services they need or have to offer. These are posted on the Bulletin Board and other students respond with individual messages in MAILBAG. *Comment:* This activity assumes honest in-tentions to exchange, so that students are engaged in meaningful communica-tion (PG4).

"Television Series": Students in small groups plan a television (or radio, play, movie, or book) series. They use a LIBRARY disk to store character descrip-tions and successive installments in their series. These could be plot summaries or actual scripts. An activity such as this could extend over a long period of time. *Comment:* As students would get feedback on their series they would revise (PG6) and when they had installments ready to share they would publish (PG3). Performing part of the series as a class play would be a special form of publishing.

"Game Review": Students discuss their favorite games, why they like them, how they're played, and special equipment needed. They write a Game Review planner and then use it to create a disk with reviews of their favorite games indexed by attributes they have decided are most relevant. *Comment:* Because students would know that other students would want to read about new games, or their opinion of old games, this activity exemplified meaningful communication with real audiences (PG4).

Activities such as these were presented in the guide simply as possibilities. We did not expect teachers to carry out the activities exactly as described. Instead, we wanted these concrete suggestions, drawn from other classrooms, to stimulate their thinking about activities that would be appropriate in their own classroom. Teacher-invented activities that drew on students' interests would be most likely to achieve goals such as meaningful communication (PG4).

SUPPORT FOR TEACHERS

Many of the QUILL teachers had never used computers before. Others had never used a process approach to writing. All of the teachers were concerned with classroom management issues. Many of them relied on a whole-group approach to teaching, which seemed difficult to integrate with having a single computer for 30 students. Teachers who did successfully introduce QUILL into their classrooms had to cope with other demands on their time and even conflicts with school or district practices. As we continued to field-test QUILL, we became even more aware of the need for teacher support, and we expanded the teacher support system. By the time we implemented QUILL in Alaska, the system included a "cookbook," teacher workshops, classroom visits, a hotline, local facilitators, an electronic mail network, monthly mailings, and a year-end conference:

QUILL Cookbook. In addition to specific activities such as producing a class newspaper, the *QUILL Teacher's Guide* contained a "cookbook" for introducing a class to the use of QUILL and to ideas such as brainstorming, planning, revising, use of keywords, collaborative writing, and electronic mail. It was not designed to be a rigid specification of how to use the software, although it was sometimes interpreted that way. We quote here from the *QUILL Teacher's Guide* (p. 59):

> The QUILL Cookbook is a twenty-step plan for introducing QUILL in the classroom. Beginning with Step 1, "Introducing the Computer," the lessons build student and teacher competency in using computers to develop writing skills. Stu-

dents will use QUILL's MAILBAG, LIBRARY, PLANNER, and Writer's Assistant programs. Each step is organized by objective, preparation, and procedure. The steps should be done in order, but they can be adapted to meet your teaching style and the needs of your class.

The QUILL Cookbook often has students work in pairs to read, plan, compose, and revise texts. Pairing not only encourages oral language skills development but also allows students to use the computer more frequently. Once you have completed the Cookbook and the students are comfortable using the computer, you can be more flexible in designing your own computer-based writing activities.

The "roadmap" to the Cookbook [Fig. 3.24] illustrates the sequencing of the steps and their relationship to one another. It will take from 4 to 6 weeks to finish the steps, depending on the amount of time allotted for using the computer, the number of computers you have available, and your students' expertise. The Cookbook schedule should help you allot time for QUILL.

Workshops. Workshops for teachers introduced both computers and the writing process. A typical 3-day schedule, such as we used in Alaska, was the following:

QUILL Workshop Schedule

Day 1	Introductions
	Overview of QUILL
	Writing workshop (see later)
	Introduction to the Apple II
	Beginning Writer's Assistant: editing a sample file
	Using MAILBAG to SEND and RECEIVE messages
Day 2	CREATE and USE a restaurant review planner
	Discussion of how and when to integrate PLANNER into classroom writing projects
	ADD a restaurant review
	SEE others' reviews
	Comment on these texts using MAILBAG
	CHANGE a restaurant review
Day 3	Teacher's Guide
	Advanced Writer's Assistant
	Utility disk
	Discussions of classroom issues

The agenda was designed to introduce teachers to the important parts of the QUILL software and curriculum by having them carry out writing activities similar to those their students might do. We chose restaurant reviews as a topic because it was an interesting one to most teachers and it permitted short pieces of writing. It was also a topic in which the teachers could be the experts. We wanted to encourage them to see writing as a form of communication in which students could talk about what they knew best.

Cookbook Roadmap

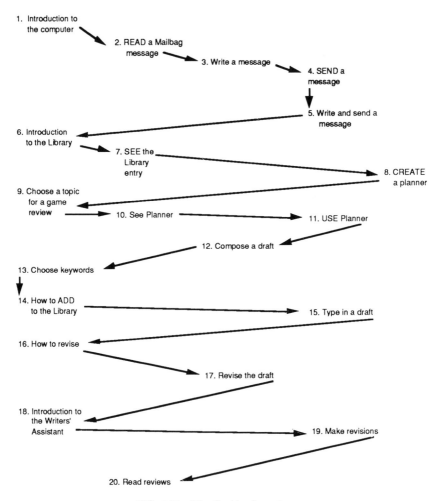

Teacher presents lesson/introduces activity	Students observe/read at the computer	Students write at their seats	Students write/revise at the computer	Teacher uses the computer alone

1. Introduction to the computer
2. READ a Mailbag message
3. Write a message
4. SEND a message
5. Write and send a message
6. Introduction to the Library
7. SEE the Library entry
8. CREATE a planner
9. Choose a topic for a game review
10. See Planner
11. USE Planner
12. Compose a draft
13. Choose keywords
14. How to ADD to the Library
15. Type in a draft
16. How to revise
17. Revise the draft
18. Introduction to the Writers' Assistant
19. Make revisions
20. Read reviews

FIG. 3.24   The Cookbook roadmap.

50

There was flexibility in the schedule to allow teachers to focus on what they felt was most critical for them. Their initial concerns were usually about using the computer, and then more specifically about Writer's Assistant. Later, concerns about how to manage QUILL activities in the classroom became paramount.

The writing workshop, designed by Don Graves (personal communication, 1983) took from 2 to 4 hours. We placed it first on the agenda in order to emphasize that QUILL was a new way of teaching writing, not just a new technology. It was intended to give teachers a brief "tour" through the writing process with an attentive partner as an audience and to model for them how a different approach to writing might look in a classroom. It thus introduced one form of collaboration in writing (PG5), and also reified the role of planning throughout the writing process (PG1). The steps of the writing workshop were the following:

1. The leader and teachers swapped a few "everyday" stories orally, as preparation for writing.
2. Each participant made a list of four things she might write about. After choosing two, she told her partner briefly about each.
3. Based on her partner's reaction, she chose one topic and wrote quickly about it on one $3'' \times 5''$ card.
4. Each person told her partner what she has written; the partner asked one question about the content of the story.
5. On another $3'' \times 5''$ card, everyone wrote her story from a different angle. (She could continue with the same angle, if it was going well.)
6. Each person made a concept web including the events that preceded and followed her story and the people involved; she told her partner about the surprises that emerged from the web.
7. On a third $3'' \times 5''$ card, everyone wrote her story again, this time bearing in mind the surprises that emerged in step 6.
8. Each person solicited some help from her partner on a troublesome aspect of her writing and wrote a fourth $3'' \times 5''$ card using that help.
9. Everyone chose four lines she had written somewhere along the way and polished them.
10. Participants were invited to share something they had written (from any of the $3'' \times 5''$ cards) with the rest of the group.

Teachers found this activity both enjoyable and enlightening; it gave them particular insight into how their students might feel in school writing situations. Some had trouble getting started, but found their partner helpful in getting them "unstuck"; they sometimes even developed a surprising bond with their partner during this relatively short workshop. But while they felt comfortable reading their writing to a partner, participants were often reluctant to share with the entire group. Thus, the workshop allowed them to experience both the power of having a real audience for their writing and the potential awkwardness that might result when a group was not yet a "literacy community." The workshop also brought teachers face-to-face with the importance of audience feedback (PG4), the connections among reading, writing, speaking, and listening (PG2), and the role of multiple revisions (PG6).

Teachers came to QUILL workshops concerned with learning how to use the new software, so they had patience for only a limited amount of off-computer writing before they got their hands on the keyboard. The first afternoon, therefore, we introduced the QUILL software by having teachers send one another MAILBAG messages. We simulated an electronic network by having each teacher send her partner a message in MAILBAG, then swap disks and read one another's message. In addition, each teacher sent a message to the Bulletin Board (the mailbox available to everyone), and read the messages that others had posted there, thus doing exactly what their students would later do.

Most of the remainder of the sessions focused on using QUILL and, in particular, on Writer's Assistant. On the third day we returned to discussions of curriculum integration and classroom management. We shared with the group some examples of writing that students in field-test classrooms had done, in particular, a TV script written collaboratively by a group of girls in a sixth-grade classroom in Hartford.

Other Support.   We followed up the workshops with 1- or 2-day visits to each classroom. This enabled us to work collaboratively with teachers in solving the myriad of practical issues that arose in introducing QUILL and to work towards activities appropriate to specific classrooms. The NETWORK maintained a hotline to provide follow-up help. Teachers could call for help with hardware, software, or classroom problems. The software included the hotline number, and would display it if an unexpected software condition arose. We also encouraged schools to identify a "local facilitator," responsible for visiting classrooms, troubleshooting, and generally supporting teachers after the initial workshops. In some schools and districts, this was the computer coordinator; in others, it was the language arts coordinator.

In the Alaska setting, there were some additional support elements. There was extensive use of long-distance electronic mail for communication among teachers, developers, and the local facilitator; the growth structure and content of this network are analyzed in depth in chapter 7. Carol Barnhardt, the local coordinator, also sent monthly mailings containing samples of student work, ideas for activities, and software tips. Finally, there was the year-end conference[2],

---

[2]Barnhardt (1984) is a conference paper that describes the Alaska QUILL project.

which served as a focal point for the teachers to discuss their re-creation of QUILL.

These support activities were designed not only to help teachers implement QUILL, but to provide them with literacy environments that mirrored those their students were experiencing. We believed that in order for teachers to establish successful functional learning environments that involve written language, they would need to think broadly and critically about a range of literacy practices. Moreover, they would need to participate themselves in similar functional learning environments. These environments are mutually reinforcing (see Fig. 3.25). When teachers engage in meaningful literacy practices they are better able to serve as mentors for student apprentices; in turn, their teaching and even their own literacy development are expanded as they observe students' learning. In chapter 7 we discuss the development of a functional learning environment for teachers based on an electronic mail community that was synergistic with the students' writing experiences.

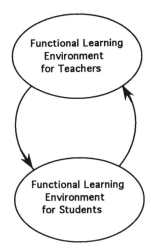

FIG. 3.25. Mutual reinforcement of functional learning environments.

SUMMARY

QUILL was a project to encourage real communication, a focus on audience and purpose, revision with a reason, and the development of a literate community. In software, curriculum, and teacher support, it embodied a particular approach to literacy development. Yet even in its most detailed form, this specification was only the starting point for the realization process. In each setting, the innovation looked different, adapted and appropriated by a particular teacher in a particular school in a particular cultural context. One of our goals in this book is to characterize these differences and to identify the reasons they arose. In the next chapter we look more closely at the settings in Alaska in which QUILL was used. This provides the background for our detailed analyses of QUILL realizations in chapters 5, 6, and 7, as we construct a situated evaluation of QUILL.

Chapter 4

The Alaskan Context

A critical aspect of a situated evaluation is an analysis of situations in which an innovation is realized. Characteristics such as classroom organization, the teacher's background and educational approach, the students' backgrounds, the amount and configuration of technology in the classroom, and the organization of the individual school have an obvious impact on what actually happens in a classroom. More global characteristics, such as the influence of state educational agencies, the relationships among schools, and ethnic and linguistic aspects of the larger community, also shape classroom practices. Any realization of an innovation develops from an interaction among these contextual features and the "packaged" innovation received by the teacher. Accordingly, in this chapter we describe our perspective on Alaska, its history, and the growth of its educational system.

A first glance at Alaska highlights its extremes—the largest area, the smallest population and population density, the highest mountain, a large number of linguistically and ethnically diverse populations, and the most northern, most western, and most eastern locations in the United States. It is thought of as "the last frontier," a state full of rugged individualists and small Native communities, where transportation challenges have played a large part in determining the flow of everyday life. Alaskans, too, see their state as separate, referring to the continental United States as "Outside" or "The Lower 48."

The possibility of generalizing from an experience in Alaska to classrooms in the rest of the United States seems at first difficult, if not impossible. But the issues central to education in Alaska in 1983 were similar to those that were becoming prominent elsewhere in the United States: increasing cultural and linguistic diversity, increased investment in technology, movements toward decentralization and local control, and shrinking community tax support for education. In fact, Alaskan schools were dealing with the implications of linguistic and cultural diversity years before they became national educational priorities. The rest of the country is just now facing the impact of the influx of recent immigrants, as their children enter the schools in growing numbers. Alaska's experiences can serve as a reference point as other states attempt to integrate bilingual, multicultural, and traditional education.

In addition, Alaska's diversity, rather than making it an exception, actually provides an efficient and useful laboratory for investigating educational innovations. Because Alaska has rural and urban schools, multiethnic and ethnically homogeneous schools, combined-grade classrooms and single-age classrooms, student:teacher ratios from 7:1 to 30:1, and districts reflecting a range of socioeconomic factors, we were able to study many different types of classrooms within a single state. These settings provided us with a microcosm of different classroom and community types that are represented throughout the United States, and situated evaluation, in focusing on the variability among classrooms, allows us to capture this diversity in useful ways.

ALASKA'S PEOPLE AND PLACES

Approximately 535,000 people now live in the state of Alaska, including 65,000 original, or native, Alaskans, commonly referred to as Eskimos, Indians, and Aleuts, or collectively as Alaska Natives. The large majority of non-native people are transplants from the "Lower 48" states, but there is a rapidly growing number of immigrants from Asia and Latin America. Alaska's citizens live in an area with one of the lowest population densities in the world (about 1 person per square mile). Seventy-five percent of the population resides in three major urban areas. These cities (Anchorage: population 250,000; Fairbanks: 75,000; and the capital, Juneau: 29,000) offer the same kinds of amenities found elsewhere in the United States. They have well-developed transportation systems, modern shopping complexes, well-equipped homes, and extensive educational facilities.

Outside of these three cities, the rest of the population lives in approximately 20 small towns and 180 villages; there, life is quite different from that in the urban areas. A few villages have as few as 25 inhabitants; most are in the range of 200 to 500 people. Most villages in Alaska are not only geographically isolated from one another, but are accessible only by air or, in some cases, by water. Even the state capital, Juneau, can be reached only by airplane or ferry, and it is as far from communities in Northern and Western Alaska as Colorado is from New York. Because of these transportation difficulties, rural residents often go out of their way to help one another get to other villages (see Fig. 4.1). Helen, the sole teacher in Telida, a village of 25, described the personal relationships that develop in the bush.

It was less than a year ago that I was sitting in my little log house in Telida, wondering if I dared run next door for a cup of tea while I waited for the airplane that had been arranged to pick me up and take me to Fairbanks for QUILL training. Would I miss a phone call or "bush message" on the local radio station, letting me know why the plane was late or telling me it wouldn't be coming? People were guessing—a plane had been seen flying over, just to the south, about the time I'd been expecting one to stop. Telida is small, seven households, a church and a school, plus a few old houses, no longer used, and the runway would be easy to miss for a pilot unfamiliar with the area.

It got too dark for a plane to land, I received a message about various mix-ups that had prevented me from getting to Fairbanks that night and new arrangements were made for the next morning. They also fell through, but around noon a friend, whose wife was attending the QUILL training, called to say he'd heard of the problems, and he was on his way in his own plane to take me to Fairbanks. This meant, for him, 6 or 7 hours of flying, with his two little girls in the plane, and because the weather turned bad, he didn't even get to see his wife in Fairbanks. I share this story because it illustrates the difficulties that life in a small village can present, but also the extraordinary kindness with which people respond to these difficulties. This was October of my third year as the teacher in Telida, and I had learned that I could gratefully rely on such kindness.

Village residents maintain a distinctive lifestyle in many ways, and in most rural communities today, one will see log cabins, dog teams, fish wheels, food caches, fishing boats, and outhouses next to modern trucks, cars, snowmobiles, refrigerators, televisions, telephones, and school buildings. Most villages have at least one store, but many native residents continue to practice a subsistence lifestyle and depend heavily on moose, caribou, seal, walrus, whale, fish, and berries for their supply of food. Sister Judy Tralnes, a junior high school teacher from Holy Cross (population 275), described her village.

Holy Cross is a village on the Yukon River. There are about 250 here . . . about 70% are Athabaskan Indians and 30% are Yup'ik Eskimo. Two years ago private phones became available for people of the village. Until that time there was only one phone in the whole village. Recently we have gotten daily mail service. Before that time, there was air service only one, two, or three times a week.

While Holy Cross is an "integrated" village including both Athabaskans and Yup'iks, the residents of most villages are either Athabaskan, Eskimo, or Aleut. In many of the villages, native culture provides an important backbone for the community. Chevak is one such community, as Ernie, an elementary school teacher, described.

The village of Chevak, Alaska is located approximately 150 air miles north and west of Bethel and 300 miles west of Anchorage. Chevak is situated on the tundra, just 17 miles from the Bering Sea. There are no roads connecting Chevak to other villages, and travel is done by boat in the summer and snowmobile in the winter. There is an airstrip, and Chevak receives daily air service from Bethel. There are phones in the village, but most communication is still done by "CBs" (citizen band radio). . . .

Chevak is a traditional village, predominantly Cup'ik Eskimo, and has a population of roughly 500 people. Chevak is one of several villages in Alaska where the native language (Cup'ik) is still the first language of the people.[1] There is, however, a growing concern that the language is losing ground to English, especially with the younger children. The village also remains strong in many other aspects of their traditional culture. Native dancing, arts, crafts, and numerous other components of the Cup'ik culture are still practiced by the village and are taught both in school and at home.

Language and Literacy

Alaska has an unusually wide diversity of languages and dialects for such a small population. English is spoken by nearly everyone in the state, though many residents are bilingual. There are four different native language families in Alaska (Eskimo-Aleut, Athabaskan-Eyak-Tlingit, Tsimshian, and Haida), which comprise twenty distinct Alaska Native languages. Even related languages among these are mutually unintelligible. All of the Alaska Native languages are linguistically very different from the Indo-European languages, and there are only a handful of non-natives, other than linguists, who have ever become proficient at speaking one of them. A wide variety of English dialects is always found in Alaskan schools, and these range from Brooklyn "accents" to Southern drawls. There are also varieties of English used in several Alaska villages, which are sometimes referred to as "Village English."

The steady influx of non-natives since the gold rush days of the early 1900's, the severe decline in population of some of the native groups, and the policy of punishment for speaking native languages in school have seriously affected the viability of many of the native languages of Alaska. Today some of the languages that are spoken only by older people are in critical danger of being "lost" forever.

The Yup'ik language, spoken by people in the Southwest area of Alaska, has the strongest chance for survival since many Yup'ik children speak it as their first language. In Chevak, Cup'ik continues to be the primary language. In the past few years, Chevak residents have become active participants in developing and providing school programs that promote the use of Cup'ik in the classroom. Chevak is also one of the few communities in rural Alaska where there are more native than non-native teachers in the school. Ernie, a non-native teacher, commented:

---

[1]Cup'ik is a language within the Yup'ik group of languages, one of the groups within the Eskimo-Aleut native language family.

All the children in my class had the ability to converse in their native language. There was, however, a growing concern that these children were losing certain aspects of their native language and a strong emphasis on Cup'ik was given both in the language class during the day and at home. Parents were asked to speak Cup'ik to their children as much as possible. Students were also somewhat fluent in English. Their speaking skills in English were good, but their ability to write in English was limited and in need of improvement.

Issues of literacy are particularly important and complex in Alaska because of the wide range of literacy skills that exists and significant differences in attitude toward the value of learning to read and write. Many families include elders who still speak their native language, grandchildren who are using computers in school, and a middle generation who are bilingual and have ambivalent attitudes toward non-native culture. Helen described how this accelerated transition from oral to technological culture manifested itself in Telida.

People are going directly from a tradition of oral literacy to computer literacy, in one or two generations. In Telida, this was quite dramatically true. None of the grandparents of the children I taught had been to school, and so all of their learning had been oral. The parents were bilingual, having learned the native language and the traditional ways at home, but having been sent away to school, where they learned to read and write and speak English, along with all the underlying "school values."

The children of the generation now in school are the first to have a school in Telida, and the school has two computers, so while they are living at home, with all of the traditional wisdom of their parents and grandparents available to them, they are also exposed to whatever effect computers have on the way we learn.

In Alaska today there are no villages that are either nonliterate or fully literate. A certain amount of literacy is now essential in every community, as adults need to read and write in order to apply for jobs, complete state and federal forms, order from catalogs, pay bills, participate in church and school activities, read medical prescriptions, vote, and complete the paperwork required of them when they serve on local and regional boards for their village corporations. Most villages are in transition between the two ends of the linguistic/cultural continuum.

Oil and Cultural Change

The last 20 years have brought major changes to the Alaskan scene that have had major effects on the political, social, and economic environment. The discovery of large commercial quantities of oil on Alaska's North Slope in 1968 quickly led to plans to build and operate the 800-mile-long Trans-Alaska Pipeline, the largest private construction project in recent U.S. history. In 1971, in response to the pressure for oil development, the Native people of Alaska won a comprehensive, far-reaching, and unprecedented legal settlement of their aboriginal claims to land and resources with the passage of the Alaska Native Claims Settlement Act (ANCSA). Through ANCSA, Alaska Natives retained ownership of 40 million acres of land, received $962.5 million in compensation for lands given up, and established twelve regional Native profit-making corporations to manage their entitlements.

Since their formation, these twelve corporations have invested in diverse activities such as hotel construction, oil exploration and drilling, and fish processing plant development. The most important aspect of their organization, however, is the stipulation that the 100 shares of stock that each member holds cannot be transferred or sold for 20 years; this leaves the corporations free to pursue "Native" development without fear of being taken over by non-Native economic interests.

The building of the pipeline and the passage of ANCSA brought both opportunities and frustrations to Alaska's natives. Alaska now had oil resources needed by the rest of the world, and the newly formed native corporations had enough money and land that people in the financial world were eager to assist with their investments. These events led to the creation of new jobs in construction work for the pipeline and business management and legal work for the native corporations. Many native people, however, were not able to take advantage of the increased employment opportunities. The pipeline jobs required workers to be away from home and family for long periods of time, and this was a particularly difficult adjustment for people from rural villages. Much of the ANCSA corporation business was related to the villages, but there was such a severe shortage of native people trained in business fields that nonnatives received many of the first native corporation jobs.

These changes brought Alaska's native people abruptly into the modern world. Native leaders who found themselves quite suddenly placed into corporate structures discovered that corporate and native perspectives on the world were often in conflict. Today they face the challenge of trying to establish a native way of doing corporate business before the 20-year deadline for the open sale of stock occurs. The current dilemma for these communities is reflected in the title of a publication from Yupiktak Bista, one of the nonprofit organizations: "Does One Way of Life Have to Die so That Another Can Live?"

Technology

Technological innovations have been a major element in the changes in Alaska cities and villages. For many years scientists and technologists have been lured to Alaska by the challenges posed by its geography, environment, and location. The majority of non-native Alaska citizens, while often defensive about their tried and true "sourdough" methods and tools, seldom resist experimenting with new technology if it suits their needs. And residents of rural communities have enthusiastically bought snow machines (snow mobiles), even while keeping their sled dogs well trained.

During the last 20 years, technological advances in telecommunications and satellites have begun to change communication patterns in Alaska, especially in rural areas. The development and accessibility of worldwide satellite systems occurred in the same period during which Alaska's state revenues increased due to the completion of the oil pipeline, so some of these new resources went into improving communications with remote villages. Many villages now have large satellite receiving dishes capable of tuning into 10 television channels. Telephone service has increased so that every town now has at least one telephone, and most have phones in individual households. In 1983, when QUILL was introduced in Alaska, communications were still constrained by the unpredictability of local power generators and the limited number of telephones, but the communication situation has continued to improve. Rural villages now have substantially more possibilities for communicating with other villages and urban sites.

One widely used communication form is the audio conference, an outgrowth of the Alaska statewide satellite telecommunications network and the installation of telephones in many small communities. Audio conferences allow several people at one site to talk with groups of people in one or more other sites through the use of a speaker and a set of microphones that are connected to one another and to a telephone. Initially a statewide audio conferencing system was developed so that residents could talk with their legislators in Juneau, but in 1977, it began to be used extensively by the Alaska Department of Education and the University of Alaska in a jointly organized instructional telecommunications network called Learn Alaska. Today, audio conferences are used for a wide variety of purposes, including university coursework, university administration, curriculum planning, in-service training, job interviews, school board meetings, and student exchanges.

An elementary teacher in Shungnak, a village of 225 where QUILL was used, took advantage of audio conferencing to provide a combined oral and written language experience for her fourth-, fifth-, and sixth-grade students. As they explained in the article below, the students got ready for the audio conference by writing letters to the other participants and preparing questions for the actual conference. The article (written collaboratively using QUILL) was the culmination of the activity and was published in Educational Technology/Alaska (1983).

Audio Link Shows New But Familiar World

We talked to Kiana and Fairbanks to learn more about different communities. To get ready for the conference we wrote letters and took pictures of ourselves, then we sent them to Kiana and Fairbanks. Two days before the audio conference we wrote our questions on a piece of paper. On the day of the conference the first thing we did was introduce ourselves, then we asked our questions.

We learned a few things from Kiana and Fairbanks. Kiana told us how to make an igloo. Fairbanks surprised us when they said they had only eight students in their whole school. The school has two or three grades and it is a private school called The Montessori School. We found out that Kiana eats the same Eskimo food we do. Some of these foods are frozen fish (quaq), Eskimo ice cream (akutuq) and dried fish (paniqtuq). When one girl in Fairbanks told us her father had a plane and she might come and visit us, we were very excited.

Towards the end of the conference we sang a song to the other school. The song was Pearly Shells. First we sang it in English and then we sang it in Inupiaq. After we sang our song, the kids in Kiana sang the ABC Song in Inupiaq and Fairbanks sang the Montessori song. We thought their songs were very good. We enjoyed talking to the kids in the other communities. We discovered we have many things in common, but also some of us do things differently. (p. 5)

ALASKA'S EDUCATIONAL SYSTEM

The passage of the Alaska Native Claims Settlement Act brought about changes in the economic lives of rural villagers. Soon thereafter, a parallel change in the organization of school systems occurred, one that placed power and responsibility for the operation of schools in the hands of village residents (Barnhardt, 1991). Until that time, rural Alaska Native students who wanted to go to high school had to attend BIA (Bureau of Indian Affairs) boarding schools in Oregon, Colorado, Kansas, New Mexico, or southeast Alaska. Several predominantly non-native-Alaskan communities had local high school programs, whereas predominantly native communities of similar size did not.

To redress this situation, Alaska Legal Services brought a class action suit against the State of Alaska on behalf of 14-year-old Molly Hootch of Emmonak, a Yup'ik Eskimo community of 400 people. The case was settled in 1976 with an agreement that the state would provide a high school program in every community with one or more secondary students. Over the next 10 years, 120 new small high schools were built in rural villages that previously had only elementary schools.

The Molly Hootch Case was important not only because it resulted in the opening of a large number of high schools, but because it occurred at the same time as the transfer of control from the centralized school system to regional and local areas. The new high schools helped to increase the demand for greater community participation in decision-making and for more flexible and culturally adaptive approaches to curriculum. In 1976, the state-operated rural school system was broken into 21 smaller regional administrative units.

School District Organization

Schools in the urban areas of Alaska are each part of a local "Borough School District," a borough being the counterpart of county in other states. Urban schools have a typically mixed group of students, both economically and ethnically. Marcia, a borough-level administrator in Fairbanks described the students in the Fairbanks schools:

> Fairbanks, the second largest city in Alaska, serves as a distribution point for the interior of Alaska. The schools serve a highly varied population from a wide range of socioeconomic backgrounds. Alaskan native students, both Eskimo and Indian, go to school with children from Black, White, Hispanic and various Oriental groups. When school lunches are provided with government subsidies, many children qualify for free lunches at the elementary schools within the city area. In contrast, another sizeable group of students have parents with high incomes, whether from business, professions or state service. The University of Alaska is based in Fairbanks, attracting an unusual number of highly educated, talented people for an area with a population of only 70,000.

Mary, an elementary teacher, described the students in her own class in Fairbanks:

> In my class here in the oldest elementary school in Fairbanks, in the inner city, I have a diverse student population. I have 7 Athabaskans, 1 Eskimo, 2 Blacks and 1 Chicano. Out of my class of 20 students, half are minorities. Economically, the students in my class come from neighborhoods where there are low-cost federal housing projects and the parents are on welfare, to blue collar and white collar neighborhoods. I love it—my students range from one little "gifted/talented" child who was excited when Santa Claus brought an Apple computer down the chimney of his eight bedroom house, to the twin boys whose mom is a single parent and works as a secretary, and on Sundays allows her kids to use her computer at work. I also have a child who has never seen a computer before, and some of my students have recently moved to Fairbanks from rural villages where they frequently used computers in their classrooms.

Most rural schools in the state are organized by districts, which have been established on the basis of geographical, cultural, and linguistic considerations. These areas (21 in 1983) are referred to as Regional Education Attendance Areas (REAAs) and include about 220 elementary and secondary schools in which the enrollments range from 7 to 350. The REAAs, like the borough school districts, are responsible for the education of children in their local area from kindergarten through 12th grade. Each REAA has its own locally elected school board and its own superintendent, and although the responsibilities of the school boards and administrators vary from region to region, many of the boards today are meaningfully involved in budget preparation, hiring processes, and curriculum development. There are state guidelines in all areas of school policy, but each REAA has enough latitude to design the educational process in ways that make it most appropriate for its particular region. Whereas previously, most villagers had felt alienated from their local educational institutions, a sense of school "ownership" is beginning to develop in several communities. Helen described how this connection manifested itself in Telida.

> I never thought of the school as "my school" or of the employees as "my aide" or "my janitor" and as much as possible, I tried not to think of the children as "my students." Rather I believed that the school belonged to the community, and that I was there to work with the community to make the school as much as it could be.
>
> It was the only building in town with electricity and running water, so people were often in and out to get water, to watch television in the evenings, to borrow books and magazines, and so forth. Everyone was very respectful of the need for the children to have uninterrupted school time and for me to have quiet time for paper work after school, but at other times, the school was always open and well used.

A small number of schools in rural Alaska, including Chevak, have chosen to pursue an even more independent status by contracting with the Bureau of Indian Affairs (BIA) to run their own schools. Ernie teaches in one such school in Chevak.

> Chevak School, also known as the Kashunamiut School District, is one of five schools in the state of Alaska that is not funded by the state of Alaska. Chevak contracts directly from the Bureau of Indian Affairs in Washington, D.C., and in effect controls its own school system. There is at present great debate over the future status of these "contract schools." The BIA has expressed the desire to relinquish responsibility for the running of these schools with the hope that the state of Alaska will take them over. The villagers, however, do not want to become part of the state-run schools. There is a fear that the local control they have at the present time will become weakened under the state. Chevak is one of the schools leading the fight against joining the state-run school system.

Postsecondary education in Alaska is handled by two small private colleges and the University of Alaska. The University is a multicampus system with main campuses in Fairbanks, Anchorage, and Juneau, and approximately 20 regional and rural centers around the state.

Classroom Organization

In the larger communities of Alaska, schools are big enough to be organized as urban schools are in the rest of the United States. The average elementary school has 600 students and the average high school 1,500; this translates to several classes at each grade level with an average of 25 pupils per teacher. In the smaller communities, however, a single teacher often teaches two or more grade levels in one classroom, and in some very small villages there are still some one-room schools where one teacher is responsible for all grade levels and subjects. The composition of Ernie's second/third-grade class in Chevak is typical of that found in many classrooms in rural Alaska.

> My class consisted of 24 students. Sixteen were third graders. I taught these students the previous year in second year. Eight students were second graders. All the students were Native children, and with the exception of one, all had attended school in Chevak throughout their entire, brief school career.

Student/teacher ratios in rural schools are often lower than those in urban classrooms, and many teachers have the assistance of a teacher aide for at least part of the day. These aides are mostly Alaska Natives and they often fill a "connecting" role for non-Native teachers working with Native students. Helen comments:

> For 2 hours each day, I had the help of Agnes Ticknor, a very competent aide, the mother of three of the children and cousin of the other six! We did most of our writing during the hours she was there.

In the recently established small rural high schools, classes have between one and twenty students, and teachers are often called on to teach a wide range of subjects. Teaching in these schools is sometimes supplemented by distance-learning alternatives.

Bilingual and Multicultural Education

Many events in the educational history of Alaska have been shaped by the controversies that have surrounded the use of native and non-native languages since Russian people first settled in Alaska in the late 1700s (Barnhardt, 1985b, 1991). Official school policies toward the use of native languages in the schools of Alaska paralleled those that developed in other places in the world. These attitudes followed a cyclical pattern and included a period of tolerance between 1865 and 1910 followed by a 50-year period of neglect and punishment. The return of an attitude of support and encouragement for language diversity was generated by the momentum of the civil rights movement of the 1960s.

At the federal level, several important pieces of legislation dealing directly with language issues were passed in the 1960s and 1970s. The 1968 Bilingual Education Act provided the first federal funds for bilingual education. In 1974 a Chinese parent took the San Francisco School Board to court, claiming the academic needs of the non-English-speaking student were not being met. The

Supreme Court ruled unanimously in favor of the parent in the landmark bilingual education case, Lau v. Nichols. Subsequently, the "Lau Remedies," a set of guidelines for implementing the Lau decision, were developed, mandating that schools provide programs designed to meet the linguistic needs of non-English-speaking children.

Alaska was one of the first states to pass its own bilingual education legislation, and today there are bilingual programs in about 70% of the rural and urban school districts in the state, serving children from nearly 70 different language groups. As in other parts of the United States, the forms that bilingual education programs actually take in Alaskan classrooms vary considerably. As Ernie pointed out, Chevak is an interesting example of a village where several factors have come together to produce a particularly strong bilingual/multicultural program.

> Chevak school has a special "Cultural Heritage Program" that also employs five staff, including two elders of the village who make frequent visits into the classrooms. The elders tell stories of long ago, work with students on Eskimo dancing, and encourage other aspects of the Cup'ik culture. In addition to the Cultural Heritage Program, students receive 1/2 hour a day of instruction in the Cup'ik language.

Although the stated objective of most bilingual programs is to provide "true" bilingual education (consistent with the intent of the original federal and state legislation), in reality the goal of many programs is to provide a more rapid and efficient acquisition of English, at the expense of the original language. Although bilingual education in the United States today is mandated by federal law, the actual implementation directly reflects the social, political, and economic situation of each school district and community.

Technology in the Schools

Alaska's students have often had the advantages of classrooms equipped with the most up-to-date educational technology. Alaskan teachers have a tradition of investing in "the latest," perhaps as a way of compensating for the perceived disadvantages of operating a school in a remote setting, or because their experiences living in the bush have taught them not to be intimidated by technology. Computers were particularly prevalent in Alaskan schools in the early 1980s because they became the new "in" technology just at the time when the schools had extra money from the oil pipeline.

A survey in 1985 showed that Alaska led the nation in the number of computers per student in public schools. The number of public school computers rose from 526 in 1982 to 4,585 in 1984, an 874% increase in just 2 years. Unlike many other parts of the United States, where computers are found more often in urban and suburban schools, rural and urban school districts had roughly the same computer/student ratio: one computer for every 21.8 students. The majority of computers (62%) were located in classrooms, with the rest in computer labs, libraries, and so on. Printers were attached to 23% of the machines and telecommunications modems to 7%.

Computer use in Alaskan classrooms is similar to that in other parts of the country, with a few exceptions (Office of Technology Assessment, 1988). Because of the distances between villages and classrooms, telecommunications have been in more extensive use than in other states. In 1984, there were already 336 modems in schools; many of these were used by teachers and administrators to share resources and to communicate within their own districts. In addition, a growing number of individual teachers were beginning to communicate with other teachers or to participate in distance-delivered university coursework. In 1983, when the Alaska QUILL project began, teachers were just starting to use networks to allow students to exchange letters and other pieces of writing. Some of them used the University of Alaska Computer Network (UACN), which was available for individual teachers to use if they were enrolled in a University course or if they were part of a University project. On the other hand, the Alaska Department of Education network was designed for administrative use and was almost never used by teachers.

Small rural high schools were the scene of another somewhat unusual use of computers. Because of the small number of students in many of these schools, the State Office of Instructional Services compiled Individualized Study by Technology courses for mathematics, reading, Alaska history, science, and health. These courses offered multimedia instruction using books, workbooks, audiotapes, videotapes, and software to students whose high schools could not support teachers in these areas.

The large number of teachers interested in using computers in their classrooms led to the formation of one of the first statewide organizations for computer-using educators, the Alaska Association for Computers in Education (AACED). The group has held an annual conference with published proceedings since 1981. The 1984 AACED conference became a focal point for all of those involved in the Alaska QUILL project.

THE PARTICIPANTS IN THE ALASKA QUILL PROJECT

In chapter 3 we included the story of QUILL's arrival in Alaska and a general description of the course of the project. Here we describe the individual participants, their classrooms, schools, and communities. Some of those characteristics are described in the chart and the accompanying Alaska map below, where we have circled communities where QUILL participants lived. The information on Table 4.1a and Table 4.1b summarizes characteristics of communities, schools, and teachers who were major participants in the project

TABLE 4.1a

Information on Participants in the Alaska QUILL Project

Name	Job Title	Community	Population	Cultural Groups	School Enrollment	Grade(s) Taught	Class Size
Lynne Ammu	Cross-Cultural Education Instructor	Bethel	4000	Yup'ik Eskimo Caucasian	(University)	University students	15
Michael Baumgartner	District Language Arts Coordinator	McGrath	500	Caucasian Athabaskan Yup'ik Eskimo	District: 400 (K–12)	K–12	N/A
Bonnie Bless-Boenish	Elementary Teacher	Shungnak	225	Inupiak Eskimo	59 (K–12)	4–6	12
Hans Boenish	Jr. High/High School Teacher	Shungnak	225	Inupiak Eskimo	59 (K–12)	7–12	23
Joe Davis	Elementary Teacher	Holy Cross	240	Athabaskan Indian	65 (K–12)	4–6	
Malcolm Fleming	District Gifted and Talented Coordinator	McGrath	500	Caucasian Athabaskan Yup'ik Eskimo	District: 400 (K–12)	K–12	N/A
Helen Frost-Thompson	Elementary Teacher	Telida	25	Athabaskan Indian	7 (1–4)	K–5	7
Lynne Grossman	Elementary Teacher	Juneau	25,000	Mixed	550 (K–5)	4	25
Sydney Hole	Elementary Teacher	Juneau	25,000	Mixed	550 (K–5)	5	28

Name	Position	Location	Population	Ethnicity	Enrollment	Grade	Class Size
Ernie Manzie	Elementary Teacher	Chevak	530	Cup'ik Eskimo	160 (K–12)	2–3	24
Alexander McFarlane	Elementary Teacher	Fairbanks	70,000	Mixed	470 (K–6)	6	24
Deane O'Dell	English Teacher	McGrath	500	Caucasian Athabaskan Yup'ik Eskimo	145 (K–12)	Junior High	15
Wilma Payne	Elementary Teacher	McGrath	500	Caucasian Athabaskan Yup'ik Eskimo	145 (K–12)	5	15
Mary Ramsaur Goniviecha	Elementary Teacher	Fairbanks	70,000	Mixed	400 (K–6)	2	22
Richard Riedl	Assistant Professor of Education	Fairbanks	70,000	Mixed	3500	University	N/A
Marcia Romick	District Gifted and Talented Coordinator	Fairbanks	70,000	Mixed	District: 14,000 (K–12)	K–12	N/A
Don Stand	Elementary Teacher	Nikolai	105	Athabaskan Indian	20 (K–8)	4–8	6
Judy Tralnes	Junior High Teacher	Holy Cross	240	Athabaskan Indian	65 (K–12)	6–8	16
Lena Ulroan	Elementary Teacher	Chevak	530	Cup'ik Eskimo	160 (K–12)	6	10
Sandra Zecchini	Cross-Cultural Education Instructor	Holy Cross	240	Athabaskan Indian	(University)	University students	N/A

TABLE 4.1b

Information on Participants in the Alaska QUILL Project

Name	Years Taught/ Years in Alaska	Previous Computer Use	School Equipment	Home Equipment	Phone Line Location	Previous Electronic Mail Use	Writing Project Participation?
Lynne Ammu	10/10	WP,EM,games	C,P,M	C,P,M	University office	UACN	No
Michael Baumgartner	12/12	WP,EM, educational software	C,P,M	C,P	District office	UACN, SOURCE	Yes
Bonnie Bless-Boenish	8/6	WP,EM	C,P,M	C,P,M	Classroom	UACN	Yes
Hans Boenish	4/4	None	C,P,M	C,P,M	School office	None	No
Joe Davis		None	C,P,M	none	School office	None	
Malcolm Fleming	5/5	WP,EM, educational software	C,P,M	C/P	District office	UACN, SOURCE	No
Helen Frost-Thompson	9/3	WP,LOGO	C,P,M	none	Classroom	None	No
Lynne Grossman		none	C/P	none	University Lab	None	

Sydney Hole	15/13	WP,D&P	C/P	C/P	University Lab	None	Yes
Ernie Manzie	2/2	D&P	C,P,M	C	Classroom	UACN	Yes
Alexander McFarlane			C/P		District Office	None	Yes
Deane O'Dell		none	C/P	none	Central Office	None	Yes
Wilma Payne	13/5	none	C,P,M	C/P	Classroom	None	Yes
Mary Ramsaur Goniviecha	12/12	none	C/P	none	No Modem	None	Yes
Richard Riedl	14/2	WP,EM, educational software			University Office		
Marcia Romick	8/8	WP,educational software	C,P,M	C/P/M	School Office	None	Yes
Don Stand	2/2	WP	C,P,M	none	School	UACN	No
Judy Tralnes	20/5	none	C,P,M	none	School Office	None	No
Lena Ulroan		none	C,P,M	none	Other Classroom	None	No
Sandra Zecchini	?/2	none	C/P	none	University Office	None	No

FIG. 4.1. State of Alaska.

72

during the 1983–84 school year. The tables include the following information:

Name of the participant
Job Title
Community: Name of the community in which the participant lived
Population of the community
Cultural Groups in the community
School Enrollment
Grade: Grade level taught or served by QUILL participant
Class size: Classroom enrollment, where applicable
Teaching: Total years of teaching experience
Teaching in Alaska: Total years of teaching experience in Alaska
Previous Computer Use:
    WP = Word Processing
    EM = Electronic Mail
    D&P = Drill and Practice
    OES = Other educational software used in individual schools
    Games
    LOGO
School Equipment:
    C = Computer (Apple II+)
    P = Printer (Epson)
    M = Modem
Home Equipment:
    C = Computer
    P = Printer
    M = Modem
Phone Line: Location of phone line for use with modem
Electronic Mail: Previous experience with electronic mail
    UACN = University of Alaska Computer Network
    SOURCE = The SOURCE (a commercial network)
Writing Project: Attendance at any workshop(s) of the Alaska Writing Project,
    a summer institute on process writing

The tables highlight the diversity of settings in which QUILL was used, in terms of districts, linguistic communities, schools, classrooms, and teachers' backgrounds. Participants even had varied roles in the school system—from classroom teacher to district level coordinator to rural cross-cultural educational instructor. Yet, there were also similarities. A large number of those who taught in rural schools had come to Alaska from other parts of the United States, seeking a challenging position in a multicultural educational environment. Their choice entailed a strong interest in addressing the issues of literacy in a multicultural environment; thus, QUILL fit well with their personal goals. Other specific educational priorities united the group; everyone was interested in improving their teaching of writing, in creative and open-ended uses of computers in their classrooms, or both. Helen in particular felt that teaching writing was central to her job.

> Writing is important to me—I especially love to read and write poetry—and I have noticed that teachers are usually at their best in teaching something they genuinely love.

Several of the teachers (and one administrator) had attended a Summer Writing Institute at the University of Alaska, and they recognized a link between QUILL's philosophy and that of the Institute. Mary commented on this commonality.

> Last summer I was a fellow at the Summer Writing Institute held at the University of Alaska. The project is modeled after the Bay Area Writing Project and is based on the recent research of how crucial writing is in the learning process and how it gives each writer a voice or a sense of self. I have my kids writing up a storm this year and we have monthly publications. QUILL will tie in so nicely with the philosophy of the Writing Project.

Other teachers' main interest was in using computers in their classes. Although many of them had little previous experience with computers, they saw in QUILL a different kind of educational software from other pieces they had considered. They appreciated QUILL's flexibility and felt it was well suited to the variety of situations they faced in their schools. The structure of a project that provided training and a peer group also convinced several teachers who had not known how to follow up their interest in computers to use QUILL as a first computer experience. Carol summed up her assessment of teachers' motivations in a letter to project participants in September, several weeks before the training, as follows:

> During the summer I had the opportunity to visit with several teachers and visiting professors who were in Fairbanks for summer classes. Many of them indicated that they were very anxious to respond to the public demand to improve students' ''basic'' skills, whereas at the same time they were anxious to see good educational use made of the technological tools that are now available in Alaska. With the QUILL project's strong emphasis on the use of the microcomputer as a tool for writing, it is one of the few programs available today that addresses those needs. I feel that we in Alaska are fortunate to be able to participate and offer our perspectives on the development of materials that will be commonplace in classrooms of the future.

SUMMARY

Issues facing Alaskan schools in 1983 that are increasingly relevant to schools throughout the United States are increased cultural and linguistic diversity in the schools, the growing presence of educational technology, movements toward decentralization and local control, and financial pressures. The next three chapters describe what happened in the Alaska QUILL project from three perspectives: how alternate realizations of *purpose* reflected characteristics of teachers, students, and communities; how properties of the *revision* process emerged in classrooms through the year; and how an electronic *network* fostered an evolving community of QUILL teachers. These events can be viewed as arising from an interaction of a technology (QUILL) and a social context (the Alaskan classrooms). Thus, we describe the *creation* of the QUILL innovation by teachers and students, building on their interpretation of ideas in the minds of the developers. The description of a QUILL classroom was "in the air" during training sessions; it was implied in the software and *QUILL Teacher's Guide*; it was discussed in oral and written conversations throughout the year. But only in the QUILL classrooms did it become real.

Chapter 5

Alternate Realizations of Purposeful Writing

Purpose is a slippery notion, personal in the extreme, always changeable, susceptible to context and timing, yet critical to the theory and practice of education from every perspective. At the very heart of any educational philosophy are its assumptions about the purpose, or goal, of education. During the past 300 years of American education, preparing factory workers, equipping citizens for democracy, providing adults with skills to function at least at a minimal level in society, and giving students a basis for life-long education have each been seen as primary goals for education. The goal one adopts has implications for every aspect of the educational process: curriculum design, teacher education, classroom organization, community–school relationships, and the use of new technologies.

This chapter examines purpose in education as it is embodied in classroom activities. Specifically, it explores these questions: How can legitimate purposes be fulfilled by school activities?; How does the addition of purpose change the character of educational activities?; What kinds of purposeful activities arise in the context of writing instruction?; How does technology affect the purpose of writing activities? In keeping with the structure of our situated evaluation, we examine how different teachers incorporated purpose into their QUILL-related writing activities in attempting to realize our vision of having their students "write for real purposes to real audiences."

Although in large part we left the word "real" for teachers to interpret, our view of purpose follows in general from Dewey (1966): "The aim of education is to enable individuals to continue their education. . . . the object and reward of learning is the continued capacity for growth" (p. 100). Dewey separated education from the mastery of individual skills, suggesting instead that education should help students develop both the capacity and the desire to learn. Thus, a central theme in his writing was that classroom activities should be related to students' purposes. He believed that students would be motivated to work on tasks that were meaningful to them and that, therefore, the most effective educational environments would be those that provided students with some purpose they understood. In such an environment, Dewey thought, students would not see learning skills as an end in itself, but rather as part of the process of empowering themselves to investigate and understand the world. Or, as Hawkins (1980) put it, "In a sense, you become educated when you become your own teacher."

We, and others (e.g., D. Newman, 1987), have referred to learning environments that emphasize real purposes over school purposes (e.g., getting a good grade, pleasing the teacher) as "functional learning environments," or FLEs. An FLE works as an effective educational experience both because purposeful activities are more likely to be motivating to students and because the students' learning takes place in a framework that is likely to relate to real-world tasks outside of school. Many classroom environments lack this element of purpose. They often lack the functional cues that allow students to connect an abstraction with its intended use and meaning (Brown, Collins, & Duguid, 1989). FLEs attempt to improve this situation by incorporating real purposes students can adopt as their own, turning school tasks into real tasks that students can participate in to fulfill their own goals.

These definitions and principles, however, leave many questions unanswered. Can a single specific purpose captivate an entire class? How does the social context operate to mediate group purposes? How do teachers' purposes relate to the purposes expressed in FLEs? How do students understand the purposes proposed by their teachers? Must students and teachers share the same purposes? How do the purposes of FLEs relate to those of the real world?

Newman (1987) argued that the teacher is central to the emergence of meaningful purposes in classroom activities and that her interaction with the students is critical to the creation of an FLE. He proposed that the teacher's responsibilities include suggesting tasks and presenting students with multiple interpretations of problems they encounter in working on the task. We follow Newman's observations by exploring in more detail the interaction between teacher's goals and students' goals in the creation of FLEs. In particular, we will examine how teachers' goals influenced the purposes for writing that arose in QUILL classrooms. What emerges from our analyses are some hypotheses about the situations in which FLEs for writing—in which students are able to *appropriate* meaningful goals for their writing—are most likely to develop successfully.

The notion of "appropriation" is central to our discussion of purpose and FLEs. Because it has been used in a variety of ways in educational writing, we need to spell out rather precisely what we intend it to mean. Broadly, we use "appropriate" to mean to adopt as one's own, to integrate into one's own views and goals. This definition is related to, but slightly different from, both the dictionary definition and the most widespread use of the word in educational writing. The dictionary (Morris, 1981, p. 64) defines the verb "appropriate" as "to take possession of or make use of exclusively for oneself, often without permission," and "appropriation" as "the act of appropriating to oneself or to a specific use or purpose." Our use has in common with these definitions the focus on "making use of," "for oneself," and "to a specific use," although we will not mean "exclusively" or necessarily "without permission." In educational writing, Papert (1987a) has interpreted "appropriate" in the context of education to mean "Make it your own. Take it up. Make it part of your life and your thinking and your culture" (p. 18). Our use has much of the flavor and force of Papert's, but whereas he talks primarily of students appropriating the *computer* as a tool for accomplishing their own goals, we will refer to students appropriating *goals or purposes* made available to them in school, then finding tools that will help them achieve their purposes.

There is an additional trickiness lurking here in the concept of purpose: Goals are, of course, personal and individual and not subject to direct inspection. Our discussion is based on our *interpretation* of student and teacher goals, on the inferences we have made from their behavior. In a few cases, we have somewhat more direct evidence about teachers, because they have described their goals in their writing. But for the most part, we have inferred students' and teachers' goals from their actions, and as such these inferences are subject to the criticism that our conceptual frameworks and biases may have entered into the description.

The remainder of this chapter describes first the view of purposeful writing that QUILL espoused and how we expected teachers to realize it in their classrooms. We then discuss a variety of classroom situations in which purposeful activities occurred to varying extents, including several where the students' appropriation of the stated goal is in doubt. We focus in particular on the teacher's role in choosing and shaping each activity, on his or her view of both writing and the purposes of education, and on how these beliefs affected students' experience of writing and computers.

PEDAGOGY OF PURPOSE IN QUILL

In conceptualizing the role of purpose and audience in writing, we were guided primarily by Graves' work on teaching students to write. In his observations and interventions, Graves (1984) insisted on the role of meaning and purpose in writing, even for very young children. "People want to write. The desire to express is relentless. People want others to know what they hold to be truthful. They need the authority that goes with authorship. They need to detach themselves from experience and examine it by writing. Then they need to share what they have discovered through writing . . ." (p. 62). But, Graves noted, most people have not developed this view of themselves as authors:

> People do not see themselves as writers because they believe they have nothing to say that is of value or interest to others. They feel incompetent at conveying information through writing. Real writing, they seem to think, is reserved for the professional. For the rest of us, writing is perceived as a form of etiquette in which care is taken to arrange words on paper to avoid error rather than communicate with clarity and vigor. (p. 63)

So in the classrooms, Graves observed, children wrote for one another, published books, and took their turns in the "author's chair" describing how and why they composed their pieces. Central to the classroom organization was the notion that children were writing to an audience of peers, not just to the teacher. As Graves put it, "too much writing is composed for just one person, the teacher. Young writers don't grow without the expanded horizons of other children's reactions; they possess too limited a concept of the effects of their text" (p. 190).

Purpose in Writing

In studying Graves' work and designing QUILL, we came up with our own analysis of the educational benefits of real purposes and audiences in learning to write. We identified the following ways that purpose in writing could contribute to a more powerful learning experience.

Situated Learning. As described in Brown, Collins, and Duguid (1989), situated learning is learning that occurs in an environment that allows students to use integral features of the task situation to help accomplish the work. In writing instruction, tasks with real purposes are likely to engage both features of the physical environment (such as other people's writing) and the social context (such as peers' assistance). Brown et al. considered the situating of learning experiences important because it is often precisely the situational and social supports that make learning both possible and generalizable. Duguid (1988) summarized this view: "To achieve the sort of utility and generality required of robust learning, students must be helped to develop concepts in the very situations that give them purpose" (p. 3).

Intrinsic Motivation. Brown et al. also discussed intrinsic motivation as deriving from purposeful activities. In a situation with true purpose, students perform tasks because they are intrinsically related to a goal that is interesting to them, rather than for extrinsic reasons related to doing well in school.

Understanding the Uses of Writing.   If the long-term goal of education is to provide students with tools for continued learning, it is crucial that they understand well when, and how, to use the tools they acquire. Writing has a variety of uses in real life, although many of them are absent from school writing experiences. Primarily, we use writing to communicate to a variety of audiences for different purposes: to persuade, to entertain, to connect, to inform. Writing is also an important tool for self-discovery and for exploring complex topics. Including real purposes and audiences in school writing experiences is the best way for students to learn the value of writing. As Duguid put it, "Education [is] seeking to help students not merely to acquire a particular tool . . . but also to use that tool in the activity for which it was intended. And the best way to learn to use a tool is to put it to use" (p. 2).

Audience Sensitivity.   Part of learning to write effectively is learning how to tailor a piece to a particular audience. In school, that audience is most often the teacher; thus, for an entire year a class may write to only a single audience—and an inauthentic one at that. Audience sensitivity in this context often amounts to espousing an opinion the teacher holds (even if the student does not) in order to get a good grade. In some cases where two people split the grading of compositions, students sometimes even modify their approach depending on the grader. But this kind of audience sensitivity is nonfunctional because it represents a strategy particularly developed to survive in school. Real purposes give students a reason to be concerned about their audience and to want to shape their pieces accordingly.

Audience Feedback.   When real audiences exist, they also provide the possibility of authentic audience feedback. In many classrooms following Graves' model, the audience extends beyond the teacher to the other students in the class. This set-up improves on the teacher-only model, but does not make use of the varied audiences that the world outside the classroom and the school can provide. When students write for students in another class, their community or even other communities, they discover how many ways they can—and must—vary what they write about and how they present it.

Structure of Activities.   Often, school writing assignments are accompanied by details such as "write an essay that is about 250 words long," "write a five paragraph essay," or "revise this paper once and turn it back in." Such conditions are arbitrary, generated by the teacher's focus on skills and schedules. In real writing, the length, form, and degree of revision in a piece are determined by its purpose and audience. Including real purposes in school writing provides legitimate ways to make decisions about such characteristics of the writing process, decisions that students will need to make as they carry their writing skills into situations outside of school.

Affecting the World. Writing with a real purpose can provide students with the opportunity to accomplish something in the world outside of school. Ordering mail-order catalogs, for example, a legitimate activity in the many Alaskan communities where there are no stores, actually brought the catalogs to the students. A group of students who published a tourist brochure for their village were able to deliver it to the town council and see it printed and distributed.

Closing the Gap Between Stated Purpose and School Purpose. In any classroom writing activity, there is a "stated purpose," for example writing a letter to a relative or friend thanking them for a gift. Yet, because this purpose is not real (there is really no relative waiting for the letter), the teacher has in mind an overriding "school purpose" that bears little direct relation to the stated purpose, for example, assessing the student's ability to write complete, grammatical sentences. Writing situations with a real purpose can close the gap because the writing is satisfying a real goal. This is not to say that writing skills such as grammar cannot be assessed or improved in purposeful writing settings. Rather, it means that students are not faced with a false goal and the necessity to figure out the real characteristics of the assignment that the teacher will assess.

Purpose in QUILL Training

In defining the activities we hoped teachers would carry out with QUILL, we emphasized both purpose and audience. In the introductory talk with which we began training sessions, we noted the six pedagogical goals of QUILL (described in chapter 2):

1. to help children develop skills of planning and critical thinking
2. to integrate reading and writing
3. to make writing public
4. to support meaningful communication with real audiences
5. to encourage writing with and for peers
6. to facilitate revision

Goals 3, 4, and 5 (and some aspects of 2) all address the real audience/real purpose vision, and, as we described QUILL in training sessions, we continued to tie the software back to the notions of audience and purpose. Our insistence stemmed partly from the fact that our view of purpose and audience in writing contrasted with the standard classroom writing environment. It also arose from our conviction that changes in the audience and purpose of classroom writing would have more fundamental learning effects than a more skill-oriented approach focusing on the cognitive processes of writing. We believed, as Becker (1986) said succinctly, that "The way people write grows out of the social situations they write in" (p. xi).

Another aspect of the social situations in which students write is the degree of collaboration they expect and experience. Pedagogical Goal 5 specified "writing with peers" as well as "for" them, and QUILL provided explicit supports for pieces with two authors (e.g., space for two authors' names). In relation to purpose, there is another meaning of "writing with peers" that we didn't explicitly talk about in training, but which turned out to be almost universal in realizations of purposeful activities. The most successful writing projects were group projects, not in the sense that students wrote collaborative pieces, but in the sense that they shared a goal and produced a single product, such as a newspaper, a collection of love stories, or a village brochure. Each student's contribution was thus seen in the context of a purpose shared by the entire class and judged differently than it might have been as a single contribution.

This is not to suggest that we didn't acknowledge the importance of writing skills; our own pedagogical goals emphasized planning, critical thinking, and revising (although we left out spelling and punctuation). And teachers certainly reminded us that their official curricula focused more on skills than QUILL did. Yet, we felt that learning those skills proceeded best in the context of purposeful writing activities, where purpose could provide the glue that gave direction to planning and drafting, and imagining an audience response could guide revision.

As much as possible in training, then, we attempted to model such writing environments. The Alaska training provided teachers with several opportunities to experience and discuss purposeful writing. Training began with the writing workshop described in chapter 3, which enabled teachers to write and read within a literacy community. Using MAILBAG in training let teachers see how software could enhance purposeful writing. Sharing writing that students had done in other field-test classrooms also modeled for them how such writing could actually work in classrooms.

The *QUILL Teacher's Guide* also contained many examples of activities that embodied our philosophy, including detailed instructions for creating a class newspaper, a set of game reviews to be shared with other students, and a classified ad exchange. Sample writing from field-test classrooms was included for several of the activities. Because teachers had reacted positively to their MAILBAG experience, we also discussed Classroom Chat. This activity is based on Confidential Chat, a syndicated newspaper column that allows readers to solicit advice from other readers without revealing their names. In the column, letters are most often signed with names such as "Lonesome in Louisiana" or "Need Advice Soon." Our classroom adaptation kept the anonymous aspects of the newspaper example (since students could easily adopt secret names in QUILL) and suggested that students could ask for advice on academic, personal, or whimsical problems.

In retrospect, we can see that although we had provided teachers with an experiential basis for their appropriation of real purposes, we had not really articulated a clear notion of purpose in classroom writing. We were clear about our purpose: getting teachers to appropriate the purpose of getting students to understand the purpose of writing by doing purposeful tasks. But beyond a general intuition about purpose and some specific positive and negative examples, we had a fairly limited and fuzzy concept. Although our vision was tilted toward solidly ''functional'' examples in which student writing had a clear purpose in a community outside of school, we knew that purpose was sufficiently individual that teachers would come up with their own interpretations. We were not wrong there. The students and teachers in the Alaska QUILL project both expanded our view of purpose and reminded us of the characteristics of schools that can constrain purposeful writing activities.

ALTERNATE REALIZATIONS
OF PURPOSEFUL ACTIVITIES

Our insistent yet fuzzy definition of purpose was subject to many influences in the process of its realization in classrooms. Paramount among these were three questions whose answers would have significant effects on the actual classroom writing activities:

1. What did the teachers think writing was useful for? How did they use writing in their own lives to accomplish personal goals?
2. What did the teachers think students should learn about writing in school? To what extent did they adopt our perspective?
3. What natural sources of goals for writing existed in teachers' classrooms or community contexts?

These three themes are woven together in the examples that follow; no one factor accounts for any particular story, but the interaction among them produced a wide variety of purposeful and semipurposeful writing experiences for students in Alaska QUILL classrooms.

MAILBAG AS A PURPOSEFUL ENVIRONMENT

Many teachers introduced ''writing as communication'' to their students through MAILBAG. Since they had used MAILBAG extensively during training, teachers appreciated the differences between sending MAILBAG messages and standard classroom writing assignments. They used MAILBAG as a way to help students see writing as a communicative act through participating in a writing activity that demanded a real audience and purpose.

In most classrooms, MAILBAG use led to more purposeful writing. Students saw MAILBAG as an unconstrained writing environment and were thus able to use it for their own purposes. But, the specifics of this use took many different forms, often surprising both us and the teachers involved. And a few teachers regarded the openness of the MAILBAG environment as a pedagogical problem, and in these cases little purposeful writing with MAILBAG occurred.

We describe below a few of these alternate implementations of MAILBAG and how the integration of students' and teachers' purposes and habits with the innovation produced different realizations. We draw and quote from writing by the teachers about their own classrooms (from which we quote in this paper), student writing, electronic mail (both from MAILBAG and from a network for teachers), and field notes from classroom observations.

Symbiosis With Teachers' Pedagogical Goals.   For several teachers, MAILBAG and its built-in assumptions were completely consistent with their current classroom practices and their attitudes toward teaching writing. These teachers firmly believed in "student-centered education" and in students' feeling ownership of the process and product of their work in school. They saw MAILBAG as a welcome extension of the way they already taught writing. They were comfortable with students' deciding when, where, why, and on what topics to write. Bonnie's multigrade, village-school classroom reflected this symbiotic use of MAILBAG. Students used the program frequently and enthusiastically from the beginning of the year. Bonnie offered the following comments about her class' early use of MAILBAG, which, she says, "began with a roar and a blast."

> Probably the best thing about mailbag is communicating. The person at the keyboard is in complete control. I never made any mailbag assignments. Students could use it or not, decide what they would say, to whom, when, how often, and why.

Below is one example of a MAILBAG message written in Bonnie's class; note its oral-language character. Students like Wanda seemed to regard MAILBAG as an environment in which they could carry out the same communicative functions for which they used oral language.

DEAR ALICE,

    WHAT ARE YOU GOING TO DO AFTER SCHOOL? IF YOU WANT TO PLAY VOLLEYBALL AFTER SCHOOL WE CAN BUT FIRST I HAVE TO CLEAN UP AT OUR HOUSE FIRT OK. WE WILL PLAY ALMOST ALL DAY. YOU OUE ME A CAN OF POP BECAUSE YOU PROMISED IF YOU WERE LATE.

                WITH LOVE
                WANDA

Although many messages contained nonstandard grammar or spelling, as did Wanda's, Bonnie never corrected any student message. She considered MAILBAG to be in the students' domain, where spelling and punctuation were secondary to just plain communicating. Ernie, a K–2 teacher who also saw MAILBAG as an extension of his classroom writing philosophy, shared Bonnie's attitude toward students' ownership of MAILBAG writing:

> I never stressed proper form with the MAILBAG program when the students were sending messages back and forth between themselves. . . . I saw this program as a fluency activity. If the receiver of the message understood it, it served its purpose in my eyes.

In Bonnie's classroom, students expressed their control over MAILBAG by deciding both when to use MAILBAG and when to stop using it. Several other teachers also found that students' enthusiasm for MAILBAG diminished as the year went on, but Bonnie's comment about this shift reflects again how her educational views easily encompassed such a change:

> By springtime the mailbag was hardly used at all. At first I was disappointed, then pleased. The students had learned that there were appropriate forms of communication for specific needs.

Especially in small classes where students knew each other well and saw one another frequently outside of school, the kind of communication MAILBAG facilitated was mostly redundant. As Bonnie implied, students had become more sophisticated about audience and purpose and were not satisfied with a communicative situation that did not increase their access to real audiences.

In one class, however, interest in MAILBAG remained strong during the entire year. Hans taught high school in Bonnie's village and used MAILBAG with his class after learning about it from Bonnie. He designated one disk as the students' private MAILBAG disk and promised the class that he would never read it. The students continued to send messages on the disk all year, and MAILBAG remained the most popular QUILL activity. As the year went on, Hans actually had to ration MAILBAG's use because he wanted students to use the computer for other kinds of writing as well. Why did MAILBAG remain so popular in this class? Certainly at least one influence was the unique audience Hans defined for MAILBAG messages. It appears that the secrecy of the disk made the communication environment unusual enough that students did not consider it redundant with face-to-face communication.

Integration with Other Innovations.   Before the introduction of QUILL, the classrooms we studied differed from one another along several dimensions: most notably, teachers' beliefs and practices related to the teaching of writing. A few teachers, in response to their own changing notions of pedagogy, had already instituted innovations that were consistent with QUILL's pedagogical goals. In most cases, the two innovations enhanced one another, but in at least one case, the earlier innovation had already fulfilled the goals QUILL set forth and thus reduced the students' and teacher's enthusiasm for MAILBAG. Alexander, a fifth-grade teacher, had for several years played mailperson for a short daily period during which he would deliver handwritten notes from student to student in the class. He described the purpose of this activity:

> NOTES is an activity that gives the students an opportunity to write notes to one another under the supervision of the teacher with the only rule being that they must address the note to someone in the class and have their name as the return address. They know that I do not read their notes and that anything goes (and it probably does). This activity is done in silence with myself as the mailperson and usually lasts anywhere from five to fifteen minutes.

While NOTES was a good introduction to MAILBAG, it also diminished Alexander's and his students' interest in the computer-based activity. Compared to NOTES, in which they could send and receive half-a-dozen messages in one session, MAILBAG was inefficient; message exchanges could take place only over the course of days, rather than minutes. The features of MAILBAG that allowed them to send messages to a group did not interest the students. In essence, students had no unfulfilled communicative purposes that MAILBAG could satisfy. In addition, Alexander felt that NOTES had already fulfilled the goal that most teachers attributed to MAILBAG—involving students in real-audience writing. Therefore, Alexander moved on to the PLANNER and LIBRARY rather quickly, where he pursued other writing goals.

Interactions with Classroom Management.   Since many QUILL classrooms had only a single computer, using QUILL required some teachers to rethink their classroom management practices. How were they to integrate a free-form activity like MAILBAG into a more structured day? Wilma, a fifth-grade teacher, invented a procedure to deal with the changes in her classroom structure. Wilma's students' excitement over MAILBAG was particularly significant to her, since one of her goals for the year was to help her students learn to enjoy writing. While she was enthusiastic about MAILBAG's effect on her students, she was troubled by its classroom management consequences:

> When we started using MAILBAG, I had a problem with my students wanting to be back at the computer CONSTANTLY checking to see if they had any mail or not. We decided we needed to devise a system that would solve the problem. We talked about what we could do, and soon came up with a mailbox poster, which worked quite well. We each wrote our computer code name on a library book card pocket, and glued the pockets to a piece of poster board. The poster board was then hung on the wall behind the computers. Another pocket was

added to hold slips of red paper. When a student left a message on MAILBAG for White Knight, he or she would put a red slip into White Knight's pocket. After White Knight read his messages, he returned the red slips to the extra pocket.

The classroom management issues were so central to teaching with QUILL that Wilma's idea spread around the community via our technical assistance visits and the teachers' electronic mail network. The classroom management problem turned out to be a common one—and many teachers adopted Wilma's solution.

Different Goals for Individual Students. Jim, a sixth-grade teacher, had always treated his students as individuals. His class was made up of Black and Hispanic students from several housing projects, and he found he sometimes had to adopt unorthodox approaches to encourage certain students to put energy into their school work. Jim used MAILBAG to support this goal by adopting two separate personae in writing to his students. When he carried out straightforward, and sometimes quite personal, written conversations with his students, Jim adopted a teacher/computer expert persona, Dr. A. The following exchange is typical. The first message was posted to the Bulletin Board, where everyone in the class (including the teacher) could read it. The second is from the teacher to Marlowe, using her computer name, Pee Wee (which was particularly appropriate in this case).

Bathroom

Marlowe B.

There is a lot of trouble in the bathroom. There's been writing on the new paint job, and there's been someone who's been peeling the paint off the radiator. If people keep messing up the bathroom, Ducky [the janitor] said that she was going to close the bathroom until we learn not to write in it. And there's been plenty of noise in there. If we don't have to go to the bathroom, don't go in.

Dear Pee Wee,

Thank you for being concerned about the girls' bathroom. I feel sorry for the girls who are messing it up. They must be a little "messed up" themselves. When I see Ducky, I'll try to remember to tell her what you said. —Dr. A.

Jim also had a second, more frivolous, persona called Dunedeen, a mischievous monster who sent anonymous messages to several students each week.

Jim tended to use the Dunedeen persona with students who were reluctant writers, since his challenging tone got them to respond in writing to his teases. As Dunedeen, Jim engaged students in a fantasy world of teasing and light sarcasm, similar to the way they might interact with their friends on the playground. His messages provoked playful replies, filled with "hahahaha" and epithets such as "Squarehead," often from students who never spontaneously wrote in any other situation. In integrating QUILL with his strategies for dealing with individual students, Jim found MAILBAG's flexibility particularly useful for his purposes.

MAILBAG and the Conventional Writing Assignment.   Not all integrations of purposeful writing with MAILBAG into the classroom grew out of symbiosis between QUILL and a teacher's purposes. In one case, a teacher completely rejected MAILBAG because it conflicted with her views of the appropriate way to teach writing. This teacher started out using MAILBAG in the usual way, and students began sending messages according to their own purposes, such as love letters to one another. When the teacher discovered this, she immediately made MAILBAG unavailable, since she felt that the messages students had been exchanging were not appropriate classroom writing. The gap between her pedagogical assumptions and those underlying QUILL was too great.

In a slightly different attempt at integration, a fourth-grade teacher attempted to combine a fairly conventional writing assignment with MAILBAG. The idea for her assignment came from the *QUILL Teacher's Guide*, where we had introduced "Classroom Chat," a classroom version of "Confidential Chat." Mixing the personal consultation idea of Classroom Chat with a more conventional teacher-directed writing assignment, the teacher sent the following message, complete with pseudonym.

Dear Classy Computer Kids,

   There are five members in my family and only one shower. Because I'm the youngest member of our family, I'm the last one in line to take a shower. By then, there's usually no more hot water and not too much time for me to wash behind my ears! It's a horrible way to start a day. What can I do to solve this problem?

Cold, late, and dirty,
I. Needabath

The following tongue-in-cheek student response hovers between reality and fantasy much as the original letter did.

Dear I. Needabath,

I think you should tell the first person that takes a shower you have to go to the bathroom. Then they should let you go before they take a shower. Quickly lock the door and take your shower. You will have enough of time to wash behind your ears.

Sneaky and Desparate,
Kerry N. and Jenny B.

An interesting problem emerged in this activity because of the conflict between the teacher's goals and the presuppositions of MAILBAG. The form of the teacher's message mimicked that of the standard Confidential Chat letter, but the students in the class all knew who had sent the letter and, even more important, that it posed a fake problem. Thus, their assignment was to pretend they were answering a real letter from a needy person, while knowing it was an imaginary letter from their teacher. While students produced imaginative replies, we observed that students were confused about their audience (their teacher or I. Needabath) and their purpose (real or fantasy) while they were writing. This lack of clarity was most obvious when they were signing their names; many were not sure whether to use their own names or to make up clever pseudonyms. In this situation, the teacher's assignment worked only weakly as an attempt to integrate two inconsistent pedagogical goals.

Students' Goals: Affecting School, Classmates and the Outside World. Teachers were not the only ones for whom MAILBAG offered new opportunities for integrating technology with personal goals. In several classrooms, students found in MAILBAG a new and unexpected way to pursue their own purposes in school. Students in Syd's fifth-grade class in Juneau discovered that MAILBAG could serve an unexpected purpose in their relationships with others in the classroom. One of Syd's students "saw himself without friends"; Syd worried about both his academic and social development:

He chose late Friday for his time [on the computer] so he could miss it, not realizing that more often than not, late Friday was the easiest time for me to be his partner. The other children, in spite of their ugliness to one another, were able to sense his feelings and began writing him [MAILBAG] letters telling how much they liked him and that they wanted to be his friends. There is no way to describe the face of this handsome, brown-eyed boy as he read these notes, frequently slipped into his desk anonymously. He sat near me for obvious reasons and I would watch him remove one and literally clutch it to his chest.

Syd's students, having learned the power of writing, chose to use it to be kind to a troubled student with whom face-to-face communication was difficult.

Students' purposes also interacted in an unexpected way with the availability of MAILBAG in a fifth-grade class in Oregon. When the teacher included himself as a participant in MAILBAG, he discovered that his students offered him opinions on school that he had not previously heard. Notes such as "I like it a lot better when you put the schedule for the day on the board" and "I wish we had art class more often" were representative of the opinions students communicated using MAILBAG. Because students saw MAILBAG as a medium in which they had increased access to their teacher, they used it as a new way to pursue one of their own purposes: changing their school environment.

Many students in field-test sites in Alaska used QUILL to answer a pressing communicative need: they were unable to be in touch easily with people outside of their own villages, and they had no way of meeting new people. Partly in response to their needs, the QUILL project in Alaska instituted a long-distance network, implemented through a combination of human travel and U.S. mail (Barnhardt, 1984). On one of our trips through Alaska to visit classrooms, we carried a disk called "Supermail." Students in each classroom wrote messages to children in classrooms they knew we would later visit, often to students they had never met. Several eighth-grade girls saw this long-distance network as an ideal opportunity to work on their social problems.

Calling All Men

Sheila Forsythe   Althea Jones

Hi,

This note is to all you good looking guys out there in the world. There are two of us writing so we'll tell you a little bit about ourselves. Our names are Sheila Forsythe and Althea Jones. We're both 14 and stuck in a small town in Alaska called McGrath. We have a pretty big problem and we hope that you guys will help us out. We have a very short supply of foxy dudes here. So if you are a total fine babe PLEASE I repeat PLEASE write us!!!

Keywords: /McGrath/Male Order Men/

The authors worked hard on aspects of their message that would attract the attention of their desired audience. The second keyword (including the misspelling), for example, was their own invention, intended to attract male readers; their title, obviously, had the same purpose. These girls were correct in assessing what would please their audience: Groups of boys in distant classrooms, curious about the keyword and title, did read their message.

Not to be outdone, two girls in the next town, Holy Cross, wrote the following message on the Supermail disk:

Good Looking Juneau Boys

Two Holy Cross Girls   Josie and Evelyn

Our names are Josie Adams and Evelyn Fields. We like skiing, basketball, hockey, writing letters to cute boys, and we would be more than pleased
if any of you cute boys would write to us. We don't have any boyfriends.
So you don't have to worry about that! We also would like you to send
a picture when you write. (You are going to write aren't you?) We will
send you a picture too. Josie is 14, and Evelyn is 13. Well, please write
soon! We are waiting for your letters!!!

```
          xxx     xxx
        xxxxx   xxxxx
     xxxxxxxxxxxxxxxxxx
       xxxxxxxxxxxxxx
        xxxxxxxxxx
          xxxxxxx
            xxx
             x
```

WE SEND YOU OUR HEARTS!
SINCERELY, JOSIE AND EVELYN

Keywords: /Juneau Boys/H.c.r Girls/

These two girls used a slightly different strategy for attracting readers; they
knew the disk would be travelling to Juneau next, so they specifically aimed
their "personal ad" toward Juneau boys, including them in both the title and
keywords. They also spent considerable time and effort drawing the heart so
that their message would compete effectively with the one from McGrath. In-
cidentally, boys in both Juneau and Oregon, where the disk later travelled,
took all four girls' addresses with the intention of writing to them during the
summer. In these cases, students' urgent purposes found expression in the new
opportunities QUILL provided.

While most students were eager to send messages to distant classrooms, many
found the idea of writing to strangers uncomfortable. But serendipitous connections seemed to ease this transition for some students in Nikolai, as their
teacher, Don, explained:

> What made this activity fun for my class was the fact that Chip had just come
> from Telida and the most recent messages on the disk were from cousins and
> playmates upriver. This connection made the notion of sending hellos to strangers
> Outside seem less threatening.

The Supermail disk provided an opportunity for the students to be in touch with the outside world; it made the transition gradual by allowing them to expand their understanding of communication from a familiar audience to a larger and unfamiliar audience Outside.

Adapting Community Purposes

The world outside the school walls is an obvious real audience for student writing, but in most settings, it is often difficult to interest anyone beyond students' parents. Small Alaskan villages provided a welcome answer to that plight; with only a few classes in the school, and as few as 25 people in the village, anything students wrote with their community as audience was likely to be enthusiastically received. In addition, teachers felt a bond with their villages; many of them had chosen to teach in remote villages because of a commitment to Native communities, and they had few people to interact with other than their students' families. Thus, several of the projects with real purposes drew their inspiration from the presence of a convenient and attentive audience. In addition, many writing projects strengthened the link between young students and their Native culture. In the Native villages, the preservation of Native culture was also a priority in schools, and writing projects that increased students' familiarity with their Native culture or language fulfilled a purpose that was often explicit in the official curriculum.

The writing project that most clearly involved the entire village and a connection to Native language was a community calendar produced in Telida by Helen's class of nine students in grades 1 through 5. The calendar itself included the birthdays of everyone in the village, typed by the students on the computer, printed, cut out, and pasted in the calendar on the appropriate days. Each month was illustrated with a story and accompanying picture by one of the students whose birthday fell in that month. Figure 5.1 shows the calendar for April, 1984; the story is typical of other stories in the calendar in being about the natural world and in anthropomorphizing familiar animals.

The stories were written in both Athabaskan and English. The Athabaskan text, which uses a slightly different alphabet from English, was composed with QUILL using the closest possible letters, then modified by hand to the Athabaskan alphabet. Note, for example, several instances in Fig. 5.1 of "l" modified to be "ł." Later, a chip became available through InterLearn, Inc. that could print Athabaskan and Inuit alphabets directly.

Helen made enough copies of the calendar for everyone in Telida, as well as extras for the rest of us in the project, bound them, and distributed them throughout the community. For the entire year, everyone's wall or refrigerator was adorned with a calendar made by Telida's schoolchildren. And fewer birthdays were probably forgotten that year than any previous one.

Ernie found that interviewing elders to produce a collection of Native cultural heritage writings did not work in Chevak as it had in Shungnak. The story is particularly interesting because it demonstrates the interaction between a teacher's goals and the cultural context in which he tried to get students to appropriate those goals. Chevak is a very culturally-aware village, and the school program includes a "Cultural Heritage" program that employs five people, two of whom are elders who frequently visit classrooms to tell Cup'ik stories and teach Cup'ik Eskimo Dancing. In addition, students study the Cup'ik language for half an hour a day.

In this context, it made sense for Ernie to try to produce a book made up of stories—both real and mythical—that elders might tell. Ernie continued the story:

> I decided that it would be fun to interview several of the elders in the village and come up with a small book on them. We went through the bubbling [brainstorming] process in terms of what we wanted to know and each group of students picked an elder in the village to interview. The trouble came when none of the students would go and interview the elders. Several due dates came and went, as did my patience with the students. Finally Elsie (a Cup'ik aide) told me the problem was that it was not viewed as proper for younger children to go and directly ask elders for information. If the elders began the conversation this was fine, but it was not the child's role to probe for information. This was a very good lesson for me as it reminded me that I was indeed teaching in a different cultural setting than my own, and there was a different set of rules governing social organization than I was used to.

Ernie's lesson is an important one for this book, since it emphasizes the relationship between communication and community, as exemplified by the interaction between Ernie's communication goals and Chevak's community standards. Even though Ernie's purpose coincided with some explicit goal of the curriculum, cultural constraints made it an impossible task for students, whose personal goals to be socially appropriate far outweighed their commitment to any school task.

Several teachers saw writing as a way to preserve the culture that was rapidly disappearing in Native villages. Ironically, computers, part of the "new culture" that was changing traditional ways, became the mechanism through which pieces of traditional culture could be recorded. While several Anglo teachers initiated activities in this vein, Lena, the only Native teacher in our training group, put together the most extensive project with cultural content. She had her junior high students (sixth, seventh, and eighth graders) write descriptions of the roles of members of a traditional Cup'ik family. For some students, these roles were familiar, as their families still followed Cup'ik traditions. For others, the project required discussions with their parents about the changes their family and other families had gone through. Students worked in small groups discussing individual family roles, wrote a collaborative first draft, and cooperatively edited their piece. The following is part of one of the stories that resulted from this project.

Once one young bear got
married to a bear! The
young bear is a great hunter
now.

Three years later the bear
died! It had two kids.

The two kids lived sadly ever
after.

Ts'eʔdi ʔon sojeye
hine'ediyo. Idiyats'
sritodihwtan ts'e'
hinohwnish. Nidahikogh hwla'
nehwnaneyoʔ hwye'iʔ
tsedadiyok. NoteK'a srakay
ena it'aṇ. Eyt hwtɬ'wṇ
notehna srakay ena himi'
tr'ohut'ih ts'e' dihidiyok.

by Joe Nikolai

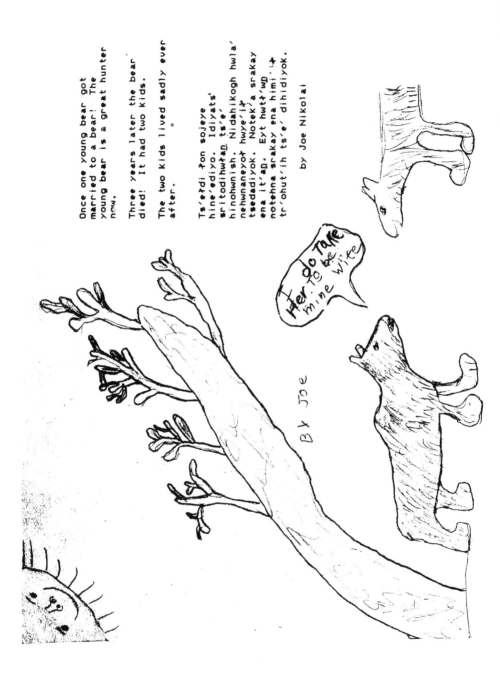

By Joe

April 1984

Dzedzano'o'

SUNDAY	MONDAY	TUESDAY	WEDNESDAY	THURSDAY	FRIDAY	SATURDAY
1 Deacon Nikolai	2	3	4	5	6 Heldina Eluska Steven Nikolai	7
8	9	10	11	12 Edward Ticknor	13	14
15	16	17	18	19	20	21
22	23	24	25	26 Thera Ticknor	27 Winchell Ticknor Steve Eluska Joe Nikolai	28
29	30					

FIG. 5.1. Telida calendar.

95

> Mother makes the mukluks by handsewing. She first makes the soles and part of the trimming. The last thing she puts on are the mukluk's laces, which are made from the sealskin that has no fur on it. It takes one to two days to finish making the mukluks with long hours spent on the pairs.
>
> Mother makes mittens out of rabbit skins. Mother cuts the rabbit skin first in the shape of the mitt then she starts sewing the mittens. After she sews the mittens she then places a cloth material on the outside of the mitten. The last thing that she sews onto the mittens is the strap that would go around the neck of a person.

Lena also worked with the high school students to integrate LOGO into her cultural perspective. These students created LOGO procedures to draw Cup'ik artifacts, such as ulus (seal knives), to go with the family stories. Following the LOGO syntax, each procedure name started with "TO," and the bulletin board was filled with pictures and procedures sporting names such as "TO ULU," "TO KAYAK," and "TO IGLOO."

School and Community Newspapers.   The most popular community-oriented writing activity in Alaska was producing a newspaper. Students in over half of the QUILL classrooms in Alaska put out classroom newspapers. On the surface, a newspaper sounds like an ideal project to incorporate real audiences and purposes into students' writing. Newspapers generally have a particular audience in mind and various articles fulfill different purposes: provide information, entertain, persuade, review. But since classroom newspapers are produced in schools, they often have purposes other than those a real newspaper embodies. Often they are merely a cover story to structure or enliven a writing assignment; often there is a school purpose to teach a particular genre (e.g., editorial) or just to practice basic skills. Looking at the set of articles included in a classroom paper can reveal just how much real purpose and audience have found their way into the writing process.

For example, a newspaper produced using QUILL in a classroom in Massachusetts included four separate articles (out of 16) on the same class field trip. In a commercial newspaper, multiple articles on a single topic usually address different aspects of a situation. In contrast, these four articles covered similar aspects of the same topic from similar perspectives. Articles throughout were mixed in the kind of audience they assumed. Some wrote as if their audience were their classmates, who knew a large number of critical details about their subject (e.g., writing about their baseball team as "Gallager's," without identifying the town or league). Others wrote as if they were addressing a larger audience who would need to know at least what town the teams were in (e.g., "Derans, a baseball team in Ridgeport"). These inconsistencies resulted from the confusion between stated and school purposes in producing the newspaper. The paper fell into a genre somewhere between a cumulative writing folder and a real newspaper, so students could not be sure how to interpret audience and purpose.

The Alaska newspapers were somewhat more successful in adopting the genres and purposes of real newspapers, yet they, too, differed from real newspapers in format, audience, and purpose. Papers published by older students tended to be most like real models, with several sections (news, sports, reviews) and greater attention to audience. Many others were more like literary magazines, composed mostly of students' stories and illustrations. Some assumed the rest of the school as an audience, while in smaller communities, the newspaper sometimes served the entire village. Teachers differed in how much they participated in editing and production; several teachers specifically considered newspapers a place where students could decide on their own standards, while Alexander, the staff advisor for the fourth–sixth grade newspaper in his school, took a more proactive role. (See chapter 6 for a detailed discussion of classroom standards and revision.)

In general, Alaska teachers saw newspapers mostly as a device for organizing a group writing project that would result in a concrete product that students could feel proud of. The teachers seldom used the newspaper context to discuss specific audience considerations, such as taking into account what the audience might or might not know about the students and their classroom. In smaller villages where most people knew one another, this was less of an issue, but even where larger audiences were involved, teachers did not use the newspaper activity to work directly on audience sensitivity.

Several teachers wrote explicitly about this view of the newspaper activity after their year working with QUILL. Wilma, for example, described the content of her class's 5th Grade *DIRTY* News. (DIRTY is an acronym made up by her class standing for Dig Into Reading Today, Yeah!)

> Students chose topics about which to write each month, and we also incorporated classroom writing projects. We studied how to write editorials, and put out one issue that included fifteen editorials that covered just about everything around McGrath and the school.

The newspaper that resulted was a mixed genre, found almost exclusively in schools; Figure 5.2 is the first page of one of the early issues. It contained news stories (mostly about the class' new computer equipment and disks!), book reviews, sports stories, health and safety notes (e.g., "people who ski at night should stay on the left side of the road"), seasonal stories (e.g., seven Christmas stories), word puzzles, and hand-drawn cartoons. There was no attempt to match the common format of a real newspaper, other than borrowing the most obvious features, such as a masthead and staff box. But Wilma made

5th Grade DIRTY News

room 3

Quill being used in 5th grade

Quill is a computer program. Quill is a program that is made to send messages to other people. Quill can send messages to people, couples, groups, and companies. Quill is a disk used for all kinds of things. The three things that you can use with it are the Mailbag disk, the Library disk, and the Planner disk. Quill can also be used for writing reports and stories. When you write a story or report you can save it, edit it, or just throw it away. Quill is a very neat disk to me so if you ever get a disk like it I am sure you would like it very much too.

by Heather Kountz

Road Safety

People who ski at night, should stay on the left side of the road. If thay don't, thay will get hurt. If thay don't maybe a three wheel or a car will run over and it will be to late.

by Alexandra Bobby

5th Grade Reads DIRTY Books

No not a Playboy but an acronim meaning Dig Into Reading Yaa. Yes every day from 11:00 to 11:15 5th grade U S S Rs (undistebed super silently reads). Good day for today.

by Burke Mehl

The Game on Dec. 3, 1983

Friday, December 3, 1983, the Micro Knights played against the Mini Knights in a very challenging game. The Micro Knights were defeated by the Mini Knights with the score of seventeen to eight.

High scorer for the Mini Knights, scoring ten points, was Clinton Shelborne. Second high scorer for the Mini Knights was Reno Hart.

High scorer for the Micro Knights was Wayne Dick with the score of three points. Second high scorer for the Micro Knights was Shannon Baker.

The micro and Mini Knights are scheduled to challenge each other a second time on December 9, 1983. The Mini Knights have won three out of four games and hope to again defeat the Micro Knights on December 9, 1983.

by Reno L. Hart

FIG. 5.2. First page of 5th grade DIRTY News.

it clear that her purpose in producing a class newspaper was not to take into account all of the audience and purpose characteristics of a real paper. Rather, it was to give students an opportunity to construct something they could OWN by writing. Wilma included the following "Letter from the Teacher" in one of the early issues of the *DIRTY News*.

> The fifth grade class has produced this newspaper on their own. Although I help them out with some of the typing, they are responsible for the editing, revision, lay-out, etc., and the students come up with the ideas for the content. I have retained the students' spelling and structure, as I feel it would be presumptuous of me to edit their work without their knowledge or consent.
>
> I'm very proud of this class. The students show a great deal of initiative, and their writing skills are improving daily. They enjoy writing, and we can see the results of that enjoyment. We have been using the computer for word processing in all our writing, and the students have learned word processing skills very quickly.
>
> GOOD JOB, DIRTY KIDS!

The Eagle's News, published by Bonnie's multigrade class in Shungnak, was closer to a community newspaper than Wilma's. Here again the nature of the community can account for some of the difference: Shungnak is less than half the size of McGrath and there are many fewer children in school. A classroom newspaper in Shungnak would make more sense than in McGrath, where it might have competition from other classes or even from the Anchorage paper. *The Eagle's News* included articles such as the following:

QUARTERLY MEETING

The Quarterly Meeting will be in Shungnak from Wednesday, March 14 to Sunday, March 18. People from the NANA region will come here. People from Anaktuvuk Pass come here too. They will have business meeting from 10-12, 2:00 service and 7:00 service. The people are gonna be busy in Shungnak.

Notice that this article not only assumes the entire community as audience, but implicitly excludes others by leaving out explanatory phrases for "Quarterly Meetings" and "services."

The newspaper that Helen's class published in Telida was even more of a community paper. The small size of the community (75 people) made this possible, but Helen's goal of connecting the students with their community naturally led her to think of the newspaper as a community resource. She expressed her overriding goal as follows: "I believed that the school belonged to the community, and that I was there to work with the community to make the school as much as it could be." Following this philosophy, Helen refers to the Telida Current as "our first school/community newspaper."

Interestingly, it was the arrival of a copy machine in the Telida school that led to the publishing of the Telida Current, as the combined presence of QUILL and the copy machine piqued students' interest in publishing. The first issue, which appeared in November, included news articles on the arrival of TV and telephones in Telida, "Telida News in Brief," a group story by the Telida students, a page of Wish Poems, several song dedications, and a "phone book" listing all the phone numbers in Telida and in Nikolai, a nearby village. Figure 5.3 shows the staff and one article from this first issue. While the contents of the first issue clearly suggest a community focus, Helen described how the newspaper became even more connected with the rest of the community.

One Sunday afternoon I went over to the school for something, and Agnes, my aide, was working on the computer. I was surprised because I hadn't ever shown her how to use QUILL, but I saw that she was typing up a list of song dedications which various people had given me for the paper. She told me that Joe (her son) had shown her how to do it. It was a nice arrangement for everyone, as

---

Newspaper Staff

Writers and reporters:
All the Telida Students
Editors and typists:
Nancy Esai
Margie Esai
Joe Nikolai
Advisor:
Helen Frost

Telida News in Brief

1. Steve Eluska and Agnes Ticknor went to McKinley Fork and they came back the same day.
2. Bert Gregory went to Anchorage and he will be back on the 29th.
3. Agnes might go to Nikolai for a meeting.
4. Mary Mixon was visiting for awhile.
5. Helen went to Fairbanks for Thanksgiving.
6. Gretchen was here teaching us about photography and Foxfire.
7. Susan Barthel was here doing puppetry, and while she was here we did a puppet show at the school.
8. Donna MacAlpine came Monday afternoon.
9. We expect Naomi Gates on Tuesday.

FIG. 5.3. Second page of first issue of Telida Current.

there was a rule that children could not be in the school without an adult—Agnes' presence allowed Joe to be in the school working on some project of his, and he was available to help her if she needed help with QUILL. As for me, I was delighted to have someone else type the song dedications, which everyone loved to have in the paper, but which were very tedious to type. And so the paper became even more than the class paper.

In sum, most Alaska classroom newspapers served the teacher's purpose of providing students with a concrete group project and a forum for publishing. Few, if any, used the activity to focus on considerations of audience or to reproduce the mix of genres one would expect in a real newspaper. On the other hand, newspapers from smaller villages tended to be combination school/community papers and naturally served some of the informational functions of real newspapers.

While most schools are not in such small communities, the "school/community" paper may still be a relevant concept. With growing numbers of immigrant students in cities in the United States, many neighborhoods are small ethnic communities—or a collection of several such communities. In strengthening their connections to communities, schools could take advantage of this neighborhood structure to define a variety of audiences for writing. Haitian students, for example, might want to create a newspaper for their own community or Cambodian students for theirs. Before they can become a cohesive multicultural group, students need to feel secure connections with their own cultural group. Writing could serve community solidarity in urban settings in much the same way it did in small Native communities such as Telida.

The Classroom Community.   Most of the discussion above relates to goals that are readily described as "real"; they have an obvious audience beyond the classroom, serve some kind of function outside of the school, or relate to a reason or genre in which adults write. These were the kinds of situations we had originally envisioned when we spoke of "real purposes and audiences" in training sessions. We had less idea how to think about more conventional classroom assignments such as (but not as hackneyed as) "Write about what you did on your summer vacation," when everyone in class writes about the same topic. During the year, however, we saw several examples of how such a project could engage students and become purposeful for them. It was not the topic itself that made these projects important to students, but rather the way they arose from and reflected social relations in the classroom.

Ernie's class' book of love poems is the clearest example of an ordinary-sounding project that students got deeply invested in because of its relation to their particular classroom culture:

Our book of love poems started by several students laughing at my old sneakers I occasionally wore in class. I told the children that I love these sneakers, they

were my very best friends. One student quickly remarked that it was silly to love
something like a pair of sneakers. I turned the tables on him and said, "Isn't
there anything that you love that isn't alive?" He responded by saying that he
loved whale meat. Soon everybody in the class was shouting what they loved.
I told them it was time you wrote to them and told them so. Teaching children
is so much fun when you hit a responsive chord, they just take off and are absorbed in a task. That's what happened with this project. The students worked
for almost an hour on their first drafts . . . I had love letters to desks, chairs,
earrings, shoes, clocks, grass, and several other things.

Ernie had come across a "teachable moment" and had taken advantage
of it. Primed by their discussion of Ernie's sneakers, his students were curious
about their own attachments to inanimate objects and took on the goal of
producing a love story book of their own. When the time came to illustrate
the collection, Ernie cleverly expanded the community of students working on
the book, thus connecting his students with others in the school, making the
project even more important, and guaranteeing a larger audience for the finished
product.

> I was going to have the students draw a picture to go along with their letter, but
> I decided to involve the sixth, seventh, and eighth grades in the project. These
> students had been working with LOGO and I thought it would be an excellent
> project for them to illustrate our book.

The final product included 24 love stories, a table of contents of the poems
alphabetically arranged by subject, and a dedication from Ernie. It was cop-
ied for all the students who worked on it; an "archival" copy was laminated
and bound. Figure 5.4 is the Table of Contents of the book; the authors are
listed with the names they chose to use on the computer. Figure 5.5 shows
two typical love stories with their accompanying illustrations.

In the love stories project, Ernie and his student together constructed a
project that matched his interpretation of writing with real goals and audiences.
Students were invested both in the idea of a group product and in the process
of writing their individual pieces. In other classroom situations, students' desire
to work with their peers appeared to be the primary goal, while the project
itself was just a means to that end. In a field-test classroom in Connecticut,
for example, three Hispanic girls used the computer whenever possible to write
a TV series about Menudo, a Puerto Rican rock group. Our sense was that
their activity was fueled as much by the fun they had working together as by
their mutual interest in the actual project. Similarly, four boys in Wilma's room
started a series of adventure tales, starring Hunter—a fearless space-cycle rider
who tangled with fierce vegetables and many other villains—that they continued
in their sixth grade classroom the next year. Ernie also reported an incident
in which "two boys wanted to write a story about the igloo that the class built,

TABLE OF CONTENTS

PAGE

FIG. 5.4.   Love Stories table of contents.

which won first prize at our winter carnival. They were so excited and ready to write that I let them go right on the computer and have at the story. It threw the whole schedule out of whack for the rest of the day, but I felt it was all right to do this when I saw the excitement in the two boys' faces.''

By and large, these socially motivated incidents did not occur at the beginning of the year, but, rather, after students had had experience working together at the computer and had developed relationships with other students in the class. In many classrooms, students worked in small groups of two or three at the computer because it was a scarce resource that had to be shared among 20–30 students. Ernie's class of 24 students, for example, always used the computer in teams of three, with each team getting half an hour a day to write. In Wilma's somewhat smaller class, on the other hand, each student used the computer alone for 20 minutes a day. Interestingly, in both Wilma's and Ernie's classes, students spontaneously organized group writing projects. In

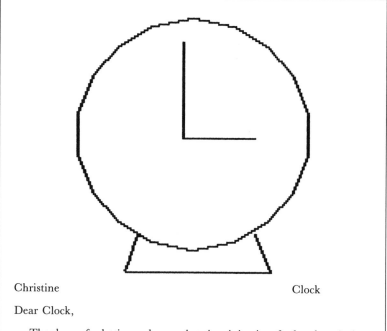

Christine   Clock

Dear Clock,

Thank you for letting us know what time it is, time for lunch and when we go home. When it is time for Reading. You have two hands, sixty little lines and a red line that moves.

Keywords: /Clock/

FIG. 5.5a.   Love Stories: Clock.

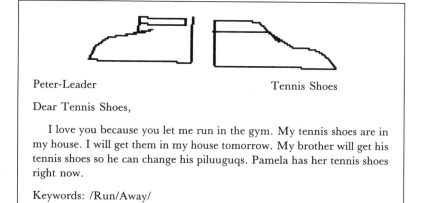

Peter-Leader   Tennis Shoes

Dear Tennis Shoes,

I love you because you let me run in the gym. My tennis shoes are in my house. I will get them in my house tomorrow. My brother will get his tennis shoes so he can change his piluuguqs. Pamela has her tennis shoes right now.

Keywords: /Run/Away/

FIG. 5.5b.   Love Stories: Tennis Shoes.

Ernie's class, the origin is clear; in Wilma's, we think it resulted more from students' collaborative experiences using LOGO (which she introduced in the middle of the year) than from their QUILL experiences, which comprised predominantly individual writing.

In some classrooms, collaborative writing arose more from a teacher's sense of its importance than from sharing limited computer resources among groups of students. Helen, in particular, thought a group writing experience was important for her young students. She often gathered her seven students around the computer and acted as scribe for a story they composed as a group. QUILL supported this activity because everyone in the group could each see the words on the screen, they could change the story easily, and each child could have a copy of the finished story. Figure 5.6, "Ellen and Kate," is a story created in this way, which appeared in the *Telida Current.*

In some Alaska QUILL classrooms, students wrote collaboratively primarily because of the low computer to student ratio, but where true writing communities arose, they resulted from such factors as the teacher's acceptance of collaborative pieces, his or her emphasis on writing for an audience, and the amount and kind of talk about writing that occurred in the classroom. Some of these ingredients were explicitly supported in QUILL (e.g., LIBRARY entries had space for multiple authors), others were discussed in training, others arose in teachers' experience with the community that grew out of their electronic network (see chapter 7 for details), and still others evolved from teachers' experiences teaching writing in new ways. The QUILL project provided a variety of supports for teachers trying to establish writing as a central part of their

---

Ellen and Kate

A group story by the Telida Students

Once upon a time there was an old lady named Ellen, and a little girl. They were walking in the woods, and a bear saw them and ran after the little girl. Her name was Kate. She said, "Help, Ellen!" She started running and the bear chased after her and caught her. Ellen kicked the bear and the bear got angry and ate her. Then he took Kate home to his den and he showed her to his cubs, two boys and one girl.

They played with her, those cubs. Kate was scared. She was crying and laughing.

Then the mother bear came and said, "Cubs, come and go to sleep. Take a nap."

While they were sleeping, Kate snuck out and went home. She told her Grandpa that the bear ate her Grandma.

After that she lived with her Grandpa. The lived sadly ever after.

FIG. 5.6.   Telida collaborative story.

classroom context, but it did not guarantee the success of their efforts. Where such communities truly flourished, they had the potential to become a prime source of purpose for student writing.

Social and Political Goals.   Sometimes a teacher's own political and social goals were so strong that they influenced every interaction he or she had with students, writing activities included. Sister Judy Tralnes, the sixth-, seventh-, and eighth-grade teacher in Holy Cross, who had chosen to devote her life to a service-oriented religious order, was such a person. In planning writing activities, she considered the village community an audience and a source of legitimate purposes, but her ultimate goal was to help her students feel a sense of power over their lives. Here is an eloquent description of her personal goal:

> One thing that struck me again and again while teaching in Holy Cross was the sense of powerlessness among the people. Their sense or apparent sense that they could do nothing to interfere with what was going to happen to them. That life was a series of things that happened, not what we made of it. So often I noticed a feeling of powerlessness and people with a very lowly opinion of themselves. There were a few exceptions but they were the exceptions to the rule.
>
> I was determined to help the youngsters that I taught to become more aware of their own personal power, more aware of their impact on one another and their possible impact in the world. . . . I hoped that they could come to a real sense of achievement and experience the rewards of their own accomplishments in becoming outstanding students. Therefore I demanded a great deal of them . . . a lot more than had been demanded of them previously. They were not disappointed in the outcome. It was a struggle in the beginning however.

Sister Judy first found an unexpected opportunity to help her students find a sense of power through coaching a newly formed junior high basketball team. Basketball is the most important competitive sport in rural villages; as Sister Judy said, "nothing is more real in life than the basketball court." After two excellent seasons, she decided "to show them that they really could affect the village." The team had been wearing cast-off uniforms from the senior high school and sometimes looked ridiculous on the court. So they decided to ask the city council for new uniforms. They planned persuasive speeches and delivered them at the next city council meeting. The city council not only awarded them basketball uniforms, but also warm-up suits. Sister Judy continued the story:

> Were these youngsters empowered. They had the world in their hand . . . they were just delighted. An emotional high soon passes. I figured it was time to do something truly concrete. Since the people are so closely bound to the land they occupy, they draw a part of their self concept from the land in which they live. So I decided we would do a brochure on Holy Cross village. I'm a big bug on

saying "thank you" in concrete ways, so I presented this as a way that they could say thank you to the city council and to the village for the uniforms and warm-up suits. . . . The youngsters were divided into groups of twos and threes to work on different topics. One group took history, another group took businesses, another group described the homes, another group described employment, one group described their basketball winnings.

The youngsters did the composing. We edited, edited, edited, and re-edited. And finally were ready to put it on the paper. It was just a thrill to me to find out that you could set up any size margin you wanted. You could single space or double space or triple space. It was just glorious. So we got the brochure laid out. The youngsters did their own illustration of it and we sent it off to the central office in the district to have it printed. We figured probably 200 copies would be enough. The people were absolutely delighted. When it came back, we had the most winsome chamber of commerce brochure that they'd ever seen. It was a delight. And the youngsters again had the rewards of their own labor, had the admiration of the village for doing something that was really attractive and really admirable and they said thank you in a very tangible way.

The brochure contained such down-to-earth descriptions as these:

Holy Cross is in the interior of Alaska. When the mission was founded, it was built on the banks of the Yukon River. Now, because the River moves, we are about one mile away from the main Yukon river.

POPULATION: Holy Cross has about 275 people; most are Athabaskan Indians and Yupik Eskimos. There are also some white and black people. Everyone here speaks English.

CLOTHES: Holy Cross people wear different clothes in the winter than in the summer. In the winter we wear mukluks, Native hats, home made mittens, knitted scarves, and sometimes we wear home-made parkas. In the summer we use shorts, pants, short-sleeved shirts, tennis shoes, and little jackets.

In producing the Holy Cross brochure (one side of which is shown in Fig. 5.7), Sister Judy started from her life's purpose to help others, particularly her students, feel empowered. She found expression for that purpose in many arenas—in sports, in local politics, and in writing. She realized that language is a central tool in taking responsibility for one's life and convinced her students of that by arranging situations where their words—either spoken or written—had impact. As with Helen's Telida calendar, the village provided a convenient and relevant audience. But Sister Judy had a more complex goal than Helen, both to give students the opportunity to produce something for a familiar and appreciative audience and to get them to learn the strategies of reciprocal interactions by saying "thank you" to the city council.

Sister Judy did not stop with the village community. She knew that her students needed to know they could wield power in the larger world as well. Early

SCHOOLS

When the Jesuit priests first came to Holy Cross there weren't any people here. In 1886 the Jesuits started a mission which had a little school. People came from different villages and small cities. The town started to grow gradually. The Sisters of Saint Anne came and looked after the pupils of the mission. People built houses. More people started to hear about the establishment in Holy Cross and then more people started to bring their children here. People from nearby had to bring their children here when school started and then come back and get them when it was summer. Holy Cross Mission School eventually became one of the most respected schools in Alaska.

Today Holy Cross has two schools; one is for the Headstart students, one is for Kindergarten to Grade 12. There are about eighty-five students in the two schools. Holy Cross School is a REAA school in the Iditarod Area School District. The present acting-Superintendent is Mr. Terry Chase.

We will soon have a day-care center, also.

Most of our houses are one story houses. We have a few two-story houses and a two unit apartment. Most have plumbing, running water and electricity. Some have to carry their water from other places. The houses are scattered through the village. Some of the houses are made of plywood, with only a few log houses. They usually have two or four bedrooms. Nearly every house has a porch that is closed-in because it is cold and the closed porch helps to keep the heat in the house. The majority of people in town have wood stoves; others have oil stoves.

Up to twenty visitors can rent a room or apartment at the lodge.

We have one steambath house. The older men use it once in a while.

FIG. 5.7.   Holy Cross brochure.

in the year, her basketball team had watched *The Day After* (a drama about nuclear war) together and spent several hours discussing how upset they were at the state of international relations. A few months later, Sister Judy learned that the next Trident submarine was going to be called *Alaska*. When she passed this information on to her class,

The youngsters were positively chagrined, just overwhelmed. So they had influenced their school, they had influenced their families, they had influenced the city council and the whole village. Now, with that background, it was time for them to influence their state. A team spirit with the people of the village was a wonderful thing to work with because it comes from their very roots, their very culture. It's not really proper to stand out, to call attention to yourself. But in working as a group, unified as a team, you can do a lot. . . .

They sat down and typed out letters to every Junior High class in the whole state asking them to gather petitions and send them to our congresspeople, to our governor and to our state senators, and our representatives. . . .

The youngsters said in that letter how they felt about Alaska and how they felt about the Trident II submarine and let them know that the meaning of Alaska and the Trident submarines were so different that the Trident II in their estimate should not bear the name of the state of Alaska. [Their letter is Fig. 5.8.]

Shortly after graduation I received a phone call from a woman who said a junior high youngster had come to her in Anchorage asking her to sign this petition, and they were going to have a press conference that evening and wanted some more information from my class on how it all got started. This story hit AP and UPI, it was wonderful. The youngsters received confirmation that they really could be of power. . . .

Sister Judy's interpretation of writing for a real purpose came straight from her life purpose of serving whatever community she found herself in. That translated into helping her students to take control of their lives, to feel self-confident and powerful. She found ample opportunities to plan activities through which her students gained a sense of power—through action, speech, and writing. Writing for her was one more instrument through which her students learned that they could affect the world. While she did not neglect the mechanics of writing (and, in fact, insisted that her students practice penmanship as well as writing on the computer), her primary purpose was educational in Dewey's sense—to equip her students with tools for learning and the confidence to use them.

The students' whole-hearted participation in the brochure and letter-writing projects—and the quality and sincerity of the writing they produced—seems to indicate that they appropriated Sister Judy's goal as she had appropriated ours. Their junior high commencement speeches that year diverged from the common list of thank-you's; as Sister Judy said, "This year they had something to say."

Practical Writing

One common interpretation of "writing with a purpose" is "practical writing"—filling out job applications, writing business letters in the right format, ordering merchandise. In several Alaska classrooms, students engaged in such activities, partly because of their functional value, but partly because teachers saw them as a context in which it made sense for students to practice mechanical skills such as capitalization, spelling, and punctuation. As such, these activities had both a legitimate stated purpose (e.g., to order from a mail-order catalog) and a school purpose (e.g., to practice certain writing skills). They differed from common school activities, such as book reviews, whose stated

TRIDENT SUBS

JUNIOR HIGH CLASS

HOLY CROSS SCHOOL
P.O. BOX 210
HOLY CROSS, ALASKA
99602

APRIL 17, 1984

JUNIOR HIGH STUDENTS

DEAR JUNIOR HIGH STUDENTS,

JUNIOR HIGH STUDENTS ARE VERY IMPORTANT AND SOME DAY WE CAN GROW
UP TO BE GREAT LEADERS. WE WANT TO BE ADULTS AND HAVE FAMILIES. WE ALSO
WANT OUR LAND TO BE A VERY BEAUTIFUL PLACE. WE WANT TO LIVE AND GROW
UP TO BE BETTER PEOPLE THAN THERE ARE TODAY IN THE WORLD. WE WANT TO
HAVE A FUTURE. I THINK THAT WE SOON CAN BE THE LEADERS OF THE WORLD
IF WE TRY. LETS WORK TOGETHER AS A TEAM. WE COULD ALL BE VERY POWER-
FUL IF WE DO. WE ARE CONCERNED ABOUT PEOPLE AND CONCERNED ABOUT WHAT
OTHER PEOPLE ARE DOING. ALASKA IS IMPORTANT TO US AND WE KNOW THAT
IT IS IMPORTANT TO YOU TOO.

IT IS FULL OF LIFE. EVERY TIME YOU TURN YOUR HEAD YOU SEE LIFE ALL
AROUND YOU, BIRDS SINGING, TREES SWAYING, RIVERS FLOWING, ANIMALS PLAY-
ING, AND CHILDREN GROWING AND ENJOYING LIFE. WE LOVE THE ELDERS TELL-
ING OLD STORIES ABOUT THEIR ADVENTURES HERE. ALASKA IS A PRECIOUS STATE.
MORE PEOPLE ARE TAKING CARE OF ALASKA NOW THAN THEY DID BEFORE. PEO-
PLE BEING MORE RESPONSABLE FOR THEIR COUNTRY. THE TRIDENT TWO SUB-
MARINES THAT THE NAVY IS BUILDING COST OVER 2 MILLION DOLLARS EACH. THE
NAVY IS PLANNING TO GET 31 SUBMARINES. EACH SUBMARINE IS 560 FEET LONG
AND 4 STORIES HIGH. ONE SUBMARINE CARRIES 24 MISSILES AND IT HAS 408 WAR-
HEADS IN THOSE MISSILES. EACH WARHEAD HAS 5 TIMES THE POWER OF THE BOMB
THAT WAS DROPPED ON HIRASHIMA. ONE SUBMARINE WEIGHS 18,700 TONS. ONE
SUBMARINE CAN DESTROY EVERY MAJOR CITY IN THE NORTHERN HEMISPHERE.
IMAGINE EVERY MAJOR CITY IN THE WHOLE NORTH HEMISPHERE.

THE NAVY WANTS TO NAME ONE OF THE TRIDENT SUBMARINES USS ALASKA.
NOW, HOW DO YOU FEEL ABOUT THAT?

I'M GLAD I LIVE HERE IN ALASKA BECAUSE IT SEEMS LIKE WHEN YOU WATCH
THE NEWS EVERY NIGHT ALL OF THE WARS, BOMBS, DEATH SQUADS, AND ARGU-
MENTS ARE IN A VERY DIFFERENT WORLD. IT IS SO PEACEFUL HERE. AND I CAN
SAY TRUTHFULLY RIGHT NOW THAT THE TRIDENT SUBMARINE NAMED USS ALAS-
KA IS A FAR CRY FROM WHAT THE TRUE MEANING OF THE WORD IS. THEY SURE
DID'T NAME OUR STATE "GREAT LAND" FOR NOTHING.

WHAT ARE WE GOING TO DO ABOUT IT? LETS ALL WRITE LETTERS TO SENA-
TOR FRED MURKOWSKI, SENATOR TED STEVENS, PRESIDENT REAGAN, AND GOVER-
NOR BILL SHEFFIELD. LETS GET ALL OUR FRIENDS TO SIGN PETITIONS ASKING
THAT THE SUBMARINE NOT BE NAMED AFTER ALASKA. WE COULD WORK
TOGETHER AND GET THEM TO CHANGE THEIR MINDS ABOUT NAMING IT ALAS-
KA. SO ARE YOU UP TO IT?

SINCERELY,

HOLY CROSS JR. HIGH CLASS

Keywords: /Subs/

FIG. 5.8.   Trident letter.

purpose often has no legitimate function. Within these practical contexts, students appropriated both the stated and school functions (at least initially) because correct mechanics actually made a difference.

Helen found, for example, that embedding "language exercises" in the legitimate task of addressing newspapers made a difference to students.

> We made a list of everyone we thought would like to receive [a newspaper], and I wrote the names and addresses on index cards and gave them to Chris and Joe to copy onto the newspapers. Just a few days earlier I had assigned them some "language exercises" about how to address things, using proper punctuation and capitalization, and they had found it boring and tedious. However, when faced with the actual task of addressing the newspapers, they were relatively enthusiastic about getting the details right.

Still, while the newspaper addressing task was more interesting than the book exercises, students, understandably, didn't find it an absorbing writing task for long. They came up with a clever solution that enabled Helen to stress mechanics in a natural way.

> Still, it was a job they would have preferred to avoid if possible, and as they were working on it, one of them said to me with great excitement, "We could do all these on QUILL and then next time we can make a copy and cut them up and tape them on the newspapers!" So we did that, and because it was something that would be used more than once, it was natural to stress the importance of correct punctuation and capitalization. I was pleased to see that QUILL was perceived as a tool that could make things easier, and that all the ideas about how to use it didn't have to come from me.

The reciprocity between a functional goal and a school goal is delicate; the functional goal must be truly useful to the students at the present time, not just practice for the future. The school goal must naturally fit the functional goal as seamlessly as possible. And if there is a short-cut to performing the functional goal, it must be permissible; otherwise, the school goal becomes paramount. Another case where such a balance worked well was also in Helen's class. Since there are no stores in Telida, mail order catalogues were the only way to buy anything. Helen used mail orders as an appropriate place to emphasize mechanics, since a misspelling could result in a long delay or in receiving the wrong item. The experience also served as a way for students to legitimately share a writing task with their parents, who did most of their shopping by mail—in writing.

Audience as Purpose

The classroom community writing experiences described above had some audience in mind, but did not focus particularly on audience characteristics as a driving force. Some writing done in QUILL classrooms, on the other hand, derived its purpose almost completely from the existence of a special audience. In at least two of the three cases we will describe here, the structure of the QUILL community and the teacher's resulting awareness of the importance of audience played a significant role in the definition of the writing activity. These are examples where the environment offered an opportunity, and the teachers grasped it as a situation in which students could find a specific audience—and therefore an identifiable purpose.

A purpose for writing is sometimes difficult to define for very young students, but Mary Goniwiecha took advantage of her student teacher's departure to create an opportunity for writing with a purpose for her second-grade students. Each student dictated (or wrote, if it was short) a good-bye letter and illustrated it; Mary assembled them into a book called "WE WILL MISS YOU MS. HILDEBRAND." The most elaborate letter was from Dolores:

DEAR MISS HILDEBRAND,

I LIKE YOU AND HOPE YOU WILL COME BACK TO OUR CLASS AGAIN. I AM VERY SORRY YOU HAVE TO LEAVE THIS WEEK AND GO TO ANOTHER CLASS. WE WILL NOT TELL YOU THE SECRETS THAT WE PUT ON THE BOARD EVEN IF YOU BREAK OUR ARMS. I HAVE BEEN GETTING MY WORK DONE MONDAY AND TODAY. I HOPE YOU HAVE A NICE WEEK THIS WEEK. ARE YOU GOING TO BE HERE WHEN WE GO TO PIZ-ZA HUT AT THE END OF THE YEAR? ARE YOU GOING TO GIVE OUT AWARDS TO THE PEOPLE THAT GET ALL THEIR WORK DONE ALL WEEK LONG? AND ARE YOU GOING TO GET THOSE PINS AND THOSE PRIZES THAT YOU GOT FOR US FOR FINISHING OUR WORK ALL WEEK LONG? ARE YOU GOING TO BE HERE WHEN OUR MOMS AND DADS COME FOR CON-FERENCE DAY FRIDAY?

LOVE,
YOUR FRIEND,
DOLORES

Bonnie used the QUILL community in a similar way. Chip had visited Shungnak after the first training session in the fall, so Bonnie's students remembered him. He and Bonnie had also told them about Andee. We were thus some of the only people they knew who did not live in Alaska; we were different in a significant way from most other people who might be an audience for her students' writing. Bonnie took advantage of this special situation by having pairs of students write something about Shungnak to send to us on the network. A fourth and fifth grader wrote the following:

We'll tell you some things about Shungnak. In the winter it is very cold. In the summer it is very warm. A lot of people in Shungnak like to go hunting and go get wood. They shoot a lot of animals and bring them home and share. A lot of people go camping in the summer. If they sain they will get a lot of fish. They smoke salmon fish for the long winter. Some people make dried fish for fish for the winter. In the winter we have dog races. Sometimes we need water. We just get ice. Next we put hot water so it could melt. We go ice fishing in the winter. It is fun playing slide in the winter on top of steep hills.

These two students show a remarkable sensitivity to their audience, it seems, describing details that are truly interesting to people who do not live in Alaska. We don't know if this is coincidental, if Bonnie prompted them, or if they had already learned, from their experiences with Chip and student teachers from Fairbanks, what distinguished Shungnak from most other places. We do know that using the QUILL developers was a clever way for Bonnie to create a salient audience for her class, one that provided an opportunity for real communication, in which the reader can really be informed by the writer.

Bonnie (with the help of Jim Levin) expanded her class' audience even further by establishing an electronic penpal connection with a primarily Latino class in San Diego. For several months, the students exchanged messages, discovering unfamiliar facts about one another's cultures. While electronic penpals often fizzle due to lack of interesting information to convey, this pairing maintained energy for a while, because each environment was truly "exotic" to the other class. Here is a typical early message from San Diego to Shungnak.

Dear Lloyd,

We read your message. What kind of dogs do you have? What color are they? What does it mean that you run 6 to 8 dogs? Is it fun having snow? Do you make snowmen? We haven't seen any snow. Because it doesn't snow in San Diego. Do you like to have some vacations in San Diego? It's fun living in San Diego. Because you could play in swimming pools. What's the name of your school? The name of our school is Balboa. Write back soon.

A final example of purpose driven by audience comes from Ernie's class. It also shares some characteristics with the Love Poems that his class wrote, since it arose in an unplanned way from a classroom conversation. The difference is primarily in the designation of audience. With Love Poems, the students did not have a particular audience in mind when they started writing; "the other students in the class" was an unspoken but sufficiently specific audience. In the Red stories described below, the audience (kindergarten and first grade students) was quite specific and provided important constraints on what the older students wrote.

> . . . our first annual Red Day. It began by one reading group reading a poem about the color red. We read it and discussed several other red things that were in and around Chevak. Soon the entire class was involved in the conversation. We decided to write red stories with the specific purpose of writing for the first grade and kindergarten students. It was an excellent activity and reinforced the concept of writing for a specific audience. The stories were very well written and several students did many rewrites to make sure everything was properly written. As one student said, "We have to make sure these make sense to the little kids!" We put the stories into a book and made enough copies for all the first graders and kindergartners. On Red Day we decorated the room in red and everybody was required to wear the color red. We then went into the other rooms and read our stories to the students. It was a fun day for all involved.

These examples illustrate two advantages of writing situations where the audience is the purpose. The focus on audience provides students with a natural way of truly informing, persuading, entertaining, or connecting with others, rather than addressing only their teacher. In addition, it provides a genuine need for audience sensitivity, beautifully illustrated by Ernie's cross-grade project.

Writing to Learn

In calling this section "Writing to Learn," we do not mean to evoke the narrow meaning of the phrase: for example, writing a social studies report about an explorer in order to learn about the exploration of the New World. Rather, we mean to investigate the role of writing in the pursuit of richer educational goals such as the development of self-concept and problem-solving skills. Or, as Ernie put it, "We wrote constantly in the class, in all different subjects. The students saw how writing fit in with other subjects; it was no longer taught as an isolated skill."

Ernie's experiences with QUILL were most clearly in the category of "writing to learn," and there was little interpretation needed on our part to describe them that way. In addition, though, we were led to viewing some other writing activities as "writing to learn" through our attempts to understand teachers' choices of incidents to share—both with us and with other teachers. Since teachers' self-reports are a primary source of the examples in this chapter, it is not surprising that many of the projects they talked about clearly exemplify the notions of "audience" and "purpose" we had discussed in training. Some of the assignments teachers chose to discuss, however, seemed more conventional and less clearly purposeful, at least within our initial concept of purpose. Yet, their descriptions of these projects and their students' reactions were no less enthusiastic. This category is thus the result of our trying to "read between the lines" of the teachers' descriptions.

Ernie's realization of "writing to learn" was unique among Alaska QUILL classrooms in explicitly including other teachers and a variety of subjects usually not connected with writing. He used planners extensively in other subjects in his own classroom. One of the most successful was a planner for a plant unit in science. He described the process as follows:

> First, the students and I bubbled [brainstormed] on the board all the questions we would want to know concerning the growth of a plant. The students came up with such things as: how big was your seed, its color, its length, its weight, when did it germinate, when did it break through the soil. . . . Every other day the students would take their notebooks to the Science lab and record anything of interest, then take their notebooks and record pertinent information on the planner. . . . Over the course of three or four weeks the students had answered all the questions on the planner. Their next task was to go through their planners, (some students had as many as five planners), and write up a rough draft of the entire experiment.

But beyond this, Ernie spread the philosophy and use of QUILL to several other teachers in his school. He had the opportunity to do this because there was a high school in Chevak. In contrast to urban classrooms, the high school was in the same building as the elementary school, and the two sets of teachers often worked together as a single team. In addition, Ernie had intended from the beginning of the project to do a bit of subtle proselytizing:

> I decided that instead of pushing my enthusiasm for QUILL on other teachers, I would let the students' work speak for the program. I published as much of the students' work as possible and was always willing to answer questions about QUILL to anybody interested. As the year progressed several of the teachers in Chevak became interested in the whole idea of word processing and the role of computers in their classroom. Carol Barnhardt offered a class teaching the Writer's Assistant (the word processor used in QUILL), and seven other staff members in Chevak took the class. . . . There seemed to develop an overall atmosphere among the entire staff that we should stress writing more in our classrooms and that the computer should play an important role.

Ernie's most noteworthy success in spreading writing and QUILL tools into an unusual area came with Fred Esposito, the woodworking teacher, who wrote two planners for students to use in his shop class. Fred used QUILL to produce the planners, then printed them out for students to fill in while they worked. One planner was on woodshop safety; the other, included as Fig. 5.9, was

WOOD

WOOD—TREES AND WOOD CAN BE DIVIDED INTO TWO MAIN CLASSES, SOFTWOOD AND HARDWOOD. SOFTWOODS ARE PRODUCTS OF NEEDLE LEAVED TREES AND HARDWOODS PRODUCTS OF BROAD LEAVED TREES. THE TERMS HARDWOOD AND SOFTWOOD HAVE NO DIRECT APPLICATION TO ACTUAL HARDNESS OR SOFTNESS OF THE WOOD. SOFTWOODS AND HARDWOODS MAY IN TURN BE DIVIDED INTO THE GENERAL CLASSIFICATIONS OF OPEN GRAINED OR POROUS WOOD AND CLOSED GRAINED OR NONPOROUS WOOD. OPEN GRAINED WOOD IS POROUS AND THE PORES OR MINUTE OPENINGS ARE EASY TO SEE. IN CLOSED GRAIN WOOD THE PORES ARE NOT READILY VISABLE.

1. *WHAT KIND OF WOOD DO YOU HAVE IN YOUR HAND?*
   mahagany

2. *WHAT KIND OF TREE DOES THIS WOOD COME FROM, NEEDLE OR BROAD LEAVED?*
   broad leaved

3. *IS IT A HARDWOOD OR SOFTWOOD?*
   hardwood

4. *IS IT OPEN OR CLOSED GRAIN?*
   closed

5. *RELATIVE TO ITS SIZE IS IT HEAVY OR LIGHT?*
   light

6. *WHAT COLOR WOULD YOU SAY IT WAS?*
   black

7. *DO YOU FEEL THIS IS A STRONG WOOD OR WEAK?*
   strong

8. *FROM THE ANSWERS TO THESE QUESTIONS WHAT USES MIGHT YOU SUGGEST FOR THIS TYPE OF WOOD?*
   jewelry box

FIG. 5.9. Planner for identifying wood.

on identifying various pieces of wood. (The answers included in the figure are just one example of how the planner could be filled in.)

Two other writing projects seem to be best interpreted as filling a teacher's purpose to have his or her students "write to learn"—autobiographies and "cures for baldness." Autobiographies were a popular project for a few months, one of those "contagious" assignments that started in one classroom and caught on in several others. Their popularity led us to think that teachers saw them both as a fun way to find out about their students and as a valuable exercise in self-knowledge and self-concept. Alexander, for example, used an "Auto-biopoem" assignment as a way to introduce both PLANNER and LIBRARY to his fifth-grade students. It was a relatively simple exercise in which students had to answer several questions about themselves and combine the results into a poem. Howard's autobiopoem follows (with a mysterious title):

Howard's !''#$%$&'(){} * = }) + <

Howard
Shy,rich,kind,helping
Sibling of Ralph & Sally & Edward & Jeanne & Kathy
lover of video games, chocolate, spinach, waffles
Who feels bord sometimes, and who feels embarass sometime
Who needs a education, and family, video games
Who gives toys and presents, smiles, madness
who fears nothing but horror movies
who likes to see things blowing up, and happieness
resident of fairbanks, wilbur st.
Allen

Alexander's final goal was an Autobiography/Yearbook, so he regarded the autobiopoem as a preparation for that project. Somewhat later in the year, students wrote one more preparatory autobiographical piece: autoballoons. Students drew pictures of themselves and connected them to several colored balloons, in each of which they wrote several important things about themselves.

The class then started on the autobiographies themselves. As a group, they generated a PLANNER to use as a guide for writing an autobiography; they stopped at 40 questions only because they ran out of time. Students chose which of the 40 questions to answer as they researched and wrote their autobiographies. After writing an initial draft, each student read his or her piece to another student. The listener jotted down questions about the autobiography, which the writer used as a guide for revision. The revised second draft was then edited for spelling and punctuation. Finally, students printed out their final drafts. Alexander noted that, "All the students did some editing, but none did a complete job. They all decided on what they were satisfied with and stopped at that. . . . Also it is interesting to note that some chose to write in all caps and some in upper and lower case." In the example included as Fig. 5.10 Howard occasionally used capital letters for emphasis; other students wrote their entire piece in capitals. Alexander assembled the final book by pasting in a school photograph of each student and making copies of the document for the entire class. On the last day of school, each student received a copy, and the class had a signing party similar to those seniors have for their yearbook.

At about the same time during the year, Bonnie was writing her own auto-

WHEN I WAS BORN, a couple of seconds . . . I was born in Fairbanks memorial hospital in 1972 19:30 I think. I weighed 10 lbs. and 2 foot tall. My godfather called me the chunk because I was so chubby. Clara was one of my mom and dad's friend, she called me chunky instead of chunk. My godfather was kind of round too. There was this church I was the first baby to be baptized at that church. I was born with a red face.

WHEN MY SISTER WAS BORN

I was only 2 years old . . . My sister was born in 1974 the same place I was born. I was happy, but when my sister was born I was jealous. I use to make fun of her.

MY FORTH SCAR

Age 9 or 8: One day there was these two Indian kids asked
if they could ride my bicycle.
they seemed nice so I said OK.
then the girl asked. then the boy ect.
then they came back to the park.
My sister was there.
I decided to run up the slide.
I tripped over the concrete and gashed my head at the end of the slide.
It was very painful.
I started to yell. I put my hand over where it hurt. Then I took my hand off of my head, my hand had blood on it. I started to holler even more. The Indian kids started to stare at me. I told my sister to guard my bicycle. I went home I made a trail of blood from the park to the doort of my house. My dad heard me screaming. He opened the door. It scared the heck out of him. Oh! Howard he said surprised. My mom came home. She was scared half to death. She said what happened to you. I told them. Our neighbor who lived in apt. A5 came over in her exersizing suit. She came over with a band-aid. I think he will need stitches. My dad said. NO! I said startled. AH! SHAT UP! My dad said. My brother took us to the hospital. The doctor look like a nice doctor. The doctor said that I needed 4 stitches. Oh! No! I groaned. The nurse said if it hurt real bad to squeeze her hand real hard if it didn't hurt to not to squeeze her hand that hard. The doctor took a big neetle and stuck it in my head.
I squeezed the nurses hand real hard.
He put this blanket like thing over my head.
He started to sew.
I thought you were going to put 4 stitches in.
My mom said.
One side was crushed so I only put in three.
The doctor answered. The doctor took his rubber glove and blew it up in a balloon. I started to laugh. this is what you get for being such a good boy.

FIG. 5.10. Howard's autobiography (from Alexander's booklet).

biography along with her class in Shungnak. She described it as "the most successful QUILL writing activity so far," and went on to share her thoughts about it with the other teachers on the network:

> Cora (the student teacher) and I put together a planner, and shared our autobiographies with the students. They REALLY wrote and now are bringing in photos from home to be displayed with the printed copies. The pictures are really great! It's fun to see what interesting events they choose to put in their life stories.
>
> We plan on doing the second edition of the Eagle's News within the next two weeks and then do biographies of folks here in Shungnak next. It sure is a fun way to learn about writing. I've been thinking that I should do more of the assignments right along with the kids . . . kids don't often see the adults write . . . I'm having mom send some old pictures of me to put up with my autobiography.

Later, Lynne Ammu in Bethel, who worked with student teachers, asked Bonnie for the planner she had used for her class's autobiography and wanted to know how to put one together for biographies as well. Bonnie's answer:

> Lynne, I don't have a planner with me right now, but will try to send it. . . .
> As I remember them, these were the questions . . .
> Intro—answer the following questions and use your answers to write your autobiography.
>
> 1. When were you born?
> 2. Where were you born?
> 3. Where are you in your family? (oldest, middle, youngest . . . sisters? brothers? etc.)
> 4. Where have you lived? traveled?
> 5. List three exciting things that have happened to you or stories that your family tells about you. . . .
>
> We printed out copies of this Planner and had the kids write answers and then do a draft on paper, edit, enter on the computer. I think a similar format would work for the biographies. . . . You might want to suggest that the kids and teacher brainstorm questions that they want to include in the interview on chart paper and then type that into the Planner, print it out, take it on the interview. I'd also suggest that on many of the Planners we've included in the introduction that the kids could choose x number of questions to answer . . . that way all the writing isn't exactly alike and the kids have some choice and they can also add more.

The teachers who did autobiographies with their class never discussed (at least on the network or in their writing) why autobiographies were such a satisfying assignment, but we can infer several possible reasons. Bonnie commented explicitly that it was "fun" to read her students' compositions, and it is certainly true that autobiographies are bound to vary more than pieces such as book reviews. In this sense, the teacher is an honestly interested audience for the students' writing. And so are the rest of the students in the class; most fifth graders are curious about their classmates' lives, and Alexander formalized this interest by creating an explicitly public document for his class. Equally important to teachers, we believe, is a sense of autobiography as a tool for students to reflect on their lives and to develop their own life stories. Alexander's students' pieces are full of intimate revelations that suggest students trying hard to come to terms with their lives. For example,

> After about 4 I moved to Fairbanks for a year or two. I had a mean teacher my mom got so mad at her for brusing my arm for acting like an airplane. Soon we moved. Mom had her fired.

> when i was in first grade i had no friends. nobody liked me. it's alfull not to have any friends, and thats why i am writing this paragraph.

> WHEN I WAS IN FIRST GRADE MY DAD GOT CANCER. HE WENT TO THE HOSPITAL IN SEATTLE FOR THREE MONTHS SO MY MOMS FRIENDS FLEW DOWN WITH US TO SEATTLE. AFTER WE LEFT SEATTLE MY MOM AND DAD CAME UP TWO WEEKS. HE STAYED IN THE HOSPITAL IN FAIRBANKS, AK. WERE WE LIVED. ABOUT A MONTH AFTER THAT HE DIED. I FELT REALLY SAD.

There is a long tradition of using writing as a way to learn about oneself; some youngsters keep diaries and it seems that many famous writers spent much of their time writing in journals (which are eventually published or dissected by biographers). Writing served the students in these classes as a way to reflect on, analyze, and accept their lives through both writing about them and sharing their stories with their peers.

Another assignment that is not at first glance clearly "purposeful" is the "cures for baldness" project. As with autobiographies, this idea, first introduced by Ernie, spread to several classrooms. After Ernie described it on the electronic network, Bonnie gave her class the same assignment. Here is one example of a Shungnak student's solution:

> Shungnak's Baldness
>
> One morning I woke up and I look in the mirror. I saw my head was bald. In Alaska even in Fairbanks and Kotz. They said we have to find the cure

> to grow our hair back to normal. One boy said "How are we going to
> put our hair back to normal? With the poition I can make the worlds greatest
> poition. I said what will you give me if I make the poition. so I made it
> than everything went back to normal. Than we lived happy ever after.
>
> The End

We think this assignment's popularity was due to its emphasis on problem-solving. The teacher presented an amusing situation and asked students to use their imagination and problem-solving skills to solve a dilemma. Since "problem-solving" was a popular educational topic in 1983 (and still is today), teachers were attracted to this project as a way to merge two important aspects of their curriculum.

This final category of purposes—teachers' desires to have their students "write to learn"—is identified explicitly only in Ernie's writing, yet it appears to be a quiet but significant force in teachers' choices of writing activities for their students. It is worthwhile as a perspective through which to examine other teachers' decisions about writing experiences in their classrooms.

SUMMARY

QUILL's attitude toward purpose was simply stated: to create a writing environment in school where audience and purpose were real and paramount. But even with such a simple goal statement there were a great variety of realizations, as the software capabilities interacted with students' and teachers' purposes and institutional realities. As students and teachers attempted to integrate their purposes, beliefs, and habits with the innovation, many new innovations were in fact constructed.

The above stories of different ways teachers attempted to create real writing contexts shed light on the questions posed at the beginning of this chapter. Teachers generally integrated the kinds of writing assignments they had already been using with their QUILL-based understandings of the purposes of writing; mostly, these combinations yielded creative new writing situations, but sometimes they did not meld successfully. We saw an important influence of both classroom and community on the specification of writing purposes; in small villages, especially, the community was a natural and influential audience. In terms of the software, MAILBAG played an important role in many classrooms as an early reification of writing with real purposes and audiences, but it served its purpose only for a limited time, as students' communication requirements grew beyond its bounds. Most emphatically, teachers' uses of writing in their private lives affected what they chose to emphasize as purposes and genres in their classes; the most striking example of this was Sister Judy, who saw writing—and many other skills—as empowering tools for improving the world.

Chapter 6

Revision

The idealization of QUILL called for a classroom writing environment in which students would become proficient in all aspects of the writing process and be free to develop in unique ways as writers. Within this environment, students would use writing to communicate with real audiences and to satisfy purposes that made sense to them. Revision in such a context would occur, not because students had to adhere to arbitrary linguistic standards, but because their own writing goals and the feedback they received from readers would make them want to improve their writing. They would focus on making meaning through their writing.

When we compared QUILL's idealized view of revision to its realizations in classrooms, striking differences emerged. Although the computer was used at times for meaning-centered revision, it was more often used for copyediting. We saw the emergence of alternate editing standards for different audiences, but the way these standards evolved surprised us. We were intrigued by the ways the social organization of the classroom influenced revision activities. An increase in revision activity was often mediated through such changes, rather than through direct effects of the technology.

Observations such as these revealed properties of QUILL that were not inherent in its definition, but emerged only as it was implemented in specific settings. The emergence of these properties implies new ways of thinking about the use of computers for writing and, in particular, their influence on revision. In this chapter we discuss the idealization of revision in QUILL. Then, we examine three major trends we observed in the realization of editing and revision practices in QUILL classrooms.

QUILL'S VIEW OF REVISION

Writing can be viewed as a form of problem-solving (Flower & Hayes, 1981a, 1981b; Rosebery et al., 1989). For example, the initial problem might be to select a topic. Any choice (and, of course, the topic decision is always subject to change) generates a new set of problems. Suppose the writer wants to write a review of a school play. Should the review cover all aspects of the play or focus on a particular actor? Should it highlight deficiencies or strengths of the play? Should the style be a straightforward account of the performance or a use of the performance as a touchstone for a broader critique? How should the review begin and end? Each of these and innumerable other questions are answered, at least implicitly, as the writer creates the text. But the creation process not only answers the questions; it is what generates them.

To complete a piece, writers try out solutions in their minds, or in text, evaluate them, and change them to meet their communicative goals. And even the goals are subject to revision. Revision is thus a necessary part of the process of producing a well-written text. It is also important as a learning process, for it is through examining and rethinking ideas that a learner grows. There was evidence at the time of QUILL's development that little revision of this kind was occurring in most classrooms (Graves & Murray, 1980; Scardamalia, 1981; Stallard, 1974). Since then, the situation has begun to change somewhat as a result of the impact of various writing projects and new writing curricula.

Definitions of revision vary, but most researchers describe it as a multifaceted process:

> Revision means making any changes at any point in the writing process. It is a cognitive problem-solving process in that it involves detection of mismatches between intended and instantiated texts, decisions about how to make desired changes, and making the desired changes. Changes might or might not affect the meaning of the text, and they might be major or minor. Also, changes might be made in the writer's mind before text is written on paper, while text is written, and/or after text is written (cf. Beach, 1984; Bridwell, 1980; Faigley & Witte, 1981; Flower & Hayes, 1981; Nold, 1981; Scardamalia & Bereiter, 1983, 1986). [And revision is] . . . integrated with other aspects of writing (e.g., planning and evaluating). (Fitzgerald & Markham, 1987, p. 4)

The notion that writing is a process of revision is central to many educational innovations concerned with improving writing, and QUILL was no exception. In QUILL classrooms, we expected to see students reworking drafts of their pieces many times before they published them. We also expected to see many types of revision—changes in word choice, stylistic changes, and major reorganizations of texts.

We emphasized in our materials and thinking that revision should be meaning-centered, that is, done in order to satisfy the writer's purpose and to address a particular audience. A central tenet of QUILL was that writing is a form of social interaction. Our fourth and fifth pedagogical goals (meaningful communication with real audiences; writing with peers) both emphasized social interaction. The software was designed to facilitate reaching an audience, to make the writer more aware of the potential audience, and to promote collaboration in writing, thereby fostering establishment of a reading/writing community.

Each of these goals has a close relationship with revision. Feedback from readers is one important input to revision-related decisions; conversations with coauthors is another. The QUILL software reflected these goals by creating an environment (LIBRARY) in which students could easily read one another's writing, providing a means of commenting on each other's writing (MAIL-BAG) and facilitating collaborative writing (automatically recording two authors for each piece). QUILL's view of revision was also articulated in the *QUILL Teacher's Guide*, teacher training, and classroom visits. Several points were central to the idealization:

Meaning-Centered Revision Versus Simple Copyediting

The description of revision within QUILL was consistent with Fitzgerald and Markham's description above, with one important difference. In QUILL training sessions, we made a critical distinction between *revision* and *editing*.[1] By revision, we meant meaning-centered changes to a text, often involving major reorganizations, additions, or deletions or wholesale changes of focus or goal. We connected revision intimately with considerations of audience and purpose. Some examples of revision that students might carry out include the following:

1. Add another argument to a persuasive piece because of an imagined counterargument.
2. Find a new lead for a narrative to pique the reader's curiosity.
3. Recharacterize the protagonist of a story to make her more rounded.
4. Rearrange the order of details in an expository piece to make the structure more comprehensible.
5. Change a word to evoke new images.
6. Delete a paragraph that doesn't make sense.
7. Change sentence structure to improve the rhythm of a piece.

By editing, we meant copyediting-like changes, typically done with little consideration of audience and purpose, entailing smaller changes to the text, such

---

[1]To emphasize the revision/editing distinction, we sometimes used the terms "meaning-centered revision" and "copyediting" during QUILL training sessions, and we use them in this chapter as well.

as corrections of spelling or punctuation. Editing tends to be focused on individual words or, at most, sentences. It is the kind of function copyeditors fulfill; notice that they are not called copy revisers! The following are typical of the kinds of editing students might be expected to carry out:

> freind → friend
> i went to school → I went to school.
> him and me were friends. → He and I were friends.
> She was short I was tall → She was short, but I was tall.
> We was having fun. → We were having fun.

But the distinction between revision and editing depends on the textual and social context of the modifications and not the extent of the textual changes. Sometimes changing a single word modifies the tone of an entire paragraph. Sometimes splitting a sentence into two is copyediting; at other times it is revision. For example, suppose a student made the following sequence of changes:

> (1) The rabbit ran. →
> (2) The rabbit ran quickly. →
> (3) The rabbit scampered.

If the change from "ran" to "scampered" were motivated by considerations of audience and purpose and were informed by audience feedback, it might be considered revision. If it were instead preceded by a lesson on "exciting verbs" and motivated by an assignment to change common verbs to more exciting ones, it would be more akin to editing.

The Computer Can Facilitate Revision

Professional writers recognize the importance of revision, but the writing process in schools sometimes fails to reflect this. Few teachers give their students an opportunity or a reason to revise, and those who do usually face a chorus of moans and groans from their students who hate "copying over." In these classrooms, students rarely understand all that revision can entail, possibly because of their long exposure to a focus on mechanics and neatness (Scardamalia, 1981). In contrast, computers have the potential to change the role of revision in students' writing process:

> For most children rewriting a text is so laborious that the first draft is the final copy, and the skill of rereading with a critical eye is never acquired. This changes dramatically when children have access to computers capable of manipulating text. The first draft is composed at the keyboard. Corrections are made easily. The current copy is always neat and tidy. I have seen a child move from total rejection of writing to an intense involvement (accompanied by rapid improve-

ment of quality) within a few weeks of beginning to write with a computer. (Papert, 1980, p. 30)

Alexander, a teacher in Fairbanks, made a similar comment:

> But there was a big snag to the Writing Project's process: EDITING. Every time we wrote and got to the editing step, cries of terror, pain, and agony would be heard throughout the classroom. And it didn't matter what grade I was teaching that day, only the creativity of the agony changed. The familiar lament, "You mean I have to copy this thing all over again, I only had to change a little bit! Why can't I leave it the way it is?" was heard over and over again. Unfortunately, there were times when I agreed and I knew that if I were in their shoes as a student I too wouldn't enjoy rewriting something I had already written.
>
>   So the year went on and I followed what I had learned about the writing process except the editing part. It was too mundane and tedious for the students and like pulling teeth to get them to do the editing.

Perhaps the most obvious role QUILL played in the classroom writing environment was as a text-editing system that could make revision easier. While the presence of a text editor does not guarantee informed revision, it does make it possible for students to revise without the undue hardship that results from rewriting entire texts.

As another aid to the revision process, we recommended that students use PLANNER as a guide to decisions about changes to the text. A student could use the questions in a planner to trigger a rethinking of a piece after completing a first draft. A revision planner might include questions such as, "Did I provide a setting for my story?" or "How could someone argue against what I've said?" PLANNER, in this way, was intended to encourage meaning-centered revision that the text editor portion of QUILL would then facilitate.

The CHANGE option in LIBRARY was a further articulation of QUILL's emphasis on meaning-centered revision. Originally we included CHANGE so that students would have to state explicitly that they wanted "to change" as opposed just "to see" a text, and thus they would be less likely to alter a text accidentally.[2] But it also served to highlight the function of revision and remind the writer that another student might soon come along to "SEE" his or her text. As one teacher (Alexander) said about his class:

> The best part of LIBRARY in my opinion, was that it helped the students realize that writing is not a half hour affair, but rather an ongoing process of revising and editing. With LIBRARY, their work was always there and could be changed with very little effort.

---

[2]Remember that students were not just editing files on their private disks, but, rather, looking at texts produced by others on a shared LIBRARY disk. Since there was no security system, we wanted the software to have different editor modes ("look, but don't change permanently," versus "ordinary editing") and to alert students to these modes.

In the workshops, we also suggested that students use the keyword facility in LIBRARY to keep track of their progress revising a piece, using entries such as "notes," "draft," and "final" to indicate different points in moving toward a finished product.

Teachers of Writing Should Be Writers Themselves

Believing that it is difficult to teach something if you cannot or do not do it yourself, we encouraged teachers to see and experience themselves as writers. We expected that direct experience of composing and revising would have major implications for how teachers implemented writing instruction in their classrooms. One was that teachers would know more about what it means to revise a text. They would experience both the difficulties and the satisfactions. They would also know more about when and in what ways the computer would be useful for revision. Another was that we expected teachers to use their experience as writers to help in deciding how QUILL was to be used. Their own beliefs and values about writing were important resources. Another was that teachers should see QUILL as a tool that could be applied to solve specific problems as they arose, including problems in teaching writing that they had identified prior to the introduction of QUILL.

The Alaska teachers were especially responsive to the idea of being writers, and some had been active writers long before QUILL.[3] We encouraged their writing in the QUILL workshop and in classroom visits. The electronic mail network became a new outlet for this writing. Teachers also wrote research papers about their own classrooms.

Revision Should Be Student Initiated and Student Controlled

An important tenet of QUILL was that revision should grow out of a student's concern with communication. Thus, the decision of whether and how to revise would be a student's responsibility rather than one prompted by the software or determined solely by the teacher. This view applied to both copyediting and revision. The MIX command, for example, made revising easier by making structural problems more visible, but still left the revision decision and task to the student. We used examples from other QUILL classrooms to illustrate student-centered revision.

Our modeling of the revision process in the workshop, as well as the formulation in the *QUILL Teacher's Guide*, emphasized peer response and student-controlled revision. In the workshop, teachers worked in pairs on a writing

---

[3]A side benefit of this writing was that we are fortunate in having a large corpus of teacher-written articles and electronic mail messages, which have informed our analyses of the uses of QUILL and have provided a greatly appreciated source of quotes to substantiate our observations.

task. (See chapter 3 for a complete description.) Each member of the pair alternated being the storyteller and the respondent through several versions of a story. Through each step of the workshop, revisions were initiated by the writer, with help from the respondent. We, as workshop leaders, acted as facilitators, rather than teachers. In the *QUILL Teacher's Guide*, we discussed a process in which students worked together to revise their writing.

The Focus in Writing Instruction Should Be More on Process and Less on Product

Closely related to the focus on meaning-centered revision was a shift from a product emphasis to a process emphasis. This meant that, using QUILL, students should have time for brainstorming, for thinking about their writing, for revising, perhaps many times, and for discussing their writing with others. We wanted to move away from the idea of the goal being simply to produce an error-free product.

The computer made it easy for students to sit and write without concern for neatness or correctness. They could even turn off the screen display and do invisible writing. Thus, the technology supported what Elbow (1973) called *free writing*. If students decided to reuse what they had written in a free mode, they could treat the free-written text as a first draft and revise it.

The QUILL workshop and *QUILL Teacher's Guide* emphasized moving away from a model in which teachers would red-mark a student's paper for spelling, punctuation, capitalization, and grammatical errors. Instead, students should think about their audience and purpose and revise their text accordingly. More generally, they should come to see different genres and audiences for writing as implying different criteria for style, content, and need for correctness.

REVISION BECOMES COPYEDITING

Given QUILL's emphasis on meaning-centered revision, and the various ways in which it was communicated to the teachers through the software, *QUILL Teacher's Guide*, and training, we expected to find many classrooms in which more frequent and richer revision took place. And, in fact, there were many occasions on which students genuinely revised their pieces. Often these classes were taught by teachers who had stressed revision for their students prior to the advent of QUILL—either because they were writers themselves or because they had recently attended an Alaska Writing Project summer workshop. The addition of QUILL to such classrooms often increased the amount of revision students carried out primarily because the computer facilitated the process.

In other classrooms, both planned and inadvertent changes to the classroom social organization appeared to underlie the increase in revision. However, in many of the QUILL classrooms we observed, copyediting predominated over meaning-centered revision. This section describes pressures that pushed revision aside. In these classrooms, a variety of factors transformed the idealization of revision we had constructed—and tried to communicate—into a realization that focused more on copyediting than we had hoped.

Definitional Problems

We learned through observing the uses of QUILL that our distinction between revision and editing was problematic. The statement that "word processors take the sting out of revision" (as one of our QUILL Alaska participants put it—Romick, 1984) remains true if "editing" is substituted for "revision." Text *editing* programs are used for both editing and revision. Both editing and revision denote the process of making changes to a composition that are intended ultimately to make it more effective at communicating. Each is consistent with the often-described practice of producing multiple drafts of a composition. "Peer editing" and "peer feedback" could both consist of comments that promote either revision or editing. Teacher-student conferences could likewise focus on either process. Thus, many of the practices identified with writing-process techniques apply to both revision and editing. As a result, our emphasis on revision was easy to ignore.

We inadvertently contributed to an emphasis on copyediting by including only relatively abstract descriptions of revision in training sessions and in the *QUILL Teacher's Guide*, since the major point we wanted to communicate was the dependence of revision on considerations of audience and purpose. While we spent considerable time describing the relationships among audience, purpose, and revision, we expected teachers to get practical experience with revision primarily by using QUILL to work on their own writing during training. When they began to use the software, however, the teachers naturally were most concerned with details of its operation and ended up performing mostly editing operations while they learned to use the program. Thus, many of the teachers had little opportunity during training to get a practical sense of what revision entails—either in general, or with QUILL as a tool.

Correcting Mistakes

In thinking and talking about changes to text, QUILL teachers clearly appreciated the significant power of Writer's Assistant to make such modifications easier, and their students often produced multiple drafts of their compositions using the computer. In general, however, teachers described this process both to their students and to other teachers as "correcting mistakes," thus characterizing it as an editing task rather than as one that involved revision. For example, Wilma, a fifth-grade teacher in McGrath, wrote about teaching revision in her classroom as follows:

> Chip had also spoken about response groups, sharing, and revision. I wasn't sure how to set up response groups and get the students revising on their own, so we started to share as a large group. I read the stories out loud, at first not giving any names. We talked about the things we really liked, and the *mistakes* we were able to hear—me and mom, the same word repeated all the time, no periods, run ons and fragments, and so on. And then, while we had real examples of fuzzy communication, I taught "language arts" lessons about the things we had noticed. [italics added]

Teachers regarded this increased ability for students to correct mistakes as an opportunity for them to create perfect pieces of writing, and a paper without mistakes was often the goal of computer-based composition. In a fifth-grade classroom in Juneau, the teacher (Syd) would ask her students to do the following:

> Pick a piece periodically for editing and final copy which means it will be *perfect*. They do so without fear. . . . Their typing skills are slow, but they are seeing and correcting many *errors* automatically as they see them on the screen, but are still getting all their ideas down as they want. [italics added]

These teachers' comments exemplify common practices. When discussing the students' revisions, most of the teachers described a similar editing process. They valued the computer because by making the text more readable than texts in students' handwriting, it could reveal mistakes, and because it could facilitate correction of those mistakes. Students did multiple drafts of compositions with the goal of producing a perfect paper.

Prior Beliefs and Practices of Teachers

Teachers came to QUILL with well-established beliefs about learning and teaching. Some had been teaching writing with correct spelling and grammar as the primary goal. Changes to these established practices were difficult. For example, Wilma described her background in the following:

> Often I would collect all the rough drafts (which we usually did with paper and pencil) and type them myself after school. When I did this, I took great pains to type them EXACTLY as written. (That ain't easy when you've been an old-fashioned English teacher as long as I have!)

Others had little experience teaching writing and, hence, based their method for teaching on the way they had been taught, which typically was a copyediting approach. Ernie, a second-grade teacher in Chevak, described his experiences teaching writing prior to his involvement to QUILL:

> I never felt comfortable teaching writing. It was always difficult for me to write when I was in school. I didn't like to write. I believe this attitude was reflected in my teaching of writing. . . . If the children spent time writing their spelling words ten times then I felt that I had done writing for that day. . . . I thought that the entire writing process consisted of assigning a task, having the students write about it, neatly of course, then hand it in to be corrected.

Ernie's reference to ''assigning a task'' highlights a central conflict between QUILL's goal of meaning-centered revision and many teaching practices. The need for revision is lessened when the task is defined precisely, as it is in what are commonly regarded as ''good'' writing assignments (Griffin, 1983). Moreover, the notion of assignment usually carries with it the idea that the only real audience is the teacher and the only real purpose is to meet the teacher's standards.

Many of the QUILL teachers had seen ''correctness'' in spelling and grammar as problem areas for their students; they regarded these skills as important, but difficult to teach. Several of the teachers felt that they had been trying for years to encourage students to correct their spelling, punctuation, and grammar; they were thus predisposed to think of QUILL as a tool to help them with their already-identified teaching problems. One teacher (Wilma) described a student's previous problems with spelling and how the computer helped him to change:

> Chuck, an atrocious speller, was entranced by the keyboard. He would labor over the keyboard until recess, which was one of his favorite times of the day, and often continue while his friends went outside. . . . Chuck soon saw that letter reversals and spelling mistakes were very apparent on the monitor's screen, and seldom rested until he had corrected everything. He discovered a myriad of ways to find out how to spell what he had misspelled. He asked our classroom spelling experts. He started using a dictionary. He started keeping his own word book with words that I spelled for him. He started sounding out words more carefully. Chuck is still a poor speller, but I feel there was a great deal of improvement during the course of his fifth-grade year.

Using the computer for copyediting thus helped teachers solve a problem they recognized as difficult and important: getting students to spell correctly and to write grammatically correct sentences.

Student Initiation and Control

The domination of meaning-centered revision by copyediting arose ironically in part because teachers faithfully implemented an important point QUILL had made about revision: that the process should be student-initiated and student-controlled. There are several indications in teachers' writing that students were initiating and controlling the editing process and using the computer to become more proficient at it. They were not making changes in their texts only to respond to a teacher's red-penciled corrections, but because they were developing individual standards of quality. The result of this development was, in fact, more time spent trying to produce mistake-free papers. Wilma noted this in her fifth-grade class:

> Then I started to notice something interesting—the next stories we wrote didn't seem to have those same mistakes. Soon we started talking about style—active verbs, vivid adjectives and adverbs, more concrete details, pronoun and verb agreement. These are things I had never gotten to when teaching out of the grammar book the year before, and if I had, I'm sure it wouldn't have meant much to the students. But now we were talking about their writing. It was personal. They owned the problems, and it was up to them to correct the problems. And they did.

Alexander also created a classroom environment in which students had responsibility for their own revisions:

> When we finished our second draft, we were ready to polish or edit. Each student was required to check over his or her paper for spelling and punctuation errors and correct them. And to varying degrees, they did.
>
> Rather than teach them all the capabilities of Writer's Assistant, I demonstrated only the drop, add, and mix features. I also told them that I would not make any changes at all. Whatever they put into the computer, would be what got published. If there were any mistakes, they would still be there for all to read.
>
> All the students did some editing, but none did a complete job. They all decided on what they were satisfied with and stopped at that. And actually that's all I felt I could ask for. Also it is interesting to note that some chose to write in all caps and some in upper and lower case. That is still true this year.

Even young students in their first year of writing could learn to be their own editing monitors if the teacher set the right context. Third grader Sandra was described by her teacher, Helen:

> Within a few months, when she brought me a story, I could say something like, "This would be easier to read if you put periods and capital letters in it." And she would go back to fix it, working towards perfection.

From an adult perspective, the focus on low-level formal details of a text seems misplaced. But from a developmental perspective, this focus may be entirely appropriate, and not so distant from meaning-centered revision as it seems.

This seemed evident in an episode we observed early in the QUILL field test in a sixth-grade class in Hartford, Connecticut. Two boys were writing a review of Donkey Kong, a video game. This review was to be stored on a LIBRARY disk, available for all their classmates to read. Their joint writing proceeded smoothly until they wanted to say, "The object of the game is to rescue Mario's girlfriend." The question they faced was where to place the apostrophe in "Mario's." One student said before the "s" and the other said after. They argued for a while and then one went to get his grammar book to look up the rule for apostrophes. This student-directed activity proceeded with no prompting from adults and no monitoring, even as students in the rest of the class were resisting a worksheet assignment on grammar by throwing wads of paper, getting up to wander around, and looking out the window. The students using QUILL were not only more engaged, they were practicing writing skills as the need arose in their writing, an integration of doing and learning most likely to result in real growth.

Managing with Limited Resources

A central idea within QUILL was that students should have equitable (not necessarily identical) access to the computer. We were particularly concerned that the less academically successful students have ample opportunities to write, revise, and publish. We designed QUILL using the heuristic: "Look at the computer tools and environments that adult writers find useful; adapt them for classroom use." In many respects this heuristic was a good one. The general emphasis on purpose and audience is valid in both the adult and the classroom worlds. But in detail, there are significant differences between these two worlds that must be considered.

One obvious quantitative difference, which has qualitative implications, is that the resources in our adult models were more extensive. We were familiar with situations in which an adult would have effectively unlimited access to computer resources—a terminal or microcomputer in one's own office, for example. In contrast, most of our classrooms had 25 students using only one computer. Even when there was a lower student–computer ratio, for instance a class of 15 students having two computers, there was still a major difference in accessibility. Moreover, the constraints of a school day—with activities such as recess, assemblies, lunch periods, testing, whole class discussions, and so on—exacerbated the limited access. It was typically the case that students had less computer time than they wanted and needed for writing.

We had not sufficiently anticipated the impact of these management problems and spent little time during training addressing many of the issues that arose when teachers tried to integrate a computer and revision as part of the writing process into their classrooms. In fact, the *QUILL Teacher's Guide* devoted only 6 out of 96 pages explicitly to classroom management issues. Unfortunately, this left to teachers the challenging task of figuring out how to organize their classrooms to permit computer-based revision.

Without a clearer specification of revision and the way to manage signifi-cant revision using only one computer, teachers were left to invent their own solutions. How could teachers with only one or two computers and 20 to 30 students manage their classrooms so that individuals or pairs of students could revise their work on the computer? Teachers were forced to address a con-tradiction that was inherent in the use of QUILL in a setting with scarce com-puter resources.

They communicated frequently about this issue on the network, especially at the beginning of the year. For example, Syd described her use of time blocks in order to fit the use of QUILL into a busy schedule:

> I scheduled around violin, band, gifted programs, resource programs, reading classes, and then P. E., library, and so on. We set up 20-minute blocks required once a week and even ended up with lots of extra spaces so many times they could get a second turn at it. . . . The technicalities of setting up a space for the com-puter to be the least disturbing but at the same time most accessible by me for assistance required trial and error.

Ernie addressed the same problem through the use of learning stations:

> I spent a great deal of time planning how to implement QUILL in the classroom. Quite frankly this was my biggest worry concerning the program. Even with El-sie (an aide) in the room full time, how was I going to get 24 children on the computer in a fair way? Maybe the students who were stronger academically should use the computer more and the students having trouble with various sub-jects could get more smaller group instruction from Elsie and myself. . . . After a great deal of thinking, I decided on a plan that worked very well. First I devel-oped various learning stations. (In addition to the computer stations) there was a library station containing books, tapes, and film strips, a game table . . . a typing station consisting of two manual typewriters, a language station, which consisted of five sentences with various mistakes in which the students had to recopy the sentences correctly, and an art station.

With one computer and 25 students, teachers often felt the best use of the computer was as a polishing tool or as a printing press. In a fifth-grade class-room (Wilma's), the process was described as follows:

> Because of time limitations, they did the rough draft, rewrite, and editing on paper before entering it on the computer. They then edited again with a partner and printed out the results.

Limited computer resources in the school thus had implications for time management that were different from those found in the office or the home. Students could not wander to the computer whenever they felt the need to add to or revise a composition. They could not afford to use their time at the machine simply thinking about their writing task; they needed to press keys. This time-management issue alone led to realizations that differed from the QUILL idealization of revision.

Parental Attitudes

The use of the computer as a copyediting machine was reinforced by parents' expectations regarding the teaching of writing. Parents saw the computer as a way for their children to produce error-free writing. They viewed computer output differently from the handwritten pieces that their children brought home, expecting it to be perfect, like the professionally produced pieces they resembled. They assumed the computer had a spelling checker, which it did not, and perhaps checkers for grammar and punctuation as well. And, just as teachers and students could more easily see mistakes in a text, parents saw problems they probably would not have noticed in handwritten drafts. At times, their desire to see correct compositions was far greater than that of the classroom teacher or the students. Ernie found he sometimes had to explain his writing philosophy to parents who were dissatisfied with their students' work:

> One parent made the comment that her daughter was coming home with papers that were not corrected for spelling and punctuation errors. I had a conference with the parent and explained how I planned to teach writing and the whole concept of form, fluency and correctness, and whereas she said she understood, from time to time she would still comment on how her daughter needs to work more on grammar and spelling.

Editing as a Complement to Free Writing

A focus on editing continued in part because it was consistent with QUILL's suggestions about free writing. In fact, copyediting is a logical complement to the notion that it is sometimes useful to write without concern for grammatical correctness, because at least in some cases, the writer may wish to use the freely written text later on. Teachers realized that the ability to change text later in the writing process allowed students to compose without being distracted by considerations of mechanics. They worked hard to get students to concentrate on ideas in their first drafts, rather than on spelling and punctuation. Syd described her attempt to communicate this concept to her students:

> [My students] write daily and what they have discovered is that the idea "uncorrected first draft," don't worry about spelling, sentences, capital letters, and so on, means they can write ideas. No one is going to get on them for forgetting to indent a paragraph. They write willingly and fluently.

Interestingly, permission to write a draft for which mechanical correctness did not matter was a new experience for many students. Ernie noted that his second- and third-grade students were already trained to worry about spelling when they wrote.

> It was amazing to see how conditioned students were in terms of spelling. They constantly asked the eternal question: "How do we spell . . . ?" At first the students had a hard time figuring out what their teacher meant by "Don't worry about spelling on this copy, just get down your ideas and we will worry about spelling later."

Many teachers emphasized copyediting because they wanted to convince their students that writing a composition included a time when mechanics were secondary—and a later time when editing was appropriate.

An Unintended Emphasis on the Writing Product

A paradoxical aspect of some realizations of QUILL was that whereas QUILL emphasized the *process* of writing, the computer presence brought about a focus on the *product*. While the computer was a tool that facilitated quick creation of imperfect drafts and multiple revisions, students and teachers often focused on the final draft, giving short shrift to the earlier drafts and the revision process.

One reason for this was that the computer printouts resembled professionally produced texts. We saw this capability as one that would lead students to regard their writing as important and worthy of effort; at the same time, it led them to see their work as "perfectible" in the categories of neatness, spelling, and grammar. Thus, given the opportunity to satisfy their teacher's requests for technically accurate compositions and their own search for correctness, students concentrated on copyediting. A high school teacher (Judy) described one appeal of the computer for herself and her students as follows:

> It could be an instant attractive piece, even with misspelled words and all the rest; it looked neat when it came out in draft form. We could decide how it was going to be corrected . . . do all of the corrections needed and revise it again and revise it again and revise it again and not have to take all the labor of writing it again and again.

There was a thin line between the computer's support of an audience emphasis, which would have led to meaning-centered revision, and its support of attractive products, which led to copyediting. Often the latter dominated the former.

ADJUSTING WRITING STANDARDS
TO FIT THE AUDIENCE

A product emphasis implies that the goal of writing is to produce a "perfect" piece, free of spelling or grammatical errors. But if teachers and students become attentive to variations in audiences, departures from the perfection pattern can occur. The basic idea of adjusting standards to fit the audience was highlighted in the QUILL software by the fact that MAILBAG messages could not be revised; the first draft of a mail message was also the final draft. This distinction in the software reified the difference between the audience for a message, typically a classmate, and the audience for a story, which might include parents, the teacher, or the whole school.

As QUILL was realized in different classrooms, interesting patterns occurred in adjusting writing standards to fit the audience. Even teachers who had emphasized perfection in most of their class' writing assignments made a specific point of leaving the determination of "good enough" to students when they were producing a joint project whose audience was the entire class, the school, or some audience outside of the school. For example, Alexander's class put together an autobiography book near the end of the year:

> Each student was required to check over his or her paper for spelling and punctuation errors and correct them. And to varying degrees, they did. . . . I told them that I would not make any changes at all. Whatever they put into the computer would be what got published. If there were any mistakes, they would still be there for all to read. All the students did some editing, but none did a complete job. They all decided on what they were satisfied with and stopped at that. And actually that's all I felt I could ask for.

Syd organized her class newspaper in a similar fashion:

> They were to work with a partner for any and all corrections—learning in the process that best friends do not always make the best partners. . . .
>
> Finally everything was put together onto a legal-size format and copied on the school copier. There were many mistakes, admittedly, but the paper was absolutely theirs.

Helen, in Telida, summed up her own attitude toward "perfection" in student publications with the following story:

> We tried to produce a newspaper each month, and I began to feel pressured to get everything typed up and laid out in a way I thought looked best. . . . I was grateful for QUILL in getting all that typing done, but so many things at once began to feel like too much.
>
> My solution was to change my standards for the newspaper. I don't say "lower" because I did it more as a change in perspective, letting my reasoning take

me along these lines: "I don't have time to do this the way I think it should be done, but it is important to the children to get it done somehow. Well, I'll let them do it to their own satisfaction, and see how it comes out."

For example, here is a story by John Paul (second grade), one of his first independent attempts at using QUILL:

---

a moose and a wolf
john paul nikolai

One A Time There Was a Moose and a Wolf. The Wolf tried to kill the Moose But It Was a Bull Moose. But It Was Three Wolves And By The Time When It Was April The Moose Was Dead.

This was an edited version. His first version had been difficult to understand, and when I pointed out some of the problems he was eager to fix them. When I read this version, I said something like, "I can understand this now, but there are still some mistakes with capital letters. Do you want me to help you fix them before we put it in the paper?" He said cheerfully, "No, it's o.k. like that." Joe had by that time been chosen as student editor, and he agreed with John Paul, so it went into the newspaper just as it was.

That issue of the paper is so clearly the children's own work, so full of their life and exuberance, that I wonder, in retrospect, why I ever felt a need to pressure them into "correct form." But at the time I remember feeling some concern that other teachers and perhaps my supervisors would think that my standards were not high enough. I believe that this is a false pressure, which we, as teachers, often put on ourselves. In fact, I received more compliments and delighted responses to that issue of the paper than the earlier ones.

As I look at that third issue of the *Telida Current*, I am struck by the deep advantages of relinquishing control. I never thought of the school as "my school" or of the employees as "my aide" or "my janitor" and as much as possible, I tried not to think of the children as "my students." Rather, I believed that the school belonged to the community, and that I was there to work with the community to make the school as much as it could be.

In classrooms such as Helen's, teachers relinquished control of editing for those pieces of writing that were intended for the largest audiences. The same teachers might apply strict editing standards to essentially private pieces of writing—those written just for the teacher. This policy appears at first contrary to that in the world outside of school, where published pieces are usually edited closely, by several parties, and informal writing—the hasty note to a friend—may be left in a raw, unedited state.

But for the students, the teacher was an important public audience, more significant and more critical in many ways than their classmates or an unknown reader of the school newspaper. So they did edit for that significant public audience. At the same time, they knew that the readers of the school newspaper would accept their apparently unpolished writing. Thus the students did adjust writing standards to fit the audience, using their own ideas of the status of the audience.

Whereas many teachers relinquished the responsibility for the final decision in the editing process in the context of a newspaper—a product whose audience was primarily within the school—they changed their demands yet again when the final product was to be disseminated to a more public audience. The brochure that the Holy Cross high school class produced for their town council to send out in response to tourist inquiries contained no errors. Neither did the calendar that the Telida class prepared for their entire community. The change in audience implied a return to the "perfect" standards teachers set for their students in regular classroom exercises—but for a totally different reason, as Helen described:

> In Telida there were no stores, so mail order catalogues were very important, and the children learned early that accuracy was essential in placing an order. A misspelling or miscalculation could result in long delays or in receiving the wrong item.

Thus, once teachers got away from the straightforward connection between the computer and a polished piece, there were interesting variations in the amount of editing and revising they expected their students to carry out. For some in-class writing designed to develop skills, they emphasized correctness. For newspapers and similar documents with a small school audience, they felt it was appropriate to let students decide how much editing was enough. When texts were to be used for serious communicative purposes outside of school, however, teachers were careful to coach students to correct their pieces—especially in the case where errors would have undesirable consequences, such as getting the wrong shirt in the mail.

THE WRITING PROCESS AS A FUNCTION OF THE SOCIAL CONTEXT

There has been much speculation and writing about the potential of word processors to help students learn to revise (Daiute, 1986; Haas, 1989). The conventional hypothesis has been that students do not revise partly because of the mechanical difficulties presented by copying over a piece, and that the computer is a powerful way to overcome this barrier. But, as we saw above, in many classrooms the computer is still used primarily for copyediting. Clearly, the copying-over task is not the only barrier to revision, and the computer alone is not a sufficient solution to the lack of revision. The question then is what besides the computer is necessary to create an environment in which meaning-centered revision occurs. In several situations, we saw revision occurring as a result of fundamental changes in the social context of the classroom.

Milling Around

The most compelling example of revision occurring as a result of changes in the social context happened in a sixth-grade classroom using QUILL in a school in Hartford, Connecticut. The following[4] illustrates how the computer's effect on the social context was the most important influence on revision in this classroom.

One afternoon during Black History Week, Jim Aldridge's sixth grade attended the annual ''Black History Show'' put on by various classes in the school ranging from kindergarten to sixth grade. Jim had encouraged his sixth graders to write critical reviews of the show, although he did not require them to do so. With this in mind, many of them went to the performance equipped with pad and pen and were observed by the researchers to be taking notes periodically throughout the performance. The next day students who volunteered to critique the show were asked to write a draft of their review on paper at their desks, bring it to Jim for minor corrections, and then be assigned a number that would determine their turn to enter their writing on the computer.

One of the drafts presented to Jim was Margaret's. Her handwritten copy read:

> I liked the Black History show because I was surprised to see the little and big children singing so well, and clearly. The best acts were Mrs. Martin's, and Miss Simpson's classes. The songs were nice and the people on stage weren't scared. The worst act was ''Famous Black People''—Mr. Agosto's + Mr. Anderson's class. Everybody messed up and forgot what to say, and they didn't speak clearly. They could have at least practiced more. The scenery was pretty good, and the light was bright enough, but the sound was not that good. Mr. Hodges was speaking very loudly and was good on the stage. I think the show deserves three stars because it was very good.

Jim assigned Margaret the number 5. Marines, her classmate, friend and generally acknowledged class ''star,'' finished soon after and received the number 7. While they were milling around the computer waiting for their turns, Margaret read Marines' handwritten, highly negative review of the show (Ma-

---

[4]A more complete version of this story is told in (Bruce, Michaels, & Watson-Gegeo, 1985).

rines' review was later published in the class newspaper). Marines' sharpest criticism was for the Glee Club:

> The scenery was very good it was excellent but the lighting was a little dull. The sound was awful in some acts but in others it was good.
> I don't know what happened to the Glee Club, they were almost all weak. The audience couldn't hear them. They sounded soft then they went loud. It was a disaster!

When Margaret had her turn at the computer, she entered her first three paragraphs unchanged, but then felt compelled to rectify and explain the discrepancy between her review and Marines's. Her fourth paragraph reflects a change in her reported opinion of the lighting as well as a socially situated explanation of Marines' criticism of the show.

> The scenery wasn't very much, and the light was kind of dull, and the sound wasn't very good. Mr. Hodges was speaking loud and clearly, and he was great on the stage. When the Glee-club was singing so nice, Marines got very jealous and asked Mrs. Evens to be in the Glee-Club. But when Mrs. Evens said no she wrote bad things about the Glee-Club on the computer up-stairs.

Margaret concluded her revised review with the same conclusion she had reached in her earlier draft, but this time set off with "But," perhaps to distinguish her opinion from Marines's:

> But I really liked the Black History show. I gave it 3 stars because it was very good.

This example demonstrates that the motivation for the revisions Margaret made in her review derived from the classroom social context rather than from the availability of the computer per se. In "milling around" the computer waiting for their turn to get on, students read each other's writing and interacted over it. These interactions affected both the content and form of student writing. For Margaret's review, it was these interactional factors—rather than the ease of typing at a keyboard and revising electronically—that influenced her final product most. A different classroom organization, incorporating one computer per student or constraints against reading fellow students' work, would have produced a different outcome for Margaret's review; her computer-assisted piece might have looked much more like her hand-written draft.

Other Changes in Social Context

Our experiences in other QUILL classrooms are suggestive of the same influence of social context. Alexander, a sixth-grade teacher in Fairbanks, had been a participant in a 4-week Writing Project workshop the year before we introduced QUILL. In his first classroom implementation of the writing process, however, he did not encourage his students to edit because the mechanical aspects of revising were too difficult for them. When the computer arrived, it alleviated some of these problems, and Alexander finally instituted a procedure for peer response and revision:

> After writing their initial draft, they had to read it to someone else. The listener had to jot down questions that they had about various events in the autobiography. These questions were then used as a way of revising their work. This also was the general procedure for most of the writing in the class.

Thus, Alexander modified the social environment, providing a source of responses on which students could base their revisions, because of the availability of the technology that made revision possible. This in itself is an example of a straightforward second-order change in the writing system. He intended that this change would, in fact, result in increased revision and, to a certain extent, it did.

But as in the Black History Show example, a change made primarily to respond to the management aspects of the new technology can inadvertently lead to increased revision. A student from the University of Alaska was working with Alexander's class as part of an education course he was taking. Alexander pressed him into service as a computer expert twice a week because students often had questions about the way QUILL worked. The arrival of the University student coincided with another increase in students' revision. He became an additional audience somewhere between teacher and student. As such, he contributed to the social context by having both the time and the perspective to provide appropriate responses that led to revision.

> Students are often reluctant to ask the teacher things they think they should know about QUILL. And I found that by having Tim at the computer, not only did the students ask him questions that they probably would not have asked me, they also got more writing done. Tim would often help them with their revising and other aspects of their writing that I would not have had the time for otherwise.

Ernie also purposely changed the social structure of his classroom to encourage meaningful revision.

> We stressed students working in groups when writing. We encouraged, begged, pleaded, and anything else we could do, to get the students to help each other instead of running to the teacher for help.

The group writing work was implemented through the use of learning stations. In addition to introducing these learning stations, Ernie tried to shift students' focus from grammar to content and made a videotape of his class to observe how this new classroom organization was working.

> The peer editing idea was working. Several instances were seen of students actively involved in conversation concerning writing. In fact this aspect of the tape surprised me as I did not realize to what extent the peer editing was going on. When looking more closely at the segment of the tape concerning peer editing, I found that most was dealing with grammar and not with content. The advantage of having a video tape showing this was that Elsie and I could begin stressing to our students that more work should be done in response groups dealing with content not just with the grammatical aspects of writing.

The classroom organization that supported this peer editing had been implemented for two separate reasons: Ernie's desire to promote student talk about writing and his need when QUILL arrived to reorganize the classroom to deal with the addition of the computer. But in the end it was not the arrival of the computer that increased the amount of revision that occurred, but the changed social context that resulted from the teacher's solution to classroom management issues that enhanced students' motivation and opportunity to revise.

In some classes, the social context was modified by the appointment or emergence of a "computer expert." Several teachers chose computer experts from among their students to answer questions about QUILL and especially about Writer's Assistant. In some classes, this person assumed a larger role in the writing process itself. In Wilma's fifth-grade class, the computer expert became the editing expert as well:

> Zan was fascinated by the ease of editing in the QUILL system compared to Bank Street Writer. By that time we were putting out a newspaper every month or so, and she became my chief mistake-finder-and-fixer. Zan did not excel in her academic courses, but she was an excellent typographer. When her classmates brought rough drafts for her to edit, she often discovered things that even my top English students had missed. She gained a lot of recognition for this among her peers.

In each of these cases, it was not the presence of a text editor that resulted in an increase in revision, but a change in the classroom environment—the creation of new social roles—that resulted from a teacher's attempts to integrate the technology into the classroom.

SUMMARY

Properties of an innovation emerge as the innovation becomes realized in specific contexts. In the case of revision, we saw that copyediting was a prevalent focus despite QUILL's emphasis on meaning-centered revision. This happened for a variety of reasons, including preexisting beliefs and practices of students, teachers, and parents. For instance, meaning-centered revision conflicted with the goal of student control of the writing process, because students may choose to focus on copyediting alone. Writing standards were adjusted to fit a variety of audiences, in ways unanticipated in QUILL per se. Where we did see more revision, it was often due to changes to the classroom writing system.

These examples highlight contradictions in the interaction of QUILL with particular settings. Contradictions such as these raise new questions about QUILL and about computers and writing in general. For example, meaning-centered revision on the computer came into conflict with the goal of equity of access in settings with limited resources. If one insists on equity of access to the computer, and there is only one computer for 30 students, how can the class day be organized so that students use the computer for meaning-centered revision? Should perhaps, small groups of students have exclusive access for limited periods of time, say, 6 weeks? Or, should one conceive of equity in broader terms, so that some students have greater computer access while others have greater access to other resources? Alternatively, since meaning-centered revision can of course be done without a computer, perhaps the best use of the computer in a limited resource context *is* simply as a printing press (exactly the opposite of what we recommended). Given the constraints under which teachers must operate and the limited resources available, the use of the computer as a printing press is at least a rational choice, one which should be judged within its context.

Any innovation is likely to generate contradictions such as these when it emerges from a controlled situation. Teachers often bear the major responsibility for coming up with creative solutions to these difficulties. Studying what teachers do is the key to situated evaluation.

Chapter 7

The Alaska QUILL Network: Fostering A Teacher Community Through Telecommunication

In *Democracy and Education,* John Dewey (1966) articulates some of the complex relationships among community, education, and communication:

> There is more than a verbal tie between the words common, community, and communication. Men live in a community in virtue of the things which they have in common; and communication is the way in which they come to possess things in common. . . . The communication which insures participation in a common understanding is one which secures similar emotional and intellectual dispositions—like ways of responding to expectations and requirements. (p. 4)

These arguments suggest that the environment of any educational experience can be viewed from the perspective of community: Do students feel a bond with other students in their classroom? Are students and teachers part of the same or different communities? Do teachers feel connected in a substantial way to other teachers in their school? In other schools? The sense of being part of an educational community with shared goals, perspectives, and rituals can be as important a part of an educational experience as the content or method.

Jaime Escalante's success in teaching advanced calculus to students from a Los Angeles barrio (documented in the movie *Stand and Deliver*) was due in part to the close-knit community he created in his calculus classroom; he and the students shared jokes and ritual greetings along with a desire to learn calculus. In his description of Brazilian samba schools, an alternative educational model to traditional schools where novices and experts alike work on their samba dancing, Papert (1980) emphasized the importance of community. "There is a greater social cohesion, a sense of belonging to a group, and a sense of common purpose" (p. 178).

Yet creating communities is a difficult proposition in today's educational institutions; we hear more about alienation—of students, of teachers, of administrators, of parents. Given the intimate connection between community and communication, it is at least possible that the increased communication possibilities offered by computers and computer networks could play some part in creating and supporting educational communities. Electronic networks might alter users' social networks by introducing additional resources for information, assistance, comment, or comfort. Electronic interchange might solidify, extend, augment, or replace interpersonal contacts, leading to a more densely interconnected community.

In fact, the QUILL project in Alaska demonstrated at least one way in which telecommunications can provide a fertile environment for the evolution of a community. The participating teachers in the Alaska QUILL project were connected through an electronic network for the 1983–84 school year in which they were implementing QUILL. Our analysis of their use of the network demonstrated not only that a community did emerge, but identified characteristics of the network that were instrumental in nourishing the evolving community. The mechanisms that fostered the teacher community often surprised us. Some were merely unanticipated effects of the network setup, but others resulted from gaps in the technology that might have, under other circumstances, undermined network use. In the end, the community flourished, and the strength of the connections among teachers turned the realization of QUILL in Alaska into a community implementation.

ELECTRONIC NETWORKS IN EDUCATION

While electronic networks were introduced in the business world over 2 decades ago (Caswell, 1988), experiments with school-based networks for teachers and students were relatively rare when QUILL was introduced in Alaska in 1983. Much of the early work in educational networking had focused on helping administrators access resources and exchange information. This early focus derived from several factors: Administrators were more likely than anyone else in the school system to have computers; administrators controlled budgets and, therefore, the acquisition of equipment; there were fewer administrators to link than teachers or, especially, students; and, there was a clear function of resource sharing to be served by a network. One of the earlier networks, for example, was SpecialNet, set up by the National Association of State Directors of Special Education to promote communication among special education coordinators. The two most frequent uses of the network were for information exchanges and for gathering special education data for statewide record-keeping.

But in the early 1980's, there were few examples of networks linking students or teachers on which we could model our teacher network, so we had to make design decisions based on intuition and personal experience. As the year went on, however, our work did benefit from a project that was setting up networks to link students in widely scattered classrooms. In parallel with our QUILL network implementation, Jim Levin and his colleagues at the University of California, San Diego began to experiment with networks that allowed students of different cultures to exchange messages (Levin, Riel, Rowe, & Boruta, 1985). Our work and theirs intersected over the course of the QUILL project and the structure of both networks benefitted from the experiences of the other.

One of the San Diego group's first findings was that a straightforward penpal system did not work well for student communication. Levin and Levin (1985) set up an "electronic penpal" exchange between classrooms in Alaska and San Diego. Students in both places were initially excited by the opportunity to find out about life in a place they considered exotic. Such a communicative set-up, however, had many limitations, as Levin and Levin described in the following:

> most of the initial exchanges between San Diego and Alaska took the form of "electronic penpal" exchanges. While this is a good start-up activity, it is difficult both to manage and to integrate into the rest of the curriculum. Students generate messages like the following (written by third graders in San Diego) with great excitement.
>
> > Hi! new friend from Alaska. Our names are Karina and Manuel. I wish if you could come to San Diego. I wonder if it is cold over there. Well here its warm but some times it rains. We have some rats. Don't you have any pets? Whats your computer name? Our computer name is apple. Karina's friend is Brenda my friend is Juan. We take care of the disks and all the other things of the computer. Our printer gives us what we write. We are going to have a book fair for next week. We like to go to Balboa Park. Good bye! Write us soon.
>
> Since the messages are sent electronically, the students know the messages get to Alaska almost immediately. However, when days go by with no response, the motivation wanes. To understand why responses are delayed, the students would have to take the point of view of the other school. A set of 30 such messages arrive in Alaska, somewhat overwhelming the classroom which might only have 7 students. The Alaskan teacher has to print out the messages, distribute them to students, and then organize times for the students to get on the computer to generate responses. The whole process might take several weeks. Finally, when the set of electronic responses arrive back in San Diego, those students that get responses are excited, but those that don't are disappointed and don't want to participate further. Once the messages are read, there is little motivation to reread them. In this way, the electronic penpal activity has a limited utility in an educational setting. (pp. 8–10)

An alternative approach is a student newswire called The Computer Chronicles News Network (Levin, Riel, Rowe, & Boruta, 1985; Riel, 1985; Riel, 1987). Students at each of several sites (in the United States, Israel, Japan, and Mexico) wrote newspaper articles that were available to everyone on the network. Students at each site then constructed their own editions of the Computer Chronicles, selecting from both those articles written at their own site and those that came in over the newswire. This use of the network fostered more valuable communication than the penpal situation had, as Levin and Levin explained:

> [this newswire activity] is a way of providing a wide range of audiences for writing. The challenge of writing an article that is likely to get published in the edition put together in other sites is much more motivating for writing than simply sending a penpal letter. Similarly, it provides a functional environment for reading, since the articles that come in have to be carefully read to help decide which to include in the local edition. (p. 10)

In the years since the QUILL in Alaska networking experiment, knowledge about the use of networks in education has undergone a slow but steady growth. Several projects have used long-distance networks to create different types of student communities. The InterCultural Learning Network has grown out of the Computer Chronicles News Network, incorporating more sites and additional joint projects (Levin, Kim, & Riel, 1990; Riel, 1987). Especially successful have been collaborative science and social science projects, such as comparative descriptions of water cycles and the appearance of the moon, that take advantage of the geographically and culturally diverse nature of the network participants (Levin, Riel, Miyake, & Cohen, 1987; Levin, Waugh, & Kolopanis, 1988).

More recently, an electronic network has been used to create a distributed scientific research community. The National Geographic Kids Network™ (Foster, Julyan, & Mokros, 1988; Lenk, 1989) has given students the opportunity to contribute to a real scientific collaboration by networking hundreds of classrooms into a data-collection and analysis team studying problems such as acid rain in conjunction with a professional scientist who is also on the network. As both the InterCultural Learning Network and National Geographic Kids Network illustrate, a common trend in network environments for students has been the creation of goal-oriented projects that truly benefit from the participation of classrooms in different locations.

The uses of networks for teachers have lagged behind their uses for students, perhaps because it has not been as obvious how teachers would benefit from the introduction of electronic communication facilities. In the last few years, however, several teacher networks have been developed, so that a critical mass of experiences is beginning to accumulate. A network for secondary science teachers organized by the Educational Technology Center (Katz, McSwiney,

& Stroud, 1987) using the system Common Ground (Hancock, 1985), for example, linked 75 teachers in eastern Massachusetts to communicate about science and science teaching. The results of their study underlined the importance of personal knowledge and common goals in the evolution of networking communities. The network organizers found many participating teachers, most of whom did not know each other personally, were reluctant to write messages, viewing the network instead as a curriculum resource. In particular, more inexperienced users who knew no one else on the network personally were likely to respond only to messages about a narrow set of science topics that they viewed as central to their teaching. Katz et al. suggested that an ''activity'' approach, similar to the Computer Chronicles News Network, in which participants worked toward an explicit common goal, might have gone further toward fostering widespread network use and the growth of a community. Given the increasing accessibility of the technology necessary to support networking—for teachers, students, and administrators—analyses such as Katz' and ours are important in informing the future design of educational networks.

PRECURSORS OF THE ALASKA TEACHER NETWORK

No other QUILL implementation had an electronic network for teachers, although the role of networking in QUILL had already undergone a significant change through the field test in 1982–1983. We had begun by including MAILBAG in QUILL, with the notion of students using it to communicate with one another and occasionally with the teacher. The *QUILL Teacher's Guide* made this purpose explicit by listing three goals for the use of MAILBAG:

- Encouraging written communication to varying, but specific, audiences (for example, friends and classmates).
- Allowing different kinds of writing to occur (for example, informing, persuading, instructing, entertaining).
- Motivating students to write more by personalizing the experience. (p. 38)

We did not include interclassroom networking for students in the original QUILL design because of the difficulty schools had obtaining modems and classroom telephone lines. Some teachers, however, exchanged disks containing their students' writing either by physically handing them to one another or sending them through the US Mail. These extensions fit with our original idea of giving students the opportunity to write personal messages with a specific audience and purpose, so they further articulated, rather than altered, our conception of QUILL.

Because of our focus on writing by students, we had not originally considered the possibility that teachers would be as eager as students to write to one another. The field test, however, suggested that facilitating teacher communication was a worthwhile extension of the QUILL design. During the field test in the Northeast United States, teachers in the three experimental sites wrote letters to one another on an ever-growing "teacher communication disk," clumsily passed through the U.S. Mail. In addition, during the first 2 years of QUILL use, our colleagues at The NETWORK partly fulfilled the function of a teacher network by publishing QUILL Scribbles, a teacher newsletter, every few months. While these "networks" used more primitive technology than telecommunications, their popularity demonstrated that teachers trying out an unfamiliar and challenging innovation wanted to be in touch with others in the same situation. Implementing a teacher network fit well with our original notion of providing purposeful writing environments for students. The implementation of our writing innovation for students was the catalyst for a writing innovation for teachers.

In addition to our field-test experiences, the context in which we were about to introduce QUILL affected our implementation. Most dramatically, we recognized the need for the Alaska teachers, widely scattered around the state in groups of one or two, to remain in contact. Since developing methods to cope with geographical isolation is a familiar activity in Alaska, teachers welcomed a new communication channel. Their desire was a major reason why we made an effort to surmount the equipment difficulties and other logistical barriers to establishing a teacher network.

In Alaska in 1983, assembling a teachers' network was no small task. There were many resource restrictions. Few classrooms had telephones that could be used for telecommunications. The nearest telephone was usually in the school office; sometimes the only available phone was in the teacher's home. Except for a few teachers in Juneau and Fairbanks, using the network was not free, and each school district had to decide how much to allocate for paying networking bills. Because they were also paying a fee to be part of the project, most districts could not put aside much for this aspect of it. Finally, even the resources that existed were not reliable; both power and telephone service in the villages were more likely to be out of service than they were in the cities. One classroom even had to contend with the computer being unreliable because soot from the school's wood stove got inside the machine.

Despite these problems, we decided to include a long-distance network in the Alaska QUILL implementation for the following reasons:

1. Alaska QUILL teachers lived in widely separated villages and cities. A computer network would increase the communication opportunities for distant participants because it would alleviate many of the problems of distance, time, and space.

2. Most of the participants would have met at the 3-day QUILL training

session in October, so they would have common experiences and personal knowledge on which to base their messages. A few had known each other for several years.

3. A few of the teachers had already used the University of Alaska computer system's electronic mail system in computer-mediated classes offered by the University. Several others had had experience with audio conferences, a type of conference call common in Alaska, in which several separate locations are simultaneously connected via a telephone link.

4. In 1983, Alaska school districts were beginning to acquire telecommunications equipment and subscriptions to national networks, primarily as a way of tapping into large educational data bases.

5. Appropriate networking software that was compatible with QUILL and simple to use had become generally available ("The Network Tool" from InterLearn Inc., in Cardiff, CA, written by Jim Levin in 1983).

In other words, there was a perceived function (communication among teachers working on a common project who had little opportunity for face-to-face discussion), a facilitating technological context (users with some telecommunications experience, hardware, and software availability), and a supportive social context (users with some personal knowledge and shared experience). The teacher network we established interacted with these preexisting conditions to produce a strong QUILL teacher community.

THE ALASKA QUILL NETWORK: HOW IT WORKED

We had few specifications for the network when we started, other than that everyone whom we considered a network member be able to access the network in some way. In addition to the Alaska QUILL teachers and the two network coordinators (Carol and John), our network included three school district administrators (Mike, Malcolm, and Marcia), a University administrator (Dick), the software developers (Andee, Chip, and Jim), and the University of Alaska professor who had been responsible for bringing the QUILL developers to Alaska for a seminar in the spring of 1983 (Ron).

The network was a "Rube Goldberg" device, made up of two established computer networks, a variety of modems, and a central portaging facility that served as "communications central" for the entire network. As we examined the features of existing networks that would allow us to exchange mail, set up bulletin boards, and do computer conferencing, we discovered a maze of options, but none that met all of our needs. So we fashioned our own network.

We chose the University of Alaska Computer Network (UACN) and the SOURCE as backbones for our system. UACN is a statewide network that is available to people or programs associated with the University of Alaska. For those QUILL teachers who lived in the larger communities of Alaska (Fairbanks, Juneau, and Bethel), UACN was a logical choice because there was no charge for using it. However, teachers in smaller communities and participants in the network outside of Alaska (primarily the developers) could not use UACN without significant long-distance telephone charges. For these people, we added the SOURCE, a national consumer data bank and mail system.

The SOURCE was available to anyone in the United States and several other countries who was willing to pay "connect time" charges (which include long-distance access charges, but are far less expensive than long-distance telephone rates). In addition, the SOURCE provided a facility called PARTIC-IPATE (PARTI for short) that allows users to set up special "conferences"— groups of people who were interested in a particular topic, such as the use of computers in education. The system supported a separate exchange of messages within each of these groups, which were open to anyone in the entire SOURCE community. Interestingly, though, our decision to use the SOURCE was based less on economic and technological concerns than on social ones; several people who we wanted to be part of the network (the University of Alaska Education Department, the Iditarod School District, and Jim Levin, in particular) already had SOURCE accounts. Had the decision been based solely on cost and services, we might have chosen CompuServe as our second network, but the networking decisions made by other people became the determining factor. Because computer networks are not yet connected by a central system like that which connects our telephones, people's choices about subscribing to a network are often based on the other people who have access to it. This was just one example of the profound effect the social context had on the network; even before the network was formally set up, our choice of technology was determined by social considerations.

The advantages of using two separate networks to build our QUILL Network included financial benefits, access to the resources of two systems, and a network with wider accessibility. The obvious disadvantage was the need to transfer messages between UACN and the SOURCE: in other words, to create a network gateway. The fact that the account set-ups were different on the two systems added to the logistical complexity. On UACN, several people had individual accounts; for the project we added a group ID called "FA-QUILL," which was available to everyone in the project who had access to the UACN system. On the SOURCE there was no such group account; mailboxes on that network belonged to individuals (Carol), school districts (the Iditarod district, to which four of our participating schools belonged), or institutions (Chip and Andee shared an account). Messages intended for the entire group always needed to be transferred from one system to the other, as did messages that were written by an individual on one system and were addressed to someone on the other. This arrangement had the unintended effect of creating a large number of messages with varying degrees of ''privateness,'' all of which became more public in the transfer process.

The role of gateway fell to Carol, as part of her job as coordinator. She and her official coportager, her son John, became quite proficient at the mechanics of transferring files between the two systems. John described his part in portaging as follows:

> One of the most important jobs I had following the conference < training session > was the portaging of messages from one computer system to the other. I figured out the best system for doing this and for awhile it was fun and interesting. However, after about 2 months of endless courier service, it got to be quite boring so I taught Mom how to do it, and from then on she got to take care of all the messages that needed to be transferred. . . . I guess that during the QUILL year, I just provided lots of computer support for my mother. She didn't have the time or patience to spend several hours at a time at the computer like I did. I was happy to do the jobs that were interesting to me, and she usually paid me by giving me a certain amount of time on the SOURCE each week.

With Carol and John serving as the link between the networks, the structure became that shown in Fig. 7.1.

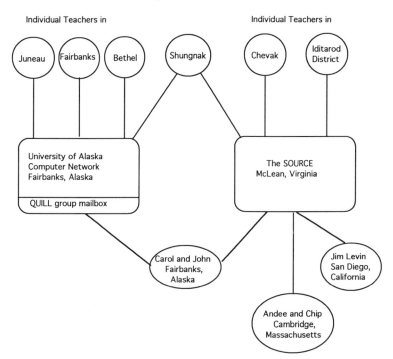

FIG. 7.1.   The Alaska Quill Network.

Teachers in Juneau, Fairbanks, and Bethel had free access to both their individual mailboxes and FAQUILL, the group mailbox. Teachers in Shungnak, Chevak, and the Iditarod District used the SOURCE because phone charges were less expensive than with UACN. Teachers on either system could send messages to any mailbox or set of mailboxes on their own network. Thus, the SOURCE users could send a message to individual addresses such as Carol, or Iditarod, or to some group of these. Similarly, the UACN users could address a message to any individual mailbox on UACN, to the FAQUILL mailbox, or to some set of these. Messages sent to the FAQUILL mailbox were always "group" mail that their senders intended to reach the audience on both networks; as time went on, in fact, they probably forgot that an intricate forwarding process was involved in getting their message to everyone.

Due to the network's complexity, many messages took circuitous routes from transmission to receipt. Figure 7.2 illustrates the path of a message sent by

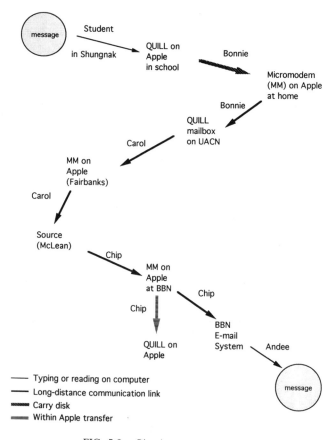

FIG. 7.2.   Circuitous message path.

students in a classroom in Shungnak, Alaska, to the QUILL developers in Cambridge.

After the students completed their message at school, their teacher took it home (next door) to the Apple she had set up for telecommunications. From there she uploaded it using Micromodem (MM) onto the QUILL group mailbox on UACN. When Carol read it in Fairbanks, she transferred it, again using MM, to the BBN SOURCE account. It was Chip's turn to check the SOURCE mail that day; in addition to reading the message, he sent a copy on to Andee on the BBN internal mail system.

The portaging technology was cumbersome, but it worked. The real challenge in portaging surfaced as Carol and John tried to develop some appropriate social protocol for exchanging the messages. Who should get messages that were addressed to an individual, but contained generally useful information? Were some complex technical messages to and from the developers better kept private so as not to confuse less technically adept users? They soon discovered there was an "art" as well as an "act" to proper portaging, an art that required sensitivity to the personal and informational needs of both the community and the individuals in it. Doing the job well required an interest in and familiarity with the information being transmitted, and an ability to provide a good deal of encouragement, humor, and moral support. They were thus an intelligent gateway that carried out tasks no automatic device could have handled. A substantial load of other managerial tasks also fell to Carol. In addition to taking primary responsibility for managing and routing information, she "cleaned" the group mailbox (i.e., saving some messages in separate files, flagging some for immediate attention, deleting others); provided the users with updated information on UACN and SOURCE commands and procedures; oriented new participants; acted as liaison to UACN, requesting changes to make it more useful for the teachers' network; and monitored the billing procedures for both networks. She developed charts to keep track of the computer-related aspects of messages (e.g., file name, account, and length), their content (subject, message), and their routing in the network (sender, sent to).

As a supplement to the computer network, Carol also sent out monthly packets of QUILL-related material to everyone on the network. Included in each packet was a paper copy of all the computer mail, copies of students' QUILL projects (newspapers, poetry, stories, booklets, etc.), a short newsletter, and copies of magazine articles that were relevant to the project. The postal mail and the computer mail, while they were somewhat redundant, turned out to serve as valuable complements to one another. Through the mailings, information was shared that would have been too difficult or expensive to send via electronic mail.

The packets often helped to ease teachers into using the computer network. Teachers who read them saw that the information being exchanged on the network was not limited to hardware and software issues. Writing standards were informal, with errors and awkwardness generally acceptable. There were many useful ideas about classrooms in general. Moreover, there was humor; the exchanges occurred within a social network that looked appealing. To be part of the group one would need to join the network.

GENERAL CHARACTERISTICS
OF THE NETWORK'S USE

The network was fully operational early in November, 1983, soon after the QUILL training ended, and was in active use throughout the school year until the beginning of May, 1984. Of the approximately twenty-five potential users of the network, about half of them used it regularly, whereas most of the other half used it occasionally. The variable that appeared to account for most of this variation in use was simply "ease of access." All of the people who used the electronic mail system routinely had a computer, modem, and phone line that was set up at school or at home so they could use the network without making any major changes to the hardware. Those who used the network less frequently had to move their classroom computer into a school room with a telephone (often the principal's office), walk to a school district office, or drive to a university computer terminal location. While these differences in access were sometimes accidental—that is the school district had independently set up a networking capability for projects other than QUILL—they were often a reflection of teachers' interest in and commitment to computers and networking. In particular, most of the teachers who had computers at home had gone to the trouble to set them up before the QUILL project so that they could figure out how to use them in their classes.

During the 6 months when the network was fully operational, more than 300 messages were exchanged among teachers, administrators, and developers through the network gateway.[1] Most of these messages through the gateway were "broadcast" messages addressed to all of the network participants; only a few were private messages sent from one individual to another. Their topics ranged from straightforward discussions of QUILL software, through exchanges of information on language arts teaching, to personal news. Teachers not only used the network to ask and answer questions, but also to share feelings about the project. The positive comments were generally glowing reports of their students' writing and enthusiastic suggestions of projects they had found successful. The negative comments were most often provoked by frustrating experiences

---

[1]Participants could and did exchange private messages. We have no way of knowing the content or even the number of such messages. The count here refers to those sent through the UACN/SOURCE gateway shown in Fig. 7.1.

with the hardware or interactions among the several pieces of software involved in sending a message over the network, which made the process much more complicated and time consuming than it needed to be. One of the more expressive messages of this type came from Ernie, late one night:

AUGHHHHHHHHHHHHHHHHHHHHHHHHHHHHHHHHHHHH!!!!! Carol sometimes I just want to throw this computer out of the window! I have been here at school for almost 3 hours trying to copy my mailbox to a file so I can keep them. . . . If you heard a loud scream Sunday night about midnight, it didn't work! (2/6/84)

During the year, the network's use went through four overlapping phases, determined by the progress teachers were making with QUILL implementation and the rhythm of the school year. The time line in Fig. 7.3 illustrates these phases.

The first phase was marked by messages about problems in getting QUILL started, as well as by greeting messages. The second phase was marked with a concern for integrating QUILL into the language arts curriculum. The third phase was marked by increased message traffic and a diversity of topics. The fourth phase saw fewer messages as the school year wound down, and a focus on the future.

Typical messages from the first phase (October to December) included:

Greetings from Shungnak! QUILL is underway. . . . We're all hanging on and going with it. The kids are learning quickly. When Chip was here we also had a visit from the supt. The students took to QUILL like a sled dog to pulling. There are a few management problems, but no major bugs with the program other than

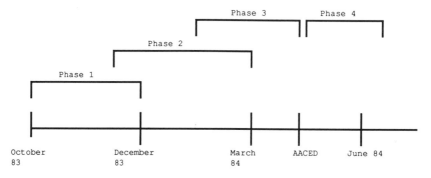

Phase 1:   greetings, hardware problems
Phase 2:   curriculum concerns
Phase 3:   high density of messages, broadening of topics
Phase 4:   focus on future

FIG. 7.3.   Phases of the Alaska Teachers' Network.

that if a student wishes to print out a mail message that they have just sent, the printer does some wierd symbols—Chip, you saw that when you were here. The only other problem has been with a kid named Johnson. For some reason part of his messages never appear when he checks mail. If we type in his name in all caps, and the sender did it in lower case would that make a difference?

Time to go send some mailbox messages. . . . Bonnie (11/6/83)

Greetings from Chevak!
This is Ernie writing to you with Lena in the copilot seat. I have begun to use QUILL (Mailbag) in the classroom with good results. I also have been doing a lot of prewriting activities with the kids. My biggest problem at the present time is how to run the computer along with a class of 24 very active second and third graders! I have the kids blocked into 30-minute slots at the computer with three kids to a group. The problem I have with that is kids don't always think in 30-minute blocks! The kids named the computer Mr. Halloween and the machine has taken on a personality of its own. More as it develops. . . .

Well that is all for now, as they say in Chevak, See you on Seair!!!! [the airline serving Chevak]

Lena and Ernie (11/9/83)

The second phase began as teachers felt comfortable with the QUILL hardware and software and the networking procedure. At this point, they had learned the mechanics of QUILL and were concentrating on integrating it into their writing curriculum. Helen, from Telida, sent this message early in January:

One thing happened in my classroom that seems to be a partial answer to the question about fitting in computer time and not neglecting regular classroom work. I had been having some standard mid-year panic about all the things the kids don't know, and my reaction to it had been to break out the old workbooks, and start handing out sheets of exercises—punctuation, capitalization, and so on. The kids' reaction was not too unexpected—"Sick!" "Boring!" "Do we have to. . . ?" and so forth. I had a hard time mustering up too much enthusiasm, and within a few days, my own insecurities had passed, and we were back at work on our class newspaper, for which there was considerable enthusiasm. When it came time to address the newspapers, it wasn't a popular task, but there was a reason for it, and it was accomplished without grumbling (apart from a reasonable request that I would do "this long one"—I had Chip and Andee on the mailing list, and the kids balked at "Bolt, Beranek, and Newman"). Anyway, while they were addressing the newspapers, I remembered that the workbook exercise, which had been so distasteful to them, involved identifying which letters in addresses should be capitalized, and why. Here was a perfect, natural, way to come at the same learning. I also suggested that they could put the mailing list on the library disk, so they wouldn't have to write it out every time, and this was accepted as a great use of QUILL.

Here there was a real reason for being as accurate as possible, and it was easy for the kids to see the need for it.

I guess I'm just trying to suggest that we let as much reality as possible into our classroom, and let the children put it together when they are ready to do so. It seems to stick better that way, and it's easier for all of us. (1/3/84)

The next few months saw the third phase: a flurry of messages exchanged among a large portion of the QUILL teachers. These included requests for and offers of curriculum assistance, complaints and exultations about the software and hardware, personal information (job changes, budding relationships!), technical discussion about features of the software, and general reporting about the progress of QUILL in their classrooms. Part of such a message sent from Wilma in McGrath follows:

We haven't been using MAILBAG much since the initial blast-off, but LIBRARY is very popular with my 5th graders. We have used it for our newspapers, reports, haiku, Christmas stories, creative writing, and lots of miscellaneous piddling around. We've used PLANNER for movie reviews, reports on American Indians, and now for reports and oral presentation planning on Heroes of the American Revolution. . . . (1/31/84)

Messages also started to arrive during this period from several "late arrivals," teachers whose equipment had been delayed, who had missed training in Fairbanks (as one entire group had, due to bad weather), or who for some other reason had taken a longer time to get involved with QUILL and the network. These messages tended to be short, intended primarily as practice with the technology—yet, they were real in the sense that an audience was truly awaiting their arrival. Here is one such message from Judy in Holy Cross:

Hello, Carol. I'm just here in Mike's office in McGrath and we're trying to learn about the SOURCE and this whole system in one easy lesson!! Do you think it will work? (1/16/84)

As April drew near, so did the Alaska Association of Computers in Education (AACED) conference, where we had arranged to present a workshop on the QUILL in Alaska project. Most of the teachers planned to attend the conference, so they regarded it as a reunion as well as an opportunity to tell a wider audience about their work. Rather than the event generating additional communication, the number of messages on the network actually dropped somewhat during the few weeks before the conference. Anticipating the opportunity to see each other in person, teachers were less likely to use the network to communicate; instead, they stored up questions and comments to share at the conference. In addition, Chip and Andee visited most of the QUILL sites either before or after the conference, so communication with them did not need to rely on electronic mail.

After the AACED conference and the round of site visits that accompanied it, network use entered its fourth and final phase. The next big event for QUILL teachers was the end of the school year. During the last month of school, several of the rural teachers were also making arrangements for new jobs, sometimes involving a move to another village. Teachers were less worried about "making QUILL work," since the year was almost over and their presentation in Anchorage was past. Thus, in this phase, communication was driven by two overriding concerns: planning for a summer training session that would extend the QUILL Alaska project and cementing individual relationships that had developed during the year. Many messages such as the following from Carol to Chip and Andee were involved in the establishment of a 2-week summer training session at the University:

> We had our "Quill Administrative Council Meeting" on Monday and all present agreed that the University ought to do whatever it can to keep Quill rolling in Alaska. We feel that the most important role that the university can play right now is to try and provide support for training this summer. The best avenue for doing that seems to be via the regular "Summer Session" that is offered here in Fairbanks. (5/1/84)

The culmination of this planning was communicated to all QUILL teachers in the following message from Carol:

> Good News! We've been able to work out an arrangement for some QUILL training for this summer. Kathleen Starr, a coworker of Chip's and Andee's at BBN, will be coming to Fairbanks in July. I've enclosed an announcement about the classes she'll be offering. There will be two levels of training . . . one for beginners and one for "experienced" people (which naturally includes all of you!). Hopefully, completion of the advanced course will lead to certification as a QUILL Trainer. It's late to be putting out announcements about summer classes, so I'd appreciate your help in passing on the information about this QUILL training.

The exchange of personal messages between people who had developed an ongoing collegial/personal relationship continued during the rest of the year. Bonnie had been developing a culturally relevant test of writing ability for the Inupiaq children using QUILL in her school. Two weeks after the AACED conference, she sent Chip a progress report on the testing, enlisted his assistance in scoring the children's compositions, and added the latest chapter to a long-standing joke between them about the weather in Alaska. Chip had always been vaguely disappointed with the lack of extreme weather during his visits to Shungnak, and professed to doubt that it ever got really cold there. Bonnie countered:

> I'd tell you that after you left the temp dropped to − 30 again, but you probably wouldn't believe me. I'd tell you that right now it's snowing up a storm like we haven't seen all winter, but you probably wouldn't believe me . . . (4/30/84)

and Chip replied:

> Your weather stories are wonderful, sometimes I almost believe them. (5/1/84)

And in between the arrangements for summer sessions and field test evaluations, some lyrical language even appeared on the network:

> Saw many cranes, and have heard spring bird songs all day. The temp is 70 in
> the sun. . . . Folks say the caribou migration is like a river on the snow. . . .
> I saw it once, won't forget it, but can't do it justice with words. . . . The sun
> only sets now for a brief time, what a place of ying and yang . . . (from Bonnie,
> 5/6/87)

HOW A COMMUNITY WAS FORMED

The content and frequency of network messages, people's interactions during and after the AACED conference, and the connections several of the Alaska QUILL teachers maintained several years after the project all evidence the fostering of a community by the Alaska network. Even though the electronic network became much less active after June 1984 and essentially disappeared later that fall, several of the individual relationships that had been established continued to thrive through the more standard communication devices of mail and telephone. In particular, some of the most interested teachers continued to be in touch with Chip, Andee, and Carol, even as they changed jobs and locations. Letters from these teachers over the next few years provided some indication of the role the network had played in their lives. For example, Bonnie wrote in May of 1985, after a difficult year of being principal/teacher in Kobuk, where she taught after the QUILL network year:

> I think a dose of the QUILL network could have helped. I didn't realize how
> truly valuable that link was to my enthusiasm. (They say phones should be in
> this summer—I need to be able to talk with some folks with the same frustrations
> and concerns.)

And a year later, she still missed the contact the network had provided, as she commented to Carol:

> I wish I had the network going still—it's like a hole now—there's nothing to replace
> it. I wish I could get hooked back into another network. In Alaska when you're
> in small places you often don't have people who share the same philosophy. You
> need someone to fuel new ideas, so you don't lose enthusiasm. The QUILL net-
> work was great because we knew we always had an audience—someone was there
> to read and respond to our ideas, thoughts, and concerns.

During the 1984–1985 school year, several of the Alaska QUILL teachers worked as QUILL teacher trainers after taking the QUILL advanced course during the summer. This gave them the opportunity to communicate with one another about substantial topics—how to organize a training session, the relationship between QUILL and the Alaska Writing Project, and so on. A letter to Chip and Andee from Helen made clear the importance of these training sessions as a way for teachers to keep in touch:

> It is great that there are quite a number of training sessions set up, and we are managing to do them all. . . . I really think I'll enjoy having this way of sharing some thoughts about teaching and writing, as well as the specifics of QUILL.

Because she had moved from Telida to Fairbanks in the summer of 1984 and temporarily stopped teaching, the training sessions were especially important to Helen as a way of keeping in touch with the teachers she had gotten to know the previous year. The following excerpts from a letter she wrote to the other QUILL trainers after a session in November of 1984 illustrate both the content of her interactions with the other teachers and the emotional connections that accompanied them.

> Marcia and Dick and I just finished a 3-day training session, and I thought it would be a good idea if, any time any of us does a training session, we make a note of things which went well or problems which arose. . . . Alex came in and gave an excellent presentation. Since we all have experience in such a wide variety of situations, I think it's important to pay close attention to each other, so that our sessions about classroom management can be as wide ranging as possible. . . . Parents need to know that QUILL doesn't make corrections in spelling and punctuation for the children. [Alex] got a lot of questions about that at conferences. . . . Happy Thanksgiving—I'm thankful for people like you in the world!

Helen also attempted to prolong the QUILL community by trying to start a QUILL Magazine in which students could publish their best writing. In a letter to Alaska QUILL teachers (both old and newly trained), she noted the need for "a real reason for students to edit their best work into a final 'polished' form" and proposed the magazine as a solution.

There is even some evidence that more long-range social connections resulted from the year of frequent communication. During the 1987–1988 school year, three teachers who were involved in the QUILL project moved to McGrath, where there were already three other QUILL veterans. It is at least possible that the social connections these teachers had formed via the QUILL network had some influence on the personal and career decisions that led to this concentration of former QUILL teachers in one village.

The effect of the network on the teachers' social context over the course of the year gradually transformed the QUILL project in Alaska from a 12-classroom implementation to a community implementation. And this change from a collection of classrooms to a community affected the way QUILL was implemented. "Contagious" ideas for writing topics found their way from one classroom to others via the network. Several teachers borrowed Ernie's "Describe a possible cure for baldness" idea, and newspapers appeared in many classrooms. A series of autobiographies and autobiopoems appeared in the middle of the year. In response to several requests delivered over the network, Bonnie shared her autobiography Planner with the rest of the group and suggested it could be used for biographies (e.g., of grandparents) as well. The network also provided a way for frustrations that may have stopped an individual teacher to be shared, absorbed, and defused in a community setting. Early in the year, questions about classroom management were posed and discussed over the network. Bonnie helped several teachers who were concerned that having only one computer meant that students couldn't read each other's work on the machine:

> In Shungnak QUILL classrooms, there never seemed to be any time for reading other students' work on the computer. We have a solution to the problem. The kids print out a copy for the QUILL book—a "magic stick" photo album. We have organized it so similar stories are on a page. The book will be placed in the library at the end of the school year. (2/3/84)

The network community also provided support for teachers when they feared the effects of their hard work wouldn't show up on standardized tests. Helen, in particular, was concerned about this, so Chip responded:

> I wouldn't worry about the test scores. We never considered looking at them in the first place as a means of evaluating QUILL because we didn't believe (nor did any one we talked to who knew about testing) that limited computer use over a short period of time would result in noticeable general achievement test score gains. [We should look instead] at things like amount of writing, attitudes, amount and types of revision, kinds of writing, use of writing in different subject areas, and so on.

Such reassurance helped teachers go on with the process of implementing QUILL, even when they were having difficulties or temporary doubts. By providing technical and curriculum resources, discussions of classroom management and pedagogical approaches, an outlet for frustration, and general support, the Alaska teachers' community supported and changed individual teachers' implementation. How did the network contribute to the growth and structure of this community? Not surprisingly, characteristics of the audience and purpose embodied in the network, the same characteristics of writing environments we emphasized in QUILL, account for much of the evolution of the community.

Writing to a Friendly Audience

Even though messages on computer networks are almost always delivered, there is no guarantee that anyone will answer them. One frequently heard complaint about computer networks and conferences, in fact, is that authors of messages often get no response at all. Even worse, they may have no idea whether anyone has even read what they have written. The lack of response is particularly frustrating if they have spent a long time carefully crafting an argument or opinion. After a few experiences that remind them of being "a lone voice in the wilderness," people often drop out of electronic networks. Communication with an unresponsive audience is not really communication at all.

In contrast, participants in the Alaska QUILL network knew that any message they wrote that needed to be portaged between UACN and the SOURCE would be read and taken seriously by at least one person: Carol. In part due to the clumsy configuration of the network and the need for Carol to reroute messages appropriately, none of these messages were without an audience. Questions that came to Carol over the University of Alaska network had to be explicitly sent on to Cambridge via the SOURCE if they were to be answered by Chip or Andee, and any message that was to be read by the entire group had to be moved from the SOURCE to UACN or vice versa. The traces of Carol's reroutings are easy to find in the messages:

I don't know about Johnson's problem, but I will send the message on to Boston, Bonnie. (11/7/87)

The following message was sent on The Source by Mike Baumgartner in McGrath and Don Stand from Nikolai. Don is going to be participating in the Quill Project and when he sent the message he was in McGrath learning how to do Quill. Some of you already know Don (from the Small High Schools Project or from graduate classes at the U of A or from his earlier participating in computer networks). As soon as he gets all his equipment, we'll be hearing from him.
Welcome aboard, Don! (Don's message follows, 1/19/84)

In addition to accomplishing the routine message transfers that resulted from the structure of the network, Carol became an "information broker," deciding for each message she reviewed whether there were portions of it that should have a wider audience. Thus, some of the personal messages she received remained private, portions of others were passed on to Chip and Andee for technical comment, and others were distributed to the entire network. Early in December, as network traffic began to accelerate, Carol faced head-on the decisions she had to make in this "triage" role. The following is a message she sent to Chip and Andee:

> I'm wondering if you do want to be barraged with ALL of the mail from up here or do you want me to screen it first and just send you the parts that you need to respond to or would you like me to send all of it to you, but indicate just those parts that I'm not able to answer. (12/9/83)

Carol's acceptance of this role meant that she had to read and analyze each message to understand what function she was meant to serve in relation to it. A consequence of that task was the fact—obvious and important to everyone on the network—that Carol was a guaranteed audience for anything they might write. In fact, some teachers who actually wanted to send group messages but were intimidated by the prospect of their writing being seen by so many different people, relied on Carol as a knowledgeable filter who could assess how appropriate it was to make their messages public.

Carol's job did not stop at the administrative task of routing messages, but extended into being a touchstone for the teacher community. In particular, she was aware of the teachers' feelings of both frustration and accomplishment and tried to use her moderator role to share the burden or the success. The following is an especially straightforward attempt at sharing the burden that Carol included in one of the mail-out packages she put together.

> Just wanted to share with you part of one of Ernie's late night messages. I think his "AUGHHHHH. . . . ." is a perfect description for the feelings of frustration and exasperation that we've ALL experienced at different times (and for different reasons) with this whole computer business. Being a pioneer in this area isn't easy, but this group of QUILL teachers sure keeps plugging away despite all of the obstacles. (Ernie's message followed this introduction; it is included earlier in this chapter, 2/6/84)

Because of the group's acceptance of Carol's triage role, the complex physical structure of the network, and the fact that sending a message required some technical effort, messages were often addressed to several audiences—both individual and group—at once. The following message from Sandy in Holy Cross is typical:

> Just a note to let you know that the X-CED computer in Holy Cross is still sick—in other words, we have not done much with QUILL as yet. Judy and Joe are moving right along however. Chip, what did you do with my flashlight when you left Holy Cross? (12/8/83)

While the above message moves from a public audience to a private one, other messages started by being addressed to an individual (often in response to a personal message) and almost imperceptibly became more public by the end. The following excerpt of a message from Andee to both Ernie and Lena in Chevak illustrates both the personalizing of a piece of a message (by using the direct address "Lena,") and its eventual shift from private to public conversation.

> Lena, your question about giving students blocks of time is a common one. Teachers have found that they have to make their classrooms a little more flexible than they have been. Some teachers structure their classrooms as activity centers in which each group in the class is doing some different piece of school work; the computer then works well as one of these activity centers. In some classrooms, teachers have used QUILL especially when reading groups were working. In others, teachers have always had someone on the computer, even if he or she missed something else in the classroom, on the assumption that it would even out in the end. Does anyone else have any suggestions? (12/23/83)

Such a private to public shift appears to be a feature of electronic mail, because of the ease with which writers can send copies of messages to many people at once. It was prevalent in the Alaska QUILL network messages because of the task-oriented nature of the network.

Occasionally, especially as experience with the network accumulated, some participants commented on the unusual assumptions about audience our messages implied. A message from Andee to Carol in February included several phrases that evidence an awareness of this pattern.

> I've just written to Helen, Wilma, Mike, Deane, and Bonnie and am finally getting around to writing to you again. . . .
>
> I don't know the details yet, but it looks as if both Chip and I will be able to attend the AACED conference—I hope that convinces a great number of you to come, too, so we can have a reunion. Let's find a really unique restaurant in Anchorage and have a rowdy time. . . .
>
> I realize this message is strange—started out being to Carol, ended up being to QUILL in Alaska—it just shows what happens when you're not sure who the audience for a text is! (2/14/84)

Besides saving on message transmission time, the inclusion of multiple audiences in the same message gave network participants the feeling of "eavesdropping" on conversations that were not really addressed to them, as if they were in a large family that held its personal conversations in the kitchen. Since network members knew their messages were likely to be read by a large group, the messages were never so personal that it was inappropriate for them to be shared, but their semipublic nature assumed a kind of familiarity and trust even before it was well established in the group. In fact, this consequence of the technology probably fostered the very sense of community that it presupposed.

"Mixed messages" (including both public and private communications) were possible in part because of another characteristic of the network audience: a set of mutually shared experiences. Almost all of the teachers on the network had attended the training session in Fairbanks, and Chip, Andee, and/or Carol had visited every classroom in the week following training. All the teachers were working with the same software and curriculum materials; many were struggling with the same implementation problems. The size of the group, too, was conducive to this sense of sharing; about 15 people were regular contributors to the network, and keeping track of their classroom and personal situations was possible.

Partly in recognition of this shared background, almost all of the messages on the network were broadcast to everyone; even if they were addressed primarily to one person. These communications further expanded the common background that the training session had begun, and network participants took advantage of this by writing messages that assumed a large amount of shared knowledge. One result was several ongoing public discussions, some about educational issues and others that were expressions of the shared (often humorous) themes that fed the group identity. One such theme focused on the weather (a frequent topic in Alaska) and, in particular, on Chip's complaints that he hadn't experienced colder temperatures. On a more serious topic, several teachers exchanged information on their use of videotape as an observational tool in the classroom. In January, Bonnie broadcast the following message; it clearly presupposes a group whose members knew each other pretty well and had all read a message Helen had sent previously about how her reaction to mid-year insecurity was to "break out the old workbooks" (1/3/84).

> Today I hooked up the video equipment and filmed us QUILLing. I haven't had much time to look at the tape yet, but have a few impressions to pass along. 1-There is a lot of good stuff happening at the computer, but I'm too busy "teaching" to get in on it. Although the audio is very hard to hear, from the nonverbal signs I can see kids very absorbed in what they are doing . . . talking over some part of the story, discussing how to move the cursor or work some command, or find a key on the board. 2-They are not afraid of the equipment at all. The kids are becoming more and more comfortable with the hardware as time passes. I know that none of this is earth-shattering news, but as Helen stated, with the coming of the second semester, there's an urge to drag out all kinds of meaningless book stuff. What is happening with kids and QUILL is making learning worthwhile. (1/18/84)

In contrast to their active participation in their own network, the Alaska QUILL teachers took little advantage of the computer conferences on the SOURCE. PARTI offered several conferences relevant to QUILL (e.g., Computers in Early Childhood, Computer Teacher) and, in addition, a QUILL conference set up by Sandy Levin in San Diego, primarily to establish pen-pal relationships between classrooms in San Diego and Alaska. Carol, in an extension of her role as network triage person, sent an introductory statement about the Alaska project to the QUILL conference and sent information about PARTI to the rest of the Alaska teachers.

These exchanges, however, never became popular with the Alaska QUILL teachers. While the PARTI community was available to Alaskan teachers as an extension of their own network, their participation in it was almost totally limited to a few messages that Carol sent, a few that Ernie sent, and an interchange Bonnie had with the Levins about her use of PLANNER. It is likely that their lack of interest in PARTI stemmed from the fact that the Alaskan network met their needs in a way the larger network could not easily accomplish, and their involvement in the Alaskan network left little time or psychological space for the effort that PARTI participation would require.

Members of the Alaska QUILL network, then, felt they were addressing a reliable and familiar audience, carefully managed and "nurtured" by Carol. They relied on a constantly growing shared background to support their communication. This sense of "being listened to" and "being known" were major contributions to a feeling of community and made them willing to put in the effort necessary to become familiar with the network procedures and to contribute on a regular basis.

Addressing Common Goals

Closely linked to the Alaska QUILL teachers' shared background were a set of common purposes that provided a starting point for the formation of the network. When the network became more robust, this set expanded, as participants realized that the network could satisfy some educational and personal goals they had not identified before.

At first the participants' most immediate goal was joint problem-solving about QUILL itself. Everyone was painfully aware that the software was less than perfect and that curriculum and classroom management details needed additional attention. The teachers needed to be in touch with one another to discuss details of the software and classroom implementation. Soon after the training session, a student in Ernie's class lost a MAILBAG message because a disk was too full. Ernie's first message, sent jointly with Lena, asked for help in avoiding the situation. Eventually, he received three separate responses to his message: one from John promising to investigate, one from Bonnie confirming that she had run into the same thing, and one from Andee explaining the source of the problem and a temporary solution.

Bonnie took it upon herself to explain to the other QUILL teachers how to move quickly through the QUILL menus to get to the word processor.

For some of you who had asked about getting into the actual writing faster, Chip showed us how to type more than one number for a command. . . . If you know the number of the choices you will be making, you can type all the numbers one after another then put in the 3 returns. The QUILL program will take all that information and do all those tasks without pausing to ask you for the information. Good luck! (2/3/84)

Teachers also exchanged ideas about using Planners to write autobiographies and interviews, evaluating the writing their students did both on and off the computer, using a cardboard "post office" and paper flags to indicate when individual students had mail in their mailboxes and specific topics for group writing (e.g., cures for baldness, ethnic family stories). Whatever the specific topic, this communication was clearly and purposefully focused on getting QUILL to work smoothly and productively in the classroom; teacher participants in the network used it as a medium for tackling their own implementation problems and sharing their solutions.

Since we were also on the network, teachers viewed us as a source of rapid feedback about the software and, occasionally, of a new version with fewer bugs. But the presence of the developers added another shared purpose: producing a piece of software that would be successfully marketable. This codeveloper sense encouraged Mike, an administrator from the Iditarod district, to make this suggestion:

Deane is using QUILL with her Jr. high class. We tried to teach it to her 9th graders, they rebeled because it takes so long to boot and to move from screen to screen to start writing in Library. Isn't there something Andee and Chip can do about that? That might be why it is billed as appropriate for grades 3-6, but it could keep the program from expanding to many classrooms. (1/30/84)

Ernie took his role as a participant in development so seriously that he wondered aloud toward the end of the year whether QUILL was really ready for the market:

This is the third time such an error has occurred with one of my disks. . . . I wonder if the program is ready for the market yet. With all the problems in McGrath and the problems with my disks I wonder if more time should be given to research on QUILL when it is used for long periods of time. I hope Chip and Andee have some suggestions. I think that the program is fantastic, my kids love it, but maybe it needs more time to smooth out the rough edges. (3/25/84)

The teachers' influence on development meant that there was at least one purpose that all network participants shared. Whereas other purposes served by the network were common concerns primarily for the teachers (e.g., figuring out how a computer influenced their classroom organization), this one universal goal made *all* the network participants into a sociologically "flat" community. Some teacher networks—such as the Educational Technology Center science teacher network described at the beginning of this chapter— have included "experts" whose main role was to provide information and answer questions. In the QUILL network, on the other hand, teachers did not see their relation to the developers as strictly one of "novice user" to "expert"; rather, there was an honest sense that everyone could make important contributions to improving the program.

Computer networks have in general been acclaimed as opportunities for participants to be less aware of the social status information obvious in face-to-face interactions (sex, skin color, ethnicity, physical handicaps) and traditional forms of written communication (letterhead, type of stationery). Because the Alaska network's participants knew each other, an egalitarian context could not grow out of ignorance; rather, it had to grow out of a shared purpose to which everyone could meaningfully contribute.

In addition to these group goals of making QUILL work, many participants in the Alaska QUILL network were fulfilling a significant personal purpose: communicating with colleagues. About three-quarters of the QUILL teachers taught in remote village schools alone or with only a few other teachers. A general lack of communication facilities also characterized several of these villages; most of the telephones in Telida, for example, had been installed only a few months before the QUILL project started. The distances between villages make teachers in Alaska more acutely aware of their needs for interaction than teachers in urban areas, whose isolation from one another is less complete, yet still significant. Ernie asked for help on a curriculum development task:

> I am going to write up or should I say attempt to write up a scope and sequence for grades K–8 dealing with writing. I want to use the QUILL and Writer's Assistant as the main ingredient of this. I also want to use ideas from the writing consortium which I am going to this week in Anchorage . . . I realize that I can't create this monster myself, but if I get the information then myself and a few other teachers in Chevak could work on it. (1/19/84)

Messages also contained birth announcements, recipes, requests for help in locating old friends, reports on extracurricular activities, travel plans, and confessions of guilt for not doing "enough" with QUILL. Bonnie clearly saw the network as an important social outlet, since she wrote on a visit to Fairbanks:

> The phones are out in Shungnak, I'm going through networking withdrawal. (2/7/84)

The dispersed community even provided a legitimate purpose for the writing that several teachers did during their follow-up training sessions. Instead of practicing using QUILL and the communications program by doing empty "exercises," teachers had a real goal: to communicate with people they had started to get to know in Fairbanks. For the teachers from Holy Cross, who had missed training because of the weather, their personal introduction to others on the system came through their initial network messages.

A cultural bond also linked most of the teachers on the Alaska network. Except for Lena, all of the network participants were Anglos and, for the most part, Anglos living in the midst of a culture that was not their own. Cultural contrasts were frequent: some were serious, some amusing. But in each village, the Anglo teachers had few people with similar backgrounds with whom to share their reactions. The network provided the opportunity to create a community unconstrained by space, time, or the traditional (and often rigid) boundaries imposed by individual schools, districts, cultural regions, and institutions. In her description of the year's experience, Helen commented:

> Being the only teacher in Telida, I really appreciated hearing from other teachers (and others involved with QUILL). . . . The important thing was the respect and support we offered each other. It's easier to put extra effort into something if you feel like someone else is interested in what you are doing.

The line begins to blur here between audience and purpose. The purposes served by the Alaska network reflected the needs of its participants, and those participants for whom the network was functional continued to be part of the audience. As in any community, common interests and common needs were the glue that held the group together. In this case, the connections were reinforced by another somewhat serendipitous parallel. Teachers were writing about writing and, as such, experiencing the writing process at the same time that they discussed it in their messages. Inevitably, they faced many of the same issues in their own writing that they observed in their students, and their own experiences writing with a computer gave them a generative perspective on their classrooms.

One of these issues was their own, students', and parents' desires for "perfect" student papers, especially when they were produced on the computer. (See chapter 5 for a more complete discussion.) As computer network writers themselves, teachers had to face a similar decision: How much effort would they put into making their messages technically perfect? At the beginning of the year, network users had to type their messages directly into the message system, which supported only the most rudimentary editing. Because they were paying telephone and/or network charges while they typed, they could not afford to spend much time editing their messages. So, their messages were full of apologies for imperfections, asides like "oops . . . I know that's not right" and retyped words, phrases, and even sentences.

By the middle of the year, the software supported composing messages within QUILL, and then transferring them to the network. Several teachers, breathing a sigh of relief, started to prepare carefully edited messages as QUILL files and upload them to the network. Simultaneously, they were struggling in their classrooms with students who worried more about correct spelling and punctuation than about meaning-centered revisions. The relationship between the requirements they imposed on themselves as computer-using writers and those they wanted their students to adopt gave teachers unusual insight into the reactions their students had to QUILL.

But the most important example of synergy between the classrooms and the network was in their sense of "purpose fulfilled by writing." The network reinforced for QUILL teachers the principles set forth for the QUILL program itself. There, by design, purpose was paramount; meaning was the mainstay of the pedagogical philosophy. So in using the network, teachers experienced themselves what they attempted to create in the classroom for their students. In the service of making QUILL work better, we created a "macroworld"—a real-world context that embodied the communicative environment we were trying to create in the classroom.

COMMUNITY AS A PROPERTY OF NETWORKS

The Alaska QUILL teachers' network "worked," in the sense that it met participants' needs by fostering a community that helped them implement QUILL more successfully. But networks don't always work; in spite of increasingly sophisticated telecommunications technology and easier-to-use interfaces, some networks never achieve a sense of self-sustaining energy. In our own experience, this is sometimes due to technological problems, but is more often a reflection of a mismatch between personal needs and what the network offers. Some networks never reach a critical mass because the purpose they might serve doesn't appeal to a coherent community. More interesting, though, are networks that continue to work for some people, but, as they mature, lose members who had originally chosen to participate. One recent example is an international discussion of pedagogy and computers that generated long philosophical discussions that effectively excluded casual users. Another is a tennis network that began as an exchange of information on tennis and a way for players to meet others of comparable skill. It evolved, however, into a mechanism for setting up formal weekly tennis events, and several more casual players removed their names from the distribution list. In both cases, the original group of participants was loosely defined as "people who were interested in the topic," but the use of the network defined a more specific community that was appropriate for only a subset of the original participants. In both cases, the critical variable that defined the evolving community was not technological capabilities, but personal needs and interests.

While the influence of personal needs and purposes on network use may be clear to the designers of general networks, they often have difficulty integrating such a perspective into their network designs. Thus, network planning has focused on technological parameters such as baud rate (at what rate can an individual receive or transmit information), bandwidth (how much information can be sent over a link between nodes in the network), network configuration, time between message sending and receiving, need for special equipment, and cost. Similarly, much of network evaluation has examined technological measures such as message volume, average response time, mean time between failures, and number of active participants.

Much of this emphasis on technological considerations is historical. The impetus for network development in the business world came from a need to access resources (e.g., programs, databases, manuals) that were not locally available. The first networks were time-sharing networks, whose person-to-machine, rather than person-to-person, connections made them utilities rather than potential communities. Even as person-to-person connections were added, the first problems to be tackled were, appropriately, designing efficient ways to route messages, dealing with complexity as networks grew large and complicated, and inventing monitoring procedures to diagnose and repair network breakdowns. Early networks sometimes acted primarily as file servers, whose main function was to facilitate the transfer of data files from one workspace to another; programs such as FTP (file transfer protocol) made this process possible without involving any communication between people. Focusing on access to remote resources made technical requirements such as high bandwidth and quick response time salient; users would not continue to use a utility that required them to read a large remote data base using insufficient networking power.

Although networks were used primarily as utilities, individual purposes and needs substantially began to affect how and how often a person used any particular network connection. Electronic mail systems added new possibilities for interpersonal interaction and issues of community began to emerge. Thus, by now, most networks in the business, academic, and education worlds involve aspects of both utility and community. The CompuServe Macinfo conference, for example, allows Macintosh enthusiasts to exchange hard-to-find tips about making the best use of their computers. Traffic in this computer conference is heavy; more than one user has even complained about its volume. However, the utility aspect of this network is bolstered by a sense of community; participants in Macinfo are energetic in their reactions to the Macintosh, feel a bond with others who are similarly inclined, and even grow to recognize some frequent contributors. This sense of community even keeps some participants from giving up in frustration over the volume of mail they receive.

The mix of community and utility is carried even further in the growing international network known as Internet, which connects many national and regional networks. With the recent increase in availability of networking hardware, constructing such a network has become simple, creating, in essence, the potential for a worldwide electronic community of university and industry scientists and engineers involved with high technology. If past use of the constituent networks is any indication, Internet is likely to be an amalgam of utility and community, with personal messages and asides mixed among the requests for information, and a variety of subcommunities coalescing over time.

A more explicit recognition of the importance of social structure in network use is in the growing number of "digests" to be found on large networks. These serve the same general purpose as conferences—allowing a subgroup of users to communicate with others who share their interest in a particular topic. In contrast to conferences, however, digests require a single organizer who—often on a rotating basis—collects all messages on the topic, organizes them, comments on them and sends out a newletter-like message once every few weeks. This structure substitutes for the deluge of messages sometimes associated with special interest discussions and works particularly well when it doesn't matter if messages are disseminated immediately.

With aspects of community showing up and even being formalized in utility-oriented business networks, analyses of the social structures that foster and are fostered by network use become even more important. For people setting up educational networks who have mainly business networks as models, an understanding of the communication characteristics that are most likely to lead to a strong community of teachers or students is especially important. And business network planners will undoubtedly find such information increasingly useful as their networks become more obviously community oriented. One study, in fact, has examined networks in both business and education to generate a list of "participant structures" most likely to lead to successful networking communities (Levin, Kim, & Riel, 1988). Their general guidelines specify that a successful network should involve:

- A group of people who work together or share interest in a task, but who find it difficult to meet in the same location and/or at the same time.
- A well-specified task to be accomplished by this group.
- Ease of access to a reliable computer network.
- A sense of responsibility to the group and/or task.
- Strong leadership and final evaluation of the group task.

Further investigation and elaboration of such criteria will need to continue as technology advances and networking resources become available to larger groups of people; the day when the effects of electronic networking on communities rival those of postal mail and telephones may not be far off.

SUMMARY

Our experience with the Alaska QUILL teachers' network provides one answer to the question posed in Riel (1989): "Can electronic networks be used
to create cooperative learning conditions for teachers as well as students?" Our
answer (as is Riel's, in describing the AT&T Long Distance Learning Network) is a resounding "Yes." The Alaska network not only created a cooperative learning experience, but beyond that a community of teachers for whom
writing was the critical link. It thus modeled the literacy environments they
were attempting to create in their classrooms. Our analysis of the structure
and strength of the network identified two categories of characteristics that help
explain its success in fostering a community, even given the imperfect nature
of the technology on which it was built. Since the network was built on communication, it is not surprising that those categories were *audience* and *purpose*.

The salient audience characteristics that led to an evolving community were
(a) previous interpersonal connections, and (b) a guaranteed, interested audience. The network participants had met and worked together during the 3-day
QUILL training, and some of the teachers had taken classes at the University
together before. The audience's interest was guaranteed to some extent by a
common purpose, but grew as well out of the unusual network structure that
made Carol a "moderator" as she transferred messages between networks. The
assurance that Carol would read and seriously consider most messages gave the
network a primarily one-to-many rather than one-to-one communication structure. The semi-public quality of the messages encouraged a "large family"
community sense, although it may have contributed to the network's eventual
demise by making participants too dependent on Carol. Still, while the network was operational, everyone knew that their messages would not go unread.

Several interacting elements of purpose also supported the teacher community: (a) common individual goals and a shared group goal, (b) a flat social
organization, and (c) a synergy between network and classroom activities. From
the beginning, participants on the network shared a common individual goal:
to implement QUILL in their classrooms. Communicating about this goal was
even more critical in the first few months, before hardware and software
problems had been solved. So, a sense of a common problem to be solved
provided an initial boost to the network. As the year went on, a group goal
emerged as well: to prepare a session for the AACED conference. Thus, teachers
shared individual goals and a group goal, both of which relied on the network
for success. In the pursuit of these goals, one kind of cooperative learning environment for teachers was supported by the network.

Teachers also shared a purpose with the wider network community that included the QUILL developers: to critique and improve the software. This "flat"
social organization added to teachers' sense of the importance of their com-

ments, because they were likely to be reflected in changes in QUILL. Finally, the network created for teachers a functional learning environment that in many ways mirrored what they were creating in their classrooms. While they were attempting to create situations for their students that made possible purposeful audience-sensitive writing, teachers had access to just such situations for themselves. What they learned about their own writing processes in that setting provided insights that could influence their work in the classroom, as they saw some of the dilemmas they faced in their classrooms reflected in their writing on the network.

These audience and purposes characteristics contributed to an environment that prompted Carol to comment in a message to Andee in February:

> It's amazing how "connected" I'm able to feel to both you and Chip, and I really do believe that this same kind of "connectedness" wouldn't occur if we were using phones or the mail system. Certainly there would be no way to share thoughts so readily with such an extended group if one were using the traditional ways of communicating. Access to you and Chip is a tremendous boon to all of us . . . both for program information and for the "pats on the back." (2/15/84)

and Mary Goniwiecha to write to the other teachers in the network:

> I must say that I have read all the letters from you all with much enthusiasm each time I've received a packet. You bush teachers are so good about communicating with us that we city folk are put to shame! I'm actually in more contact with you through the newsletters than I am with my fellow Fairbanks teachers. Tsk! Tsk!

As the community developed, it turned the network from something new and somewhat strange:

> This is the first time I've gotten connected on the SOURCE. Hi Carol and Malcolm and anyone else who's listening out there in outer space. (Helen, 12/9/83)

to a comfortable medium, quite in contrast to "outer space" in just a few days:

> Hi you guys, all is going fine and I wanted to say hello and goodnight and Merry Christmas, in case I don't get on for another week or so . . . (Helen, 12/15/83)

Chapter 8

Situated Evaluation

A central goal of this book is to contribute to an understanding of educational change. To that end we have examined how QUILL was realized in different ways in diverse settings. In the preceding chapters on purpose, revision, and network communication we studied the details of the process, because we wanted to understand how the realizations reflected the unique characteristics of QUILL as well as the particular classrooms in which QUILL was used.

Nevertheless, the general form of the realization process occurs in the introduction of any innovation, whatever the domain. The parameters, constraints, and issues related to change are in large part the same across innovations, even those built around older technologies such as books, paper and pencil, or the blackboard. What should be of greatest interest to those interested in educational change is not the fine details of the technology, but rather, the ways in which the goals, presuppositions, and attitudes of the developers of the innovation interact with those of the people who use it.

We explore in this chapter some implications of the QUILL study for the broader field of educational evaluation. We are concerned with questions such as: Why do educational systems resist change or change in unexpected ways? What is the role of innovations in encouraging change? How can we best analyze the process of change when it does occur? What are the implications of this view for the evaluation of innovations?

Implementing an innovation means introducing something new into an existing system. If the innovation is significant, it will trigger changes in the system, some of which may be easily predictable and others of which may be surprising. People involved with the system naturally want to know what those changes may be and what they mean. The notion of change that is implied by an innovation thus calls for an evaluation. We are led to a number of questions about the innovation, the two most basic being these: (a) How well does it work? and (b) How can it be improved?

In answering these questions, an evaluator must keep in mind the purpose and audience of an evaluation. Just as a student in a classroom has a variety of audiences and purposes, an evaluator has several possible audiences and purposes for an evaluation. Audiences can include teachers, administrators, parents, researchers, and developers. Purposes include helping people make informed decisions about adoption of an innovation, helping them modify an innovation, and helping them understand how an innovation might be used in a new setting. In thinking about the methods and goals of evaluation we need to take these varieties of purposes and audiences into account.

In the next section we describe summative evaluation, which addresses the first of these questions, and formative evaluation, which addresses the second. We use the evaluations of QUILL to make these descriptions more concrete. The types of evaluation discussed are useful but have many limitations. To extend their scope, researchers have proposed a variety of alternative evaluation methods, some of which we discuss later in the chapter. Each of these methods makes a contribution to the study of educational innovation and change. But even these methods fail to answer a basic question for a potential user: How can the innovation be re-created in one's own setting? This leads us to raise a fundamental issue about the nature of evaluation: What is the "it" being evaluated? An exploration of that issue leads us to call for a new type of evaluation, *situated evaluation.*

PARADIGMS FOR EVALUATION

Walberg and Haertel (1990, p. xvii) defined *evaluation,* and two major types of evaluation as follows:

> The term *evaluation* refers to a careful, rigorous examination of an educational curriculum, program, institution, organizational variable, or policy. The primary purpose of this examination is to learn about the particular entity studied, although more generalizable knowledge may also be obtained. The focus is on understanding and improving the thing evaluated (formative evaluation), on summarizing, describing, or judging its planned and unplanned outcomes (summative evaluation), or both.

Summative evaluation focuses on the impact an innovation has in terms of predefined measures, such as scores on a writing sample. It might, for example, report a substantial increase in the writing scores of students who used the innovation. As such, it addresses the potential user's need to decide whether to adopt an innovation. Formative evaluation focuses on the innovation directly, and addresses the developer's need to learn how to improve an innovation. It might detail comments from users and list changes to be made to the software.

In this section we describe the summative evaluation of QUILL, a rather standard, quantitative, objective, outcome-based assessment of changes in student writing attributable to the use of QUILL. We then discuss the formative evaluation of QUILL. These evaluations are described and then compared in some detail, both to complete our story of the QUILL experience, and to establish a baseline from which to discuss alternative methods of evaluation.

Summative Evaluation of QUILL

With *summative evaluation,* researchers look at the impact of the innovation as a whole on learning or some other outcome. They usually compare one or more experimental groups who used the innovation with control groups who did not (or used only parts of it). A measure, such as a holistic writing score, is designed to capture the educational effect of the experience of using the innovation. While many parties might have an interest in the results, a typical audience is the potential user.[1] Information is provided to a teacher, a principal, a parent, or an institution, such as a school district, regarding the effectiveness of the innovation. This information is used in making adoption or continuation decisions. Over time, the same information may lead to changes in the innovation or in the ways it is used.

Summative evaluations frequently involve any of a wide range of quantitative methods, but they are not limited to these. In this section we focus on the quantitative methods used in the summative evaluation of QUILL, as an example of standard summative evaluation.

QUILL Field Test.   A formal summative evaluation was carried out on QUILL during the 1982–1983 academic year (Bruce & Rubin, 1984). The purpose was to determine whether QUILL could be certified as effective for teaching writing and, if so, for which grade levels and which types of writing. This evaluation, done at the NETWORK, was based on data collected in a field test in Massachusetts (a rural site), Connecticut (an urban site), and New Jersey (a suburban site). The classrooms ranged from third through sixth grade. At each site there were two experimental (QUILL) classrooms and two control classrooms. The data were samples of three types of student writing:

---

[1]The term "user" is ambiguous in educational settings. Students are the ones who "used" the QUILL program and engaged most directly in the QUILL activities. But teachers also "used" QUILL in many of the ways the students did, and in addition, QUILL was something they used pedagogically. Also, principals and other administrators could be described as "users," because they were typically the ones who decided to "use" this innovation in their institutions. When we discuss summative evaluation, we have in mind administrators as users; when we discuss formative evaluation, we usually refer to the students.

exposition (e.g., a description of the procedure to follow for a fire drill), per-suasion (e.g., a letter to the principal about obtaining more computers), and expression (e.g., a story about a picture presented to the students).[2]

The goal of the evaluation was to determine for what grade levels and types of writing QUILL was effective. We judged effectiveness by assessing student writ-ing to see whether there was a significant improvement after using QUILL for 6 months. Naturally, one would expect some improvement in student writing over the course of a school year with or without QUILL. For that reason, we needed to find writing improvement for students in QUILL classrooms that was sub-stantially greater than we could reasonably expect to find in classrooms without QUILL. To do that, we also assessed writing for students in six control classrooms, each matching a QUILL class by grade level and in the same site.

We scored pretest and posttest writing samples from QUILL classes and the matched control classes using a primary-trait scoring system. This system measures the effectiveness of writing in terms of the primary goal or trait of the writing assignment (Mullis, 1980). Each writing sample was scored by two people using a scale from 1 to 4, on the basis of its success in achieving the primary goal of the task. For example, a persuasive piece should include rea-sons for the argument it makes. If no reasons were given, the piece would score 1; if several well-articulated reasons were given, it would score 4. Raters were trained for 2 days. Disagreements in the ratings, which occurred for approxi-mately 20% of the samples, were resolved by a third rater. In every case of disagreement, the first two ratings differed by no more than one unit, and the third rating matched one of the first two. Raters did not know the class from which any piece of writing came (see Bruce & Rubin, 1984, for more details).

This rather straightforward design yielded, as we show below, useful results within the framework for which it was intended. QUILL was shown to be ef-fective for teaching writing at three grade levels and for two of the functions. But it is important to interpret these results carefully. There were problems with the data collection. Moreover, as we discuss later in this section, the meas-ures captured only a small aspect of the effect of QUILL, and entirely missed unanticipated changes in the classroom.

One problem was that the data from the sixth-grade classroom pair in Con-necticut could not be considered because the teacher for the control class did not have her class complete the posttest writing sample. (As a "control group" teacher she may have felt that the posttest had little direct benefit for her class.) This was particularly unfortunate, because the corresponding experimental class was one we felt made especially interesting use of QUILL. We, of course, had other things to report about the class, but our summative evaluation paradigm could not include this classroom.

---

[2]These types of writing correspond roughly to Britton et al.'s (1975) "aims" or Kinneavy's (1971) "functions."

Preliminary analyses of the data showed greater improvement in expressive writing for the QUILL classes than for the control classes, but the difference was not statistically significant. Because the purpose of the evaluation was to certify QUILL's effectiveness and to specify precisely the areas in which it was demonstrated to be effective in the field test, we performed subsequent analyses on only the persuasive and the expository scores.

The first analysis of the data was done to determine which classrooms showed significant growth between pretest and posttest (see Tables 8.1 and 8.2). On the expository writing samples, for each of the grades three, four, and five, QUILL students achieved gains between the pretest and posttest of 0.6 to 1.3 primary-trait scoring units (0.89 to 2.3 standard deviations). All of these gains were statistically significant ($p < .01$). In contrast, only the grade four control group showed a statistically significant gain (0.5 units; 0.75 SD). Similar results were obtained for persuasive writing. All three grade levels of QUILL classes showed statistically significant ($p < .01$) gains (0.58 to 0.74 units; 0.82 to 1.45 SD), whereas only the grade four control groups did (0.52 units; 1.14 SD).

A second analysis of the data was done comparing the posttest scores of the QUILL and control groups for both persuasive and expository writing and for each grade level, to see whether QUILL students were writing significantly better than comparable control group students. A correlated t-test analysis of the data demonstrated that the differences were statistically significant ($p < .01$) in every case, including the two grade four comparisons. The pretest scores were also analyzed to verify comparability between QUILL and control classes. Only one of the classroom pairs (third grade, expository) showed a significant difference on the pretest. For that case, the control group dropped from 2.08 to 2.04 between pretest and posttest, whereas the QUILL group gained from 1.33 to 2.63. On the basis of this summative evaluation, the National Diffusion Network certified the use of QUILL for grades 3–5.

TABLE 8.1
T-test Results for Pre to Post Gains in Expository Writing

| Grade | Class | N | PRETEST | | POSTTEST | | CHANGE | | t-value |
			x	SD	x	SD	raw	SD	
3	Q	22	1.33	.565	2.63	.848	1.30	2.30	− 7.78*
4	Q	42	1.95	.668	2.55	.677	.60	.89	− 4.36*
5	Q	33	2.27	.659	3.00	.611	.73	1.10	− 4.73*
3	C	24	2.08	.504	2.04	.550	− .04	− .08	.29
4	C	28	1.60	.663	2.10	.497	.50	.75	− 3.33*
5	C	27	2.20	.925	2.44	.801	.24	.26	− 1.23

*Significant at the .01 level

TABLE 8.2
T-test Results for Pre to Post Gains in Persuasive Writing

Grade	Class	N	PRETEST		POSTTEST		CHANGE		t-value
			x	SD	x	SD	raw	SD	
3	Q	21	1.54	.509	2.28	.463	.74	1.45	− 7.07*
4	Q	42	1.97	.511	2.64	.727	.67	1.31	− 5.85*
5	Q	31	2.29	.702	2.87	.670	.58	.82	− 4.11*
3	C	25	1.50	.577	1.88	.440	.38	.65	− 2.33
4	C	29	1.72	.455	2.24	.511	.52	1.14	− 3.67*
5	C	26	1.92	.730	2.11	.766	.19	.26	− .94

*Significant at the .01 level

Other Summative Evaluations. The QUILL field test provided quantitative evidence that students in grades three to five who used QUILL improved their ability to write well for both exposition and persuasion. Other summative evaluations were also done. A study in a classroom (grades 4–6) in Shungnak also showed statistically significant improvement in students' writing using the primary-trait scoring. In contrast to the other summative evaluation, the greatest improvement was in expressive writing. Moreover, the students' posttest writing samples were almost twice as long as their pretest samples. Perhaps most significantly, at the end of the year students asked to have their writing samples back so that they could continue working on them. They no longer thought of writing as a school task to be completed in 20 minutes, but as a creative process that they had the right and responsibility to complete. This change in attitude towards writing was not, however, assessed in the summative evaluation.

Writer's Assistant (published by Interlearn), the text editor used in QUILL, was itself the subject of a summative evaluation. Levin, Boruta, and Vasconcellos (1983) worked with two classrooms, one using Writer's Assistant for 4 months, and one not. Students generated samples of writing using pencil and paper both before and after using the computer. In the experimental (Writer's Assistant) class, there was a 64% increase in writing sample length versus 4% in the control class. On a 4-point holistic scale, the experimental group's scores increased from 2.00 to 3.09, between pretest and posttest, whereas the control group decreased slightly, from 2.27 to 2.24.

Summary. These assessments are representative of summative evaluation in general. Given a well-defined measure, such as a primary-trait score for a writing sample, one can structure a study to assess whether there was a significant change following the introduction of the innovation, and contrast that change with the change found in a control group. The summative evaluation of QUILL provided evidence that QUILL "worked"; that is, for specified grade levels and types of writing, students in QUILL classrooms improved their writing skills more than did students in comparable nonQUILL classrooms. These results were useful to those making decisions about using QUILL or supporting its dissemination.

Formative Evaluation of QUILL

Formative evaluation is a second widely used method for looking at innovations. Here, the audience is not the end user, but rather the developer of the innovation. The developers introduce the innovation into a suitable context, or a small number of such contexts. They then monitor its use to determine how different features work, with the goal being to make appropriate modifications to the innovation. The methods are typically observations and interviews.

For example, suppose the developers observe that one student has difficulty deciphering a particular screen display. In the formative evaluation process this would probably be taken as a sign that the display should be examined and possibly modified. Since the developers are still engaged in shaping the innovation, they cannot afford to ignore any indicators of how the innovation functions, even without a formal statistical analysis. In contrast, in a summative evaluation, the point is to assess how the innovation as a whole achieves its goals. One takes the innovation as fixed, ignores the details, and looks for overall effects. A single student's difficulty in understanding the screen might never be noticed in a summative evaluation. In what follows, we relate several episodes in QUILL's development/formative evaluation cycle. Each of these represent changes we made in QUILL as a result of experiences with its use. Many of these changes seem obvious in retrospect but only became clear in the process of formative evaluation.

The Process Tree Interface. Early in the development of QUILL we experimented with an interface in which aspects of the writing process were made explicit (see Fig. 8.1). The user would specify where he or she was in the writing process and the computer would provide the appropriate tools. We thought this might (a) help the students develop a metacognitive awareness of the writing task, and (b) keep the students focused on writing goals rather than on computer procedures.

What we found was that our "process tree" became too bushy. The distinctions it called for were often too fine or inappropriate for the writer at a given point in the writing and multiple paths to the same computer procedure created confusion. These problems were apparent in the initial trial period and led us to revise our conception of the interface. In the end we still maintained an aspect of the original multilevel design by asking users to specify the writing

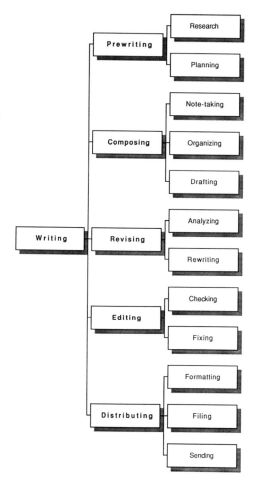

FIG. 8.1.   The writing process tree interface used in an early version of QUILL.

environment they wanted to use (PLANNER/LIBRARY/MAILBAG) rather than the tool itself (editor, mail system, keywords, etc.), but the final design was simpler to use and better in that it did not imply a fixed writing process.

Distinction Between Revision and Editing.   Another shift in emphasis came about with experience in the use of QUILL for revision. As we saw revision being reduced to copyediting in many classrooms, we realized that we had not provided a clear model for encouraging revision in either the *QUILL Teacher's Guide* or the teacher training sessions. This led us to emphasize revision more in later work with teachers. It is noteworthy that the rejected process tree had made distinctions among various aspects of revising and editing. These contradictory modifications in QUILL's view of revision and editing indicate why it is useful to think of development and evaluation as a continuous process, in which the "freezing" of an innovation occurs at a point dictated more by timing and economics than by any sense of complete knowledge about its effects.

Form Letters.   Another cycle of formative evaluation occurred in our development of MAILBAG. We originally thought that a library of forms for letters would be a useful resource for students. We considered including memos, personal letters, business letters, and perhaps, finer subdivisions of letter types. The library would then be both a handy tool to assist in the letter writing process, and a tool for instruction, since it would illustrate the ideal schemata for different writing purposes. The computer would automatically generate portions of a letter once the student had specified his or her goals.

This idea turned out to be unsuccessful. Within the confines of the Apple II computer and the need to have a simple, easy-to-use interface, we offered only a few choices of letter types. For inexperienced writers, even this selection was confusing. In order to choose the appropriate letter type, the students had to know almost as much as the computer provided. Thus many students were either confused by the options or felt them to be an unnecessary burden. Worse still, the forms constrained writers in unfortunate ways. In some cases, writers wanted to contradict the form, and their efforts often resulted in bizarre texts: Figure 8.2 shows part of a personal letter with the student's own closing ("Love,"), followed by the computer generated closing ("Sincerely,").

```
                          Love,
                            Betsy
                          Sincerely,
                            Betsy Mahon
```

FIG. 8.2.   A closing produced by an early version of MAILBAG.

Based on these experiences, we abandoned the form letter approach. In deciding to make this change, we relied on the reactions of only a few users. There was no need for a formal statistical analysis, since the difficulties revealed in practice served as convincing existing proof that our design needed reworking. This kind of tinkering is typical of the development/formative evaluation cycle. If our goal had instead been to explore general interface issues, we might have wanted to determine the reactions of a larger number of users.

Printer Form-Feeds.   The heuristic driving the original design of QUILL was that computer tools and environments that were useful in the workplace for people who write professionally might also be useful for students learning to write. In general, this proved to be a productive approach. But there were surprises.

We had set the default for the printer to do automatic form-feeds after printing each text entry. This meant that the printer turned its platen until the top of the next page of a continuous roll of paper was in place after printing each composition. Thus, users would get their texts on separate sheets of paper. In the workplace context this is done without question. Users want their products on separate pieces of paper and like the convenience of having the computer advance the pages automatically.

But in some schools there was a critical shortage of paper. When the average student text in the early grades was only a few lines long, automatic form-feeds resulted in printouts with a few lines at the top and 6 or 7 inches of blank space. This meant that the school would be using several times as much paper as absolutely necessary. Although the default setting could be overridden, several people in the school wanted no default automatic feed at all, so that paper use could be minimized without any special action being taken.

There was an additional reason for changing this default setting. Some teachers wanted to print out all the texts on one disk, or all the pieces by one student. They found it convenient to have the texts printed successively with minimal separation. Given this and the cost considerations, we changed the default to be "no automatic form-feed," something no industrial or commercial computer printing operation would have ever done.

Number of Copies.   In an early version of QUILL we had another surprise that in retrospect seems predictable, but at the time was not. When a student finished working on a piece, QUILL simply asked whether he or she wanted a copy of the piece to be printed out. Students complained. We had encouraged collaboration in writing, including working in pairs at the computer, but provided no natural way for students to get multiple copies of a collaborative piece. Although students could always make extra listings of a text, the process was more cumbersome than it should have been. We quickly changed the program so that multiple copies could be printed easily. Then, teachers complained. They discovered students were printing out many more copies than they needed, thus wasting precious paper. We had to find an appropriate compromise between cost and convenience. The "final" version of the program allowed students to print up to 10 copies at a time.

Prominence of MAILBAG.   Formative evaluation can include much more than just the acceptance or rejection of particular design ideas. It can also result in qualitative changes in how aspects of the innovation fit together. This was true of the history of MAILBAG. Originally, we had viewed MAILBAG as just one among many methods for publishing or distributing writing. As such, it played a rather minor role in our early conceptions of QUILL, not even appearing on the first three levels of the process tree. As we observed students using the program and received feedback from teachers, we came to give MAIL-

BAG an ever more central role in both the software and the activities. In the end, it was one of the three major programs in QUILL, had a prominent role in the *QUILL Teacher's Guide,* and was introduced in teacher training sessions as an appropriate first activity for both teachers and students.

Summary. These stories are but a small sample of those pertaining to changes that we made to QUILL as a result of early observations of its use in classrooms. They show how formative evaluation typically proceeds, basically as a trial-and-error process in which the innovation is repeatedly revised in response to experiences with its use. The emphasis on experience with use and the concern for modifying details of the innovation means that formative evaluation usually reveals more about the process of use than does summative evaluation. But because the focus in formative evaluation is on improving the innovation, there is little attention paid to variations in use, nor is there a concern with long-term changes in the social context of use or in the ways the innovation is assimilated. These issues cannot be ignored if we want to understand how an innovation would be realized in a given context.

Comparing Summative and Formative Evaluation

Some of the differences between formative and summative evaluation as they are usually carried out are summarized in Table 8.3. The categories listed in the first column are useful ones for examining any kind of evaluation; we will return to them when we discuss situated evaluation.

Focus. Summative evaluations are concerned with the effects of using an innovation. Thus, a summative evaluation assesses changes in, say, students'

TABLE 8.3
Differences Between Formative and Summative Evaluation

	Formative	*Summative*
Focus	Innovation	Effects of the innovation
Audience	Developer	User
Purpose	Improve the innovation	Decide whether to adopt innovation
Variability of Settings	Minimized to highlight technology	Controlled by balanced design or random sampling
Measurement Tools	Observation/interview/ survey	Experiment
Time of Assessment	During development	After development
Results	List of changes to the innovation	Table of measures contrasting groups

learning of a new concept, and treats the technical details of the innovation as if they were in a black box. In contrast, formative evaluations tend to focus on the innovation per se, and particularly on the innovation as a set of new technologies to be debugged. Although the ultimate goal may be to bring about some change in the users or the setting of use, the immediate focus is on the technology per se.

Audience.   One key distinction between the two types of evaluation pertains to the audience for the results. Summative evaluation results are often published so that any of a large number of potential users can make informed decisions about the innovation. In contrast, formative evaluation is done for (and by) the developers or implementors so that they can make improvements to the innovation. They typically make changes as needed and do not report the results outside of a small community.

Purpose.   Evaluations are done for some purpose, usually one that includes a specific action with respect to the innovation. This action is of course dependent on the audience for the evaluation. For summative evaluation, the action is the potential user's: decide whether to adopt or continue use of the innovation. In the case of formative evaluation, the audience is the developers and the action is to improve the innovation based on experiments with its use.

Variability of Settings.   In doing a summative evaluation, one focuses on the value of the innovation. Thus, one looks for controlled variation in the settings in which the innovation is implemented. If the settings are not all the same, there is nevertheless a preference for, say, a balance (e.g., among rural, urban, and suburban settings). One needs to assume that variations in use can either be attributed to fairly well-understood causal factors, or that random variation will be of no consequence with a sufficiently large sample size. The study is structured to constrain the effects of context in order to say more about the effects of the innovation itself. In doing a formative evaluation, there is a similar concern for controlled variation. Because the primary concern is to improve the innovation, one wants contexts that are typical, representative, or that at least reveal meaningful strengths and weaknesses of the innovation, one in which the innovation is used as intended by the developers. "Nonstandard" uses are not particularly informative at this stage, and could even induce changes that are inappropriate for the majority of users.

Measurement Tools.   A variety of tools can be employed for either type of evaluation, so it is simplistic to imply that there is a one-to-one correspondence between measurement tools and evaluation types. Nevertheless, certain tools are typically associated with particular types of evaluation. Because summative evaluations often seek quantitative, statistically significant results, they are usually conducted within a formal experimental design. In contrast, formative evaluation does not often call for quantitative results. Instead, the personal reactions elicited by interviews and observations are usually the most useful.

Time of Assessment. The evaluation types can also be distinguished by their time of application. Summative evaluation is performed after the development has reached a stopping point, whereas formative evaluation, by definition, is carried out during development.

Results. Summative evaluations typically yield quantitative results with quantitative bounds on the possible "error of measurement." These results can be stated concisely, and are often represented by a table or graph. Formative evaluations typically produce qualitative results, such as a list of changes to be made to the innovation.

Despite these differences, the distinction between summative and formative evaluation is not always clear in practice. Suppose, as is usually the case, that a summative evaluation identifies some strengths as well as some weaknesses of the innovation. A potential user might simply weigh these strengths and weaknesses in order to decide whether to adopt the innovation. But if the developers had insights into the *reasons* for the measured effects, they could use the same results to guide a revision of the innovation. Thus, what for the user was a summative evaluation could be viewed by the developer as a part of a cycle in which each evaluation points to areas of needed improvement. One could even think of formative evaluation as a series of microsummative evaluations of portions of the innovation, with the aim of identifying the areas in which revision is most needed. Viewed this way, summative evaluation is a feedback mechanism for formative evaluation, but only if one understands why the innovation performed as it did.

In other situations, formative evaluation can yield summative-type results. Data collected in order to guide revisions of the innovation can also be integrated for the purposes of a summative assessment. For example, the number of times a feature of the software was used would be relevant to a formative evaluation; it might be used later in a summative evaluation to stratify a sample into frequent and infrequent users.[3] One of the distinctions, then, between formative and summative evaluations is simply whether the data are interpreted as feedback to the developer for changes or as a final assessment addressed to the user.

---

[3]The more a summative evaluation attends to differences in actual use and relates those to outcomes, the less it serves the standard summative purposes, and the more it begins to take on characteristics of situated evaluation.

Problems with the Standard Evaluation Paradigm

Both summative and formative evaluation have wide-ranging and important uses. But as they are usually carried out, they also have many limitations, most of which relate to the fact that there is no provision for examining the interaction of the innovation with the situation in which the innovation is used. This makes it difficult to attend to the process of change and, consequently, to many of the concerns people have about innovations.

R. M. Wolf (1990) described three key limitations. First, most evaluations do not identify the reasons for the observed phenomena. Thus, they do not say *how* the innovation can be improved, nor what aspect of it produced the measured effects. Second, not being able to account for why changes occur means that it is questionable to generalize to other settings in which the innovation might be used. Third, the development process often continues after the evaluation, so that most evaluations are effectively of innovations that no longer exist. Again, without knowing more about the situation and process of use one cannot say whether initial results are still valid for the changed innovation.

Consider, for instance, the results in the QUILL study showing differential improvement across writing functions. The principal summative evaluation found "effectiveness" for expository and persuasive writing, but not for expressive writing. Within the framework in which QUILL was being certified, these writing function distinctions were pertinent and easily quantifiable. It is plausible that they resulted from the emphasis within QUILL activities on a variety of purposes and audiences. Students who wrote newspaper articles, letters, reviews, brochures, editorials, and other types of texts may have learned how to write appropriately for different functions, whereas students who wrote in only one genre might not have developed a sensitivity to writing function differences. And if, as we believe, writing activities of standard classrooms at that time emphasized expressive writing, then there would be less likelihood of significant improvement for that function.[4]

It is likely that the types of writing for which students show greatest improvement are those they practice. The writing function distinctions found in the QUILL evaluation may thus reflect the distribution of writing across functions in QUILL classes. If this is so, one might conclude that QUILL was generally useful for learning writing and that the areas of greatest improvement would be those the students practiced. This suggests actively promoting writing using the computer with functions in which one wants to see specific improvement.

---

[4]The contrary result in the Shungnak study, in which there were large gains for expressive writing, would still make sense under this hypothesis if the teacher gave greater emphasis to the expressive function in the writing activities for her class, and if we could assume that QUILL was a useful tool for any type of writing.

On the other hand, the results may simply reflect an overall improvement in writing ability. QUILL students probably wrote more and this alone may have made them better writers, regardless of the function. If that is the case, then active promotion of a function of writing might not produce any greater difference for that type of writing. If contriving activities to exercise that function diminished students' roles in selecting topics, their thinking about differences among purposes and audiences, or the overall amount of writing, it could even have negative effects on writing development. The summative results alone do not support a choice between these or other conflicting hypotheses, which have important practical implications. Although they highlight differences among classrooms, they do nothing to clarify why the differences might exist. A similar point holds for the grade distinctions found in the summative evaluation. There, the vagaries of data collection caused us to discard data from one of our most interesting classes, one in which the greatest amount of writing occurred. Even if we had included this classroom, the summative evaluation methodology would have provided little insight into grade-level differences.

A related point is that in order to assess before/after changes the evaluator needs to know the measure at the beginning of the evaluation period. This means that many of the most intriguing effects cannot be measured because they are unanticipated. For example, revision in some QUILL classrooms occurred not just because Writer's Assistant facilitated the mechanical act of editing, but because QUILL catalyzed changes in the social organization of writing, for example, by stimulating more collaboration (see chapter 6; also, Bruce, Michaels, & Watson-Gegeo, 1985). Yet, we did not measure the degree of collaboration in classrooms before they used QUILL, so we could not evaluate the changes that occurred.

ALTERNATIVE METHODS

Most of these limitations have been recognized by others, and various solutions have been proposed. These solutions are typically put forth as alternative methods of evaluation. They represent variations on the values for the categories in the comparison chart given in the previous section. For example, *adversary evaluation* (Clyne, 1990) and *judicial evaluation* (R. L. Wolf, 1990) entail that the audience for summative evaluation is not only the user, but other evaluators presenting an opposing viewpoint. *Decision-oriented evaluation* (Borich, 1990), *goal-free evaluation* (Stecher, 1990), and *illuminative evaluation* (Parlett, 1990) vary the purpose for the evaluation, from responding to the potential user's stated criteria to revealing whatever one can find about the innovation. *Naturalistic evaluation* (Dorr-Bremme, 1990) and *case study methods* (Stenhouse, 1990) allow for a greater variability of settings. Other methods similarly vary the types of results produced, the time of assessment, or the measurement tools.

We discuss only a few of these alternative evaluation methods here,[5] relating them to R. M. Wolf's (1990) three key limitations described above. We will look first at some methods that attempt to assess *why* changes occurred, as well as to document that they occurred. Second, we will consider the issue of generalization, looking at an approach for studying the use of innovations across settings. We will pass over the third issue, that innovations themselves change after evaluation, because little has been done to address it. Each of the methods discussed makes a valuable contribution to the evaluation problem but, when used within the standard frameworks, cannot escape their inherent limitations.

It is noteworthy that although there is considerable disagreement among all these methods over *how to evaluate* an innovation, there is a general consensus about *what is to be evaluated,* namely, that the evaluation should be of the innovation, and that "innovation" is a meaningful, well-defined term. We return to this issue in the next section.

Understanding the Reasons for Changes

Many researchers have proposed methods that address one of the primary limitations of standard evaluation, that it does not uncover the reasons for the observed changes. One approach has been to emphasize formative over summative evaluation. The argument is that traditional summative evaluation provides a summary of effects, but is removed from the way the innovation is actually used. Formative evaluation, on the other hand, is more concerned with the details of actual use since it needs to detail how to change the innovation. Thus, it is more pertinent to the question of how to effect educational change. Recognizing this, some researchers have argued that one should do formative evaluation whenever possible, both for the usual reasons, and as an alternative to standard summative evaluation.

Others have argued for broadening the range of measurement tools used for summative evaluation, specifically to include qualitative measures and results. Miles and Huberman (1984), for example, presented a variety of qualitative methods for use in summative evaluation. These methods include interviews, observations, surveys, and self-reports. They typically result in verbal descriptions of effects of the innovation; or, sometimes, visual displays such as networks to show causal relationships between factors in the situation and the implementation of the innovation; or diagrams that show variations in use along two dimensions. With these methods both the measures and the results can be qualitative.

Nevertheless, for many qualitative researchers, it is still the commonalities across cases or settings that are of interest, as it is for standard summative evaluation. Miles and Huberman (1984) stated:

---

[5]Extensive presentations of the theory and methodology of alternative evaluation exists elsewhere (see, e.g., Fetterman, 1988; Jaeger, 1988; Miles & Huberman, 1984; Tikunoff & Ward, 1977; Walberg & Haertel, 1990).

More and more qualitative researchers are using multisite, multicase designs, often with multiple methods. The aim is to increase generalizability, reassuring oneself that the events and processes in one well-described setting are not wholly idiosyncratic. . . . The researcher uses multiple comparison groups to find out the kinds of social structures to which a theory or subtheory may be applicable. Having multiple sites increases the scope of the study and, thereby, the degrees of freedom. By comparing sites or cases, one can establish the range of generality of a finding or explanation, and, at the same time, pin down the conditions under which that finding will occur. (p. 151)

The overall goal is the same as for strictly quantitative summative evaluations: to assess the usefulness of the innovation. These qualitative approaches maintain the standard summative evaluation goals, audience, and overall methodology. There is still an emphasis on generalizations rather than on contrasts, on "effects" of the innovation rather than on identifying its realizations, and a minimal concern for the details of the innovation.

In fact, many proponents of qualitative methods for evaluation (Miles & Huberman, 1984; Patton, 1980; Van Maanen, 1983) argued that the use of qualitative methods (observations, survey, interview, etc.) simply enlarges the scope of relevant data rather than changing the fundamental structure and purpose of evaluation. Both qualitative and quantitative researchers, they argue, must be concerned with data reduction, display, and drawing conclusions. The general goal in either case is to establish "findings" that are generalizable. With this general approach, if a finding then holds up across many cases it can be deemed solid or true. Idiosyncratic results can be more easily dismissed. For these reasons, qualitative methods are a useful addition to the summative evaluation framework, but they still fail to address many of its limitations.

Another alternative method is *responsive evaluation*[6] (Stake, 1990), a method that attempts to achieve a better understanding of the process of change by being more sensitive to the perspective of the users of the innovation:

Responsive evaluation is an approach to the evaluation of educational and other programs. Compared to most other approaches it is oriented more to the activity, the uniqueness, and the social plurality of the program.

The essential feature of the approach is a responsiveness to key issues, especially those held by people at the site. It requires a delay and continuing adaptation of evaluation goal setting and data gathering while the people responsible for the evaluation become acquainted with the program and the evaluation context.

Issues are suggested as conceptual organizers for the evaluation study, rather than hypotheses, objectives, or regression equations. The reason for this is that the term "issues" draws thinking toward the complexity, particularity, and subjective valuing already felt by persons associated with the program. (p. 76)

---

[6]A related method is *ecological evaluation* (Lucas, 1988a, 1988b), which seeks procedures that directly improve, rather than hamper, instruction.

Responsive evaluation is thus particularly sensitive to the interests and values of the variety of participants involved with the innovation. Formative evaluation, for example, can be done in a way that brings the users of the innovation into the development process. Their issues can then be made central to the activity of (re)designing the innovation. Similarly, summative evaluations can be made more responsive by focusing on desired educational results identified by the users of the innovation.

Differences Across Settings

The use of case studies (Stake & Easley, 1978; Stenhouse, 1990) is a common method for attending to differences across settings. One reason for the case-study approach is that variations among settings can be greater than variations among innovations. Thus, an insightful evaluation must include a wide variety of situations of use.

The need to look at variations in situations is essentially the same point as that made by Dukes (1971) in a famous article ("N = 1") on the value of psychological experiments with only one subject. Dukes argued that because situations vary greatly, a researcher may learn as much or more by observing one subject in many situations as by observing many subjects in one situation. In effect, representative sampling is applied to problems or situations rather than to subjects:

> In fact, proper sampling of situations and problems may in the end be more important than proper sampling of subjects, considering the fact that individuals are probably on the whole more alike than are situations among one another. [Brunswik, 1956, p. 39]

In the QUILL work we conducted case studies in a number of focal classrooms (Loucks-Horsley, French, Rubin, & Starr, 1985). One measurement tool we used was a *component checklist* (Loucks & Crandall, 1982; Loucks-Horsley & Hergert, 1985). The checklist defined 17 components of QUILL's use that we judged to be useful indicators of its implementation. We group these components in terms of QUILL's pedagogical goals, with an additional category for "classroom management" (see Table 8.4).

For each component, likely variations in classroom settings were identified. The component checklist scheme then called for designating which of the variations represented "ideal" implementations, which were "acceptable," and which were "unacceptable." The assignment of variations to these categories represented our judgment about which types of use were faithful to the idealization of QUILL.

For example, in terms of "frequency of use," we thought it ideal to use QUILL every day. It was "unacceptable" from the point of view of using

TABLE 8.4
Components of QUILL

QUILL PG	Component
1. Planning	Use of PLANNER
2. Integration of reading and writing	Integration with content areas
3. Publishing	Sharing writing
	Writing for different audiences
4. Meaningful communication	Use of LIBRARY and MAILBAG
	Writing in different genres
5. Collaboration	Working in pairs
6. Revision	Teacher's comments
	Teaching revision
	Conferencing
	Frequency of student revision
	Nature of student revision
Classroom management	Frequency of use
	Scheduling of QUILL
	Composing at the computer
	Students using QUILL
	Classroom structure

QUILL successfully for students to use it once a week or less. More than once, but less than daily, was "acceptable," but not "ideal." Thus, this component was defined as shown at the top of Fig. 8.3. The vertical grey line in the figure separates ideal from acceptable uses. The vertical black line separates acceptable from unacceptable uses. Note that the last variation includes daily writing by students, but no use of QUILL. In a larger context, most people would judge the daily writing to be desirable, but for the purpose of measuring QUILL's implementation, the non-use of QUILL would have to be as shown, to the right of the black line and thus unacceptable.

Component checklists can be used to generate a profile of the practices within a classroom. A teacher, for example, might use the checklist to obtain a profile of how her use of QUILL compared to the "ideal." A difference, perhaps in the amount of revision, would then stand out as an area for further work. The checklists can also be used to assess changes over time. QUILL classrooms, for example, might move from no use of PLANNER to student creation of planners. When the checklists are used to assess the overall level of implementation or to describe the innovation's impact on classrooms, they serve an essentially summative evaluation role.

In the Loucks-Horsley et al. (1985) study, practice profiles were produced for 10 teachers. Using these profiles along with other data, researchers were able to categorize teachers into four groups: "problematic," "superficial," "solid," and "super" users. This categorization was then used in an analysis of incentives and barriers to implementation. For example, they found that

Frequency of Use	Students use QUILL daily.	Students use QUILL several times a week.	Students use QUILL once a week or less.	Students do not use QUILL, but do write a. daily b. several times a week c. once a week or less
Use of PLANNER	Teacher uses PLANNER in a variety of ways: e.g., creating pre-writing activities for students; having students create PLANNERS for themselves or other students.	Students create PLANNERS for their own writing assignments or for each other.	Teacher use PLANNER to create pre-writing activities for students.	Teacher does not use PLANNER, a. but includes planning activities prior to writing b. and does not use other pre-writing activities
Writing in Different Genres	Teacher gives students QUILL writing assignments in several different genres.	Teacher gives students QUILL writing assignments in one or two genres.	Teacher does not use QUILL, but a. students typically write in several different genres b. students only write in one or two genres	
Writing for Different Audiences	Students use QUILL to write to a variety of real audiences.	Students rarely use QUILL to write to different audiences.	Students rarely use QUILL to write to real audiences.	Teacher does not use QUILL, but a. students write to different audiences b. students write to real audiences
Student Revision	Student revision reflects a balance between content and mechanics.	Student revision focuses only on content.	Student revision focuses only on mechanics.	Students do not revise.

FIG. 8.3. Excerpt from the QUILL component checklist.

"support and assistance from others can not only eliminate disincentives but can serve to maintain the influence of incentives over the course of the implementation process" (p. 74).

Summary

The standard evaluation paradigm often does not support showing why changes occur, how changes are different across settings, or how they relate to changes in the innovation. Alternative methods of evaluation address these problems to a certain extent, but as long as they are used within the standard paradigm they inherit its intrinsic limitations. For example, a set of case studies done within the summative framework often entails the need to express conclusions in terms of a summary statement about "the effects" of using the innovation. Much of the richness of the case studies is lost as users are categorized and aggregate statements are formulated. As long as the focus is on the innovation, it is difficult to circumvent this problem.

The standard evaluation paradigm presupposes the setting in which the innovation is used to be a passive system. It focuses on the innovation per se, on its properties, in the case of formative evaluation, or on its effects, in the case of summative evaluation. Papert (1987b) described this focus as "technocentrism." He related it to the child's early focus on the self:

> Egocentrism for Piaget does not, of course, mean "selfishness"—it means that the child has difficulty understanding anything independently of the self. Technocentrism refers to the tendency to give a similar centrality to a technical object—for example computers or Logo. This tendency shows up in questions like "What is THE effect of THE computer on cognitive development?" or "Does Logo work?" (p. 23)

One consequence of technocentrism is that the process of change is conceptualized as a function of the innovation alone, or else it is effectively ignored. What is needed is a different focus entirely for the evaluation process, one which we call *situated evaluation*. Before discussing it in detail, though, we need to step back and ask some fundamental questions about what it is that is being evaluated.

THE REALIZATION PROCESS

Examples such as those given in earlier chapters make it difficult to maintain a view of innovations as fixed objects that get applied to produce changes in social systems. Instead, they lead us to see innovations as processes, ongoing manifestations of social relations. This calls for an historical perspective in which we follow social changes over time, including those related to the development of innovations. We need to conceive of the adoption of an innovation as a process in which innovations are incorporated into a social system in a complex fashion that may lead to changes in the innovation, the social system, both, or neither.

It is important to make a distinction between what the developers of an innovation intend and what happens when the innovation is realized in a particular social setting. The developers may intend that the innovation modify the social system so that certain desirable characteristics are achieved. They see the innovation set in an idealized context and used in an idealized way. Their vision of the changed social system is thus an *idealization*. What happens in practice is that the social system may or may not change at all, and if it does change, it may not do so in accord with the developers' goals. Each resulting social system is a *realization*. The distinction between ideal and real suggests a process, the *realization process*, whereby the innovation leads to practices potentially different from those intended by the developers.

One possible way to think of the relationships between idealization and realization is to see the idealization as what Plato called (for reasons that do not concern us here) the "fifth entity." By fifth entity, Plato meant the real essence of an object, or the ideal form that lay behind any actual manifestation. For example, any circle one sees is for Plato a mere object with "particular qualities." It imperfectly represents the "real circle," because it has minute straight segments. Thus it is the "opposite" of the fifth entity. The real circle has no straight segments:

> Every circle that is drawn or turned on a lathe in actual operations abounds in the opposite of the fifth entity, for it everywhere touches the straight, while the real circle, I maintain, contains in itself neither much nor little of the opposite character. . . . The important thing is that, as I said a little earlier, there are two things, the essential reality and the particular quality. . . . (Hamilton & Cairns, 1961, p. 1590)

For Plato, then, the idealization would be to its realizations as the real circle is to its manifestations. From this perspective, the realization process would be seen as generating various distortions, partial maps, images, or shadows of the idealization. Realizations would then be somewhat ephemeral and inconsequential, valuable primarily as possible clues to the true structure of the ideal. This view is represented in Fig. 8.4. The solid circle on the left represents the effect of the innovation in an ideal world; the lens represents the realization process, which in this view distorts the ideal form, and the dotted figure on the right represents a particular realization that matches more or less well to the idealization.

It should come as no surprise that we consider this Platonic view to be untenable. Social practices related to the use of an innovation are not imperfect attempts to mimic some ideal form, but are rather the thing itself. Whereas

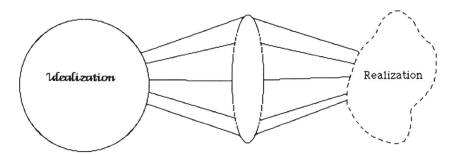

FIG. 8.4.   A Platonic view of the realization process.

we may contrast the use of an innovation with its idealization, we do not assume that users are imperfectly following preset rules. The situation instead
is more akin to Wittgenstein's (1974) language games:

> In philosophy we often *compare* the use of words with games and calculi which
> have fixed rules, but cannot say that someone who is using language *must* be play-
> ing such a game.—But if you say that our languages only *approximate* to such cal-
> culi you are standing on the brink of a misunderstanding. For then it may look
> as if what we were talking about were an *ideal* language. (p. 81)

Wittgenstein goes on to show how language *use,* not some rigid set of rules,
determines meaning. Nevertheless, many continue to search for the vacuum-
bottle ideal for language: "We think it [the ideal] must be in reality; for we
think we already see it there" (Ibid, p. 101). In a similar way, we cannot specify
the pure, or ideal, case for the *use* of an innovation, only its idealization in
the minds of the developers. Users inevitably interpret an innovation in distinctive ways, apply it idiosyncratically in their own contexts, and even re-create
it to satisfy their own needs.

Again, Wittgenstein's discussion of games is *a propos*:

> We can easily imagine people amusing themselves in a field by playing with a
> ball so as to start various existing games, but playing many without finishing
> them and in between throwing the ball aimlessly into the air, chasing one another
> with the ball and bombarding one another for a joke and so on. And now some-
> one says: The whole time they are playing a ball-game and following definite
> rules at every throw.
>
>   And is there not also the case where we play and—make up the rules as we
> go along? And there is even one where we alter them—as we go along. (p. 83)

The innovation-in-use, like the actions of people playing with a ball, is the
phenomenon we want to understand. Thus, a better view of the realization
process is that shown in Fig. 8.5. There, the solid shape on the right represents
the social practices that emerge after the introduction of an innovation. Its

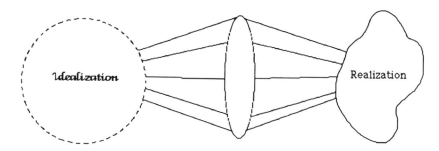

FIG. 8.5.   A Wittgensteinian view of the realization process.

characteristics reflect a history of interacting social processes, of which the innovation is only a latecomer, and one whose effects are shaped by layers and
layers of previous events. The dotted circle on the left is the idealization, an
imagined system, whose correspondence to the given realization depends as
much on the developers' understanding of the context of use as upon the inherent power of the innovation to effect change. In other words, its similarity
to the realization depends on the developers' assessment of the underlying social processes in the context of use.

The diversity of the realization process is revealed as we examine what happens when an innovation is introduced into various settings. Since the realization
of an innovation is different in each setting, one idealization can spawn an in-
definite number of realizations. Continuing our optics metaphor, we might say
that instead of the realization process being a lens, it is a prism that produces a
wide spectrum of different realizations (Fig. 8.6). As an innovation comes into
being in real settings, it acquires new and unexpected shapes because of the differences between its idealization and its various realizations. It is not only used
differently, it is re-created to conform with the goals and norms of the people
who use it. (It may be helpful to think of the prism instead as a collection of
context lenses, each of which focuses the idealization into a different realization.)

Evaluation of the Innovation-In-Use

Attending to the *use* of an entity can open up our perception to new views.
This can be seen in the case of a much simpler problem, viewing the Necker
cube (Fig. 8.7). This is a visual illusion that is usually thought of as being per-
ceivable in either of two ways. From one perspective it appears as a cube whose
nearest face is in the lower left corner of the figure; from another perspective
the nearest face is in the upper right corner. Most people tend to see the cube
in one way at first, and then, with varying degrees of difficulty, can "flip"
it so that the other way becomes apparent.

Using what he calls "experimental phenomenology," Ihde (1977) argued that

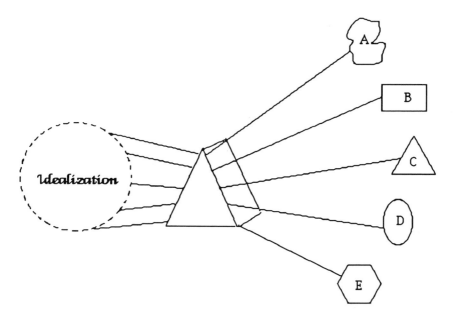

FIG. 8.6.   Alternate realizations of an innovation produced by a prism—or collection of context lenses.

most studies of the Necker cube assume in advance that there are only two ways to perceive the cube, and thus close off any possibility of understanding alternate perceptions. For example, one could also see the cube as a truncated pyramid, being viewed from the top, or alternatively, from the inside looking up. If one is interested in understanding the phenomenon, in this case, different ways of perceiving the Necker cube, then it is essential to adopt a methodology that reveals different ways of perceiving, rather than one that assumes the existence of only two ways. What is needed is, in Ihde's words, an *a priori* science, a mode of investigation done prior to more formal hypothesis testing.

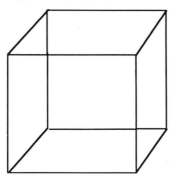

FIG. 8.7. The Necker cube.

The methodology does not measure variables, but instead is a means of identifying new ones.

A similar example was used by Wittgenstein:

> You could imagine the illustration appearing in several places in a book, a textbook for instance. In the relevant text something different is in question every time: here a glass cube, there an inverted open box, there a wire frame of that shape, there three boards forming a solid angle. Each time the text supplies the interpretation of the illustration. But we can also *see* the illustration now as one thing, now as another.—So we interpret it, and *see* it as we *interpret* it. (1974, p. 193)

Thus, the "same" object has different meanings in use, and our interpretations of those meanings shape what we see.[7]

We are interested in an *a priori* type of evaluation that is open to new variables and sensitive to alternate uses and interpretations. As Hymes (1974) said in describing "functional" linguistics, the "organization of use discloses additional features and relations [within language structure]" (p. 79). We should understand "discourse structures as situated, that is, pertaining to cultural and personal occasions which invest discourse [structures] with part of their meaning and structure" (p. 100).

A similar approach is needed for the study of innovations and change in which we recognize the situatedness of any realization of an innovation. A situated study of the uses of an innovation can disclose relations—contradictions, missing elements, patterns of sensitivity to context—within the idealization. Thus, analyses of the idealization (structure) and the realizations (function, or use) serve in a dialectical relation to each other; as we study one aspect we come to understand the other better as well. Without such an approach, one can never know if unanticipated changes occur. And these unanticipated changes may turn out to be the most significant for education.

New Questions

New realizations of an innovation arise in each setting in which it is used. This leads us to conceive of innovations and the technologies within them in an entirely new way. Moreover, our basic evaluation questions (How well does *it* work? How can *it* be improved?) need to be reformulated. The "it" is no longer the innovation (or even what we now call the *idealization*), but the innovation-

---

[7]In the examples in this book, it is important to remember that we are presenting our perspective, as developers, on the contexts and the uses of the technology, in this case, QUILL. A number of times we describe examples in which we were surprised by what occurred. It is typically in those cases that one may identify interesting differences in perspective among users and developers.

in-use, a situation-specific set of social practices. The fundamental question then becomes:

- What practices emerge as the innovation is incorporated into different settings?

Since this question has a multiplicity of answers, the "it" in our original questions becomes "they":

- How well do *they* work?
- How can *they* be improved?

Similarly, other questions one might ask about innovations and social change need to be reformulated. Above, we asked questions such as those on the left in Table 8.5. Recognizing the richness and the importance of the realization process leads us to ask new sorts of questions such as those on the right in Table 8.5.

SITUATED EVALUATION
OF EDUCATIONAL INNOVATIONS

This book is an evaluation of QUILL, but it is neither a summative, nor a formative evaluation. Instead, it is a *situated evaluation,* one that analyzes the varieties of use of the innovation across contexts. The evaluation is focused on the innovation-in-use, and its primary purpose is to understand the different ways in which the innovation is realized. We use the term *situated evaluation* to emphasize the unique characteristics of each situation in which the innovation is used. Our guiding assumption is that the innovation comes into

TABLE 8.5
Questions About Innovations and Change

Old Questions	New Questions
What *can* the innovation do?	What do people *do* as they use the innovation?
To what extent are the innovation's goals achieved?	How do social practices change, in whatever direction?
What constitutes proper, or successful, use of the innovation?	What are the various forms of the *innovation-in-use?*
How should people or the context of use change in order to use the innovation most effectively?	How should the innovation be changed and how can people interact differently with it in order to achieve educational goals?
How does the innovation change the people using it?	How does the community fit the innovation into its ongoing history?

being through use. The object of interest is not the idealized form in the developer's head, but rather, the realization through use. Situated evaluation seeks to characterize alternate realizations of the innovation and to identify new variables. It assumes that measuring predetermined variables is insufficient, no matter how well those measurements are made.

Purposes of Situated Evaluation

A situated evaluation examines the various *realizations* of an innovation in different settings. Its concern is with the characteristics of contexts that give rise to different realizations. The careful articulation of the process whereby an innovation becomes realized in different ways can be useful in several ways:

Explain Why the Innovation Was Used the Way it Was.   A situated evaluation can help *explain* what happened, as opposed to just describing effects.

Predict the Results of Using the Innovation.   This explanation can in turn provide the basis for predicting the realization of the innovation in similar contexts, providing the new context is well understood.

Identify Dimensions of Similarity and Difference Among Settings.   Examination of a realization of an innovation can reveal characteristics of a setting, such as a teacher's underlying pedagogical philosophy, that might be less visible otherwise.

Improve the Use of the Innovation.   Users of the innovation can refer to the situated evaluation as they work on improving the use of the innovation. They might find a realization whose setting has similar aspects to their own and specifically adopt practices of that setting. For example, a teacher might have students with low interest in writing start with the QUILL MAILBAG, if that strategy was found to be successful in a similar setting.

Improve the Technology.   Developers, likewise, can refer to the situated evaluation as they try to improve the innovation in terms of its interaction with different contexts. In this way, situated evaluation serves as a sort of formative evaluation.

Identify Variables for Later Evaluation.   Finally, a situated evaluation can help structure future observations of an innovation's use. One way it does this is by focussing attention on the most salient dimensions of the innovation with respect to particular contexts. This can be used to guide a complementary summative evaluation.

A Procedure for Situated Evaluation

Situated evaluation cannot be proceduralized; it is a process of discovering relationships. Nevertheless, we saw patterns in the discovery process emerge as we performed the situated evaluation of QUILL. There were three major aspects of this process. We looked first at the idealization of QUILL, in order to delineate as fully as possible what was intended by the developers. This included analyzing the theoretical underpinnings, the technology, the suggested activities, and the support system for its use. Second, we examined the settings in which QUILL was to be used. Setting characteristics included the cultural backgrounds, institutional resources and constraints, the teachers' goals and practices, the students' roles, the nature of academic tasks, and other elements of the social environment. Third, we analyzed QUILL's realizations in different settings and generated hypotheses about how and why these realizations developed as they did. In what follows, we elaborate on these aspects of situated evaluation.

The Idealization of the Innovation

A thorough analysis of the elements of the innovation independent of its use within real settings is part of a situated evaluation because it serves to characterize how participants in the setting of use might have perceived the innovation. It is also an index of the intentions of the developers, people who are often important participants not only in the initial creation of the innovation, but in its re-creation in context.

In contrast to the priorities for summative evaluation, the innovation is not privileged over any of its realizations; similarity to the idealization does not count as more successful, and non-use can be as important to consider as "faithful" use. Moreover, the innovation is not seen as an agent that acts upon the users or the setting, but rather as one more element added to a complex and dynamic system. It would be more correct to say that *the users act upon the innovation,* shaping it to fit their beliefs, values, goals, and current practices. Of course, in that process they may themselves change, and their changes as well as those to the innovation need to be understood as part of the system.

There are several aspects of the innovation that need to be analyzed critically (see Fig. 8.8). First, each innovation emerges from a theory, articulated to varying degrees in documents about the innovation. Any educational innovation has a theory of both learning and teaching. For QUILL, this was presented in chapter 2 and in earlier articles about QUILL (Rubin & Bruce, 1985, 1986, 1990). The learning theory incorporated ideas about communication and its relation to education and community. The teaching theory had specific commitments to pedagogical principles such as collaboration and purposeful writing. These were summarized in terms of concepts such as functional learning environments, and very specifically, QUILL's six pedagogical goals.

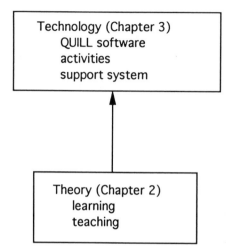

FIG. 8.8.   Elements of an innovation that need to be analyzed.

   The idealization of an innovation also includes new technologies, if only in the form of texts that imply changes in practices. We conceive of the technology broadly. First of all it includes various tools, artifacts, or apparatus, in the case of QUILL, a new software system. Second, it includes prescriptions for use of the new tools, in this case, the QUILL activities as articulated in the Teacher's Guide. Third, there is a support system for users, for those who are to carry out the new procedures or activities. Obviously, the elaboration of these elements varies greatly among technologies. For QUILL, they are described in chapter 3: new technology in the form of computer software and hardware, a set of recommended reading and writing activities, and a support system for teachers and students. These elements reify the theory; for the users, they are the innovation.[8]

   For example, QUILL called for "meaningful communication with real audiences" (PG 4). This meant that the function of "communication" in writing should take precedence over the function of "exhibiting skills for the purpose of evaluation." This was a part of the QUILL theory. The software, for example, MAILBAG, provided a technological environment in which communication in writing was not only facilitated, but seen as an appropriate activity for both teachers and students. The *QUILL Teacher's Guide,* in particular its description of specific activities such as "Confidential Chat," showed procedures and activities that emphasized communication in writing. Finally, the support system around QUILL included specific elements intended to foster these changes: The training workshop included discussions of illustrative ex-

---

[8]In fact, in most cases, the innovation is identified solely with the new apparatus, in QUILL's case, the software.

amples from other classrooms, and follow-up help in the classroom included communication-based activities specific to each classroom.

The Settings in Which the Innovation Appears

The shift in perspective from the view that realizations are distortions of the ideal to one in which realizations are creations that result from active problem-solving has implications for the sorts of questions researchers need to ask in evaluating innovations. With this perspective, the social context in which the innovation is used becomes central. Questions relating to cultural, institutional, and pedagogical contexts need to be addressed. To answer these questions in full is a formidable task, but focusing on a few specific aspects may go far in providing what is needed for a situated evaluation. In the QUILL study we found that cultural, institutional, and pedagogical contexts were all critical in shaping realizations. Of these, the pedagogical context was probably the most important.

The cultural context is another important factor in shaping how an innovation is used. That was one reason why we examined rural, urban, and suburban settings in the QUILL field test. In the Alaska project we saw a city/village distinction, and also a variety of languages and cultural traditions (as described in chapter 4). We also examined some specific factors related to socioeconomic status, home life, and previous schooling, such as:

- socioeconomic status
- dropout and transfer rates
- standardized test scores
- number of students with a computer at home
- initial student attitudes toward computers

There was a large linguistic diversity across QUILL classrooms. In addition, some classes were bilingual and students were able to write in two languages. Despite this variation, we did not have evidence that differences among QUILL classrooms could be attributed to linguistic differences. We did find that the topics and audiences of the writing were greatly influenced by the culture of the community. In addition, the city/village distinction appeared to have a major impact on how communication was viewed within the classroom. The village classrooms seemed much more receptive to the possibilities of communication as opposed to just "composition."

A second type of context that needs to be examined is the institutional. Here one needs to examine the ways in which goals and practices in the institution shape, constrain, or direct the use of the innovation, and to look at the resources available to support the innovation's use. Often, the availability of resources or the imposition of constraints at the building or district level has a significant impact on classroom practices. There are several levels of institution to consider: the school district, the school, and the classroom as a mini-institution.

In the QUILL study we looked at a variety of factors at different institutional levels, including:

Alaska QUILL project
- training workshop
- electronic mail
- end-of-year conference

District
- standardization of curriculum
- use of standardized tests
- support for QUILL use
- local facilitator

School
- # students in the school
- # computers in the school
- policies regarding student access to computers
- attitudes of the principal and other school personnel towards
    the use of computers
    the teaching of writing
    the relation of QUILL use to other ongoing curricula

Classroom
- # students in the classroom
- parent/aide involvement in the classroom
- presence of QUILL staff
- regulation of computer use
    method (lists, scheduled times, etc.)
    frequency and duration of computer use for each student
- physical layout
    number and type of computers in the classroom
    physical placement of the computer
    arrangement of computer components, charts, MAILBAG mail-
       boxes, and so on.

A third category of context turned out to be the most important—how the teachers' goals and practices related to the way they incorporated the innovation into their classrooms. A recent study (Anderson, 1989) suggests that five dimensions can be used to characterize both instructional programs and the classrooms in which these programs are implemented. These dimensions are the following:

- academic goals of schooling

- teacher's instructional role
- students' roles in promoting their own learning
- the nature of academic tasks
- the social environment as the context for individual learning

For example, in one classroom, a teacher may have adopted as a goal the improvement of scores on a basic skills test. Her own role in relation to this goal might be to convey information to students or to manage practice on these basic skills. The students' roles might be to receive this information and to apply it in daily practice activities. Tasks in such a classroom might include worksheets, and short answer quizzes that correspond to the basic skills test. Finally, the social environment might be one in which students work independently on the worksheets or respond to teacher questions, and the teacher provides feedback to the students on the correctness of their work.

In contrast, in another classroom the goals might include self-regulated learning and the use of language for communication, rather than evaluation. The teacher's role would be as a facilitator of student projects. Students would work alone or in collaboration on tasks whose functions were clear and meaningful for them. The tasks might require transformations and extensions of existing knowledge. Accordingly, the social environment would be one in which failure was accepted and stretching beyond the given was valued. Clearly, the incorporation of an innovation like QUILL would have different results in either of these extreme characterizations. But even subtle variations on these dimensions can have major effects on the realization, many of which have been described in chapters 5–7.

Characteristics of a social setting, including the cultural background of students and teachers, the institutional practices, constraints, and resources, and the classroom instructional environment—contribute to the different realizations of an innovation. In order to understand these realizations, we need to understand these settings in detail. In the QUILL study we collected information on these characteristics in various ways, including observations, interviews, and written reports by teachers. The information we gathered augmented the subsequent interpretations we made of QUILL's use. Analyses of QUILL's use in turn led us to rethink our initial assessment of the settings, even of the categories themselves.

The Realizations of the Innovation

The third aspect of a situated evaluation is to study the realizations of the innovation in different settings. The study of the realizations should attend to the three limitations of the standard paradigm described earlier. First, one should examine the ways the innovation was used and search for the reasons that changes occur. This includes examining whether the idealization was consonant or dissonant with existing social practices. It also includes analyzing how the innovation's use led to new social organizations, as in the emergence of a teacher community around the use of QUILL. Second one should look at the variety of uses across settings, treating each of these as an independent re-creation of the innovation, rather than as a data point for an aggregate statement about the innovation. Third, one should examine changes in the design of the innovation brought about by its use and the ways these changes relate to new practices.

In the QUILL studies, we had access to a rich, intertextual corpus of materials for assessing realizations. These included our own field notes, writings by teachers about their classrooms, electronic mail discussing the implementations, student writing, interviews with students and teachers, practice profiles using the QUILL component checklists, and some videotapes. Thus we relied on direct observations, but to a large extent, also on what was already written. This is the typical situation one would find in doing a situated evaluation (cf. Clifford, 1986; Clifford & Marcus, 1986). But even with large amounts of text available, observations are essential to doing a situated evaluation.

Understanding the Reasons for Change.   Extreme variations among realizations may lead one to feel that no valid generalizations about the innovation are possible. But the variations in use are actually beneficial for a situated evaluation. The reason is that our goal is not context-free summaries, but rather, hypotheses about how and why the innovation was realized in different ways in different contexts, in other words, the beginnings of understanding the reasons for change. Thus, situated evaluation seeks to identify new relevant variables to study. Through this process the evaluators may reach a deeper understanding of the idealization, elements of the settings, or the realizations, thus obtaining successively more refined analyses of the use of the innovation.

In some cases, we may observe realizations that are similar across diverse settings. This warrants the hypothesis that for that range of settings, the particular use is a shared one. An example of this was discussed in chapter 6 on revision. Recall that in virtually all of the QUILL classrooms, Writer's Assistant was used for copyediting. It was a tool for low-level correcting of texts, even when it was also used for higher level revision. Essentially, this reflects the convenient match between the text-editing capabilities of the computer and teachers' interest in having students learn spelling, grammar, punctuation, and capitalization and having them apply this knowledge in their writing. It also reflects the fact that copyediting is not inconsistent with either an emphasis on the mechanics of writing or an emphasis on its communicative functions. The practices we observed thus support an hypothesis about a common practice: All of the Alaska classrooms used the computer for copyediting.

In contrast, the use of the computer for true revision varied greatly. And when revision did occur the reasons for it also varied. Its appearance was often related to the social organization of the classroom, which in turn was affected by the presence of previous innovations (the Alaska Writing Project, Alexander's "Notes"), the availability of computers, cross-age grouping, or other situation-specific factors. Thus, to say that "some" or "many" classrooms used the computer for revising is empty without a characterization of why the revision occurred.

The characterizations produced by these analyses can be used in various ways. For users in different contexts they provide reasonable expectations about how the innovation might be realized. They also suggest what to change in the context in order to achieve particular results. For developers, the characterizations can be used in a formative way, to revise the innovation, perhaps by including more explicit ways to alter the context or to make the innovation more adaptable to different contexts.

Differences Across Settings.   As we look for the reasons for change, we describe, then compare and contrast each of the realizations. The purpose is not to rank the effectiveness of the innovation across settings, nor is it to identify problem cases that must be discarded or analyzed separately, as they would need to be in the standard framework. Instead, the variations become the objects of study.

In the chapter on purpose, for example, we discussed alternate realizations of purposeful writing using MAILBAG. We saw how teachers' pedagogical goals led to different amounts and types of in-class message writing. There were also significant variations due to the presence of other innovations, classroom management issues, and students' own goals.

We thus focus on differences in use. This leads us to identify differential aspects of the settings that lead to different uses. Variation in use may suggest a functional relationship. We saw in chapter 6, for example, that the degree to which students' writing showed attention to real audiences and purposes reflected their teacher's philosophy about the importance of that attention. In classrooms in which the teacher focused on activities involving real communication, there were abundant examples of attention being paid to purpose and audience in writing. For instance, the writing of the Holy Cross brochure (described in chapter 5) required attention to a particular type of audience: outsiders who wrote for information about Holy Cross. In some other classrooms true communicative writing was rare. In one (non-Alaskan) classroom, we saw continuous use of QUILL with multiple writing assignments, but every text had only one audience, the teacher. These variations in use lead us to characterize the effect of the innovation as a function of elements of the setting in which it is used.

In some cases, one can identify an entire set of classroom practices as a separate realization. This makes sense when the practices are significantly different from other classrooms on several dimensions, as when, for example, a

change in topic is consistently associated with a change in student collaboration patterns, a new role for the teacher, and new goals for a writing activity.

An example of this is the situated evaluation of Electronic Networks for Interaction (ENFI), an approach to teaching writing in which students communicate via terminals linked in a local area network (Bruce & Peyton, 1990).
Although there is a consistent philosophy underlying ENFI and even a model
for its use (at Gallaudet University), in a brief period it was realized in many
different ways. Sixteen distinct realizations of what some might refer to as "the
same innovation" were identified. At one site students reenacted dramatic literature using the network. At another, a professor used it for a Socratic tutoring
approach to develop thinking skills. At yet another site it was used to support
aspects of the writing process such as brainstorming and peer critiques. Each
realization formed a coherent whole and arose from identifiable elements within the setting of use. The status of the realization was evident in the discourse
of students and teachers, in the physical layout of the room, in the types of
activities students engaged in, as well as in observational and interview data.

Changes in the Innovation.   A situated evaluation should make it easier to
describe not only differences across settings, but differences across time as the
innovation changes. We have seen such changes in QUILL and in many other
innovations. Change is a normal part of the process of implementation, a process
described by Berman and McLaughlin (1975) as a mutual adaption between
an innovation and its social setting. The adaption can be to any aspect of the
innovation—its technological apparatus, the procedures for its use, or the support system. Even the underlying theory may be revised.

The focus in situated evaluation is on the setting as a complex, historically
and culturally defined system, in which the innovation is one element. Thus,
differences in versions of the innovation do not shape the design of the evaluation, but simply provide more variation to study. As a result, it is more feasi-
ble to compare and contrast cases of classrooms that use prototype versions
of the innovation with those that use advanced versions, than it would be with
summative evaluation, which is built on assumptions of a single entity being
evaluated.

Part of this analysis is to examine how new users conceptualize the innovation. Such an examination bears some resemblance to formative evaluation.
But in situated evaluation there would be no assumption that a particular setting of use was typical. Thus, the purpose would be to understand the varieties of actual use, not to identify a list of changes to the innovation.

The situated evaluation view of changes to an innovation encompasses more
than changes to the technology, even defined to include the underlying theory
and support system. Because the innovation does not unilaterally alter social
practices but, rather, becomes incorporated into them, we need to examine
the extended process of change in these practices. Thus the analysis avoids the

untenable position that measures changes during one interval of an ongoing process to account for the effect of an innovation. For example, QUILL teachers sometimes added collaboration to their classrooms first by having one student read a piece for an author while he or she typed it, acting as a "computer helper." The reader would often also watch the screen to catch typing errors and would start to make comments on the piece itself. Later in the year, the teacher might make collaboration more formal by, for example, having teams of students work on articles for a class newspaper.

The experience with the QUILL teachers' network is another example of this change process (chapter 7). It represents an ongoing creation of an innovation as part of evolving social practices.

Comparison with Traditional Frameworks for Evaluation

A key difference between situated evaluation and the standard frameworks is that its purpose is to learn first how the innovation is used, not how it ought to be changed or whether it has the claimed effects. Because it is concerned with actual use, it does not focus on the innovation or its effects, but rather on the social practices within the settings in which the innovation is re-created. This shift in focus has implications for the audience of the evaluation, the role of setting variability, the tools for evaluation, the time of assessment, and the presentation of results. For example, the goal of understanding the innovation-in-use leads to an emphasis on *contrasts* between uses rather than constancy. We can now summarize the discussion of situated evaluation by comparing it with the traditional types of evaluation:

TABLE 8.6
Comparisons Among the Three Types of Evaluation

	Formative	*Summative*	*Situated*
Focus	Innovation	Effects of the innovation	Social practices
Audience	Developer	User	User (but also developer)
Purpose	Improve the innovation	Decide whether to adopt innovation	Learn how the innovation is used
Variability of Settings	Minimized to highlight technology	Controlled by balanced design or random sampling	Needed for contrastive analysis
Measurement Tools	Observation/interview/survey	Experiment	Observation/interview
Time of assessment	During development	After initial development	During and after development
Results	List of changes to the technology	Table of measures contrasting groups	Ethnography

Focus.   Recall the Walberg and Haertel (1990, p. xvii) definition, that evaluation is an "examination *of an educational curriculum, program, institution, organizational variable, or policy.* The primary purpose . . . is to learn about *the particular entity* studied. . . . The focus is on understanding and improving *the thing* evaluated (formative evaluation), on summarizing, describing, or judging *its . . . outcomes* (summative evaluation) . . ." [italics added]. It is clear from the wording, and from most of the work on evaluation, that standard evaluation is concerned either with properties of the innovation alone or with its "effects." In contrast, situated evaluation focuses on the way the innovation becomes social practices.

Audience.   Situated evaluation results can be used by both users and developers. Users can make decisions not only about whether to use the innovation, but how to use it in their particular context. Developers can learn how to revise the innovation taking into account the variations in use.

Purpose.   For situated evaluation, the audience is broad, as are the actions. The results could lead to developers changing the innovation, to users changing their practices, to adoption of only parts of the innovation, or to deeper understanding of the process of use.

Variability of Settings.   The central concern for situated evaluation is with characterizing the way an innovation comes into being in different contexts. Because the audience for the evaluation wants to know how to improve the use of the innovation, it is important to have a variety of contexts that they can compare to their own setting or to ones they might create. Thus, there is a need for a *variety* of contexts of use, or differences across settings. This is one reason why "situated evaluation" is not equivalent to "qualitative evaluation." Often, qualitative research is applied to emphasize common patterns and to dismiss idiosyncratic results. With situated evaluation it is important to capture the idiosyncrasies and to understand their origins.

Measurement Tools.   With situated evaluation, the emphasis is on differences across contexts. This emphasis implies the use of qualitative tools, including observations and interviews that are structured to elicit information about recurring social practices in the setting and to draw out differences among realizations.

Time of Assessment.   Situated evaluation can start once the innovation is developed enough to be placed in a classroom. This is in contrast to formative evaluation, which might start even earlier, in a laboratory setting. Situated evaluation can continue well after the developers have finished. It could be done before summative evaluation as a way to identify sites or issues to study, or afterwards as a way to study the process of change.

Results.   Because a situated evaluation seeks to characterize alternate realizations, it requires multiple, detailed descriptions of specific uses. Changes need to be described using appropriate quantitative or qualitative representations, but more importantly, the reasons for changes need to be discussed and linked to characteristics of the settings of use. The process of change, including changes in the innovation, in the users, and in the setting, becomes paramount. For these reasons, narrative accounts of diverse uses are most useful. Thus, chapters 5, 6, and 7 are essentially stories of the QUILL experience.

Summary

The many realizations of an innovation reflect properties of the innovation-in-use, properties that emerge only in practice. These properties may seem ephemeral, based as they are on particularities of settings, but they are the only ones that matter for evaluation, for redesign of the innovation, for selecting appropriate settings of use, or for predicting future results of use. The examples in this book show the power of the social context to affect the ultimate uses of a new technology. How the features of the technology interact with human needs, expectations, beliefs, prior practices, and alternative tools far outweighs the properties of the technology itself. Thus, when we analyze the effects of an innovation, we must consider much more than an aggregate result such as the "average impact of the typical implementation."

We see situated evaluation as a new framework for understanding innovation and change. This framework has several key ingredients. It emphasizes contrastive analysis and seeks to explore differences in use. It assumes that the object of study is neither the innovation alone nor its effects, but rather, the realization of the innovation—the innovation-in-use. Finally, it produces hypotheses supported by detailed analyses of actual practices. These hypotheses make possible informed plans for use and change of innovations.

Chapter 9

Conclusion:
What We Have Learned

It is no simple matter to look beyond preconceptions to see what happens when computers are used in education. Perceptions are shaped by values, and just as in paleontology, there are practical limitations to obtaining evidence. The process of adopting a computer-based innovation is often a gradual one, so that characterizing the use of the innovation requires long-term study. The relevant variables are often unknown in the beginning. And much of what children learn, especially with significant innovations, is not captured by standard assessment techniques, so that new methods of evaluation must be developed.

The result is that visionary statements about the effects of computer use in schools must be questioned. Publications and presentations on the use of computers in education are often characterized by visionary images of technology, but often a close examination of how computers are really used in schools leads to the discovery that the reality of use does not match the ideal. Software developers, publishers, teachers, administrators, and researchers often describe what they want technology to be like in the classroom, not how it really works in the majority of classrooms.

At the same time, one must question broad critiques of classroom computer use that assert that no educational changes occur. It is unfortunately true that the educational system resists change, and computers alone are certainly no solution to problems of inequity, inadequate funding, cultural conflict, poverty, systemic resistance to change, and so on. Nevertheless, to see all classroom computer use as inconsequential tinkering is as unrealistic as to accept uncritically the most optimistic visions of computer use. As David Cohen (1988) said, the point is

. . . not that instructional change is impossible. It is that there are different kinds of change in instruction, and different organizational locales for it. There is a continual busy flutter at the heart of public education, as one infatuation after another holds sway. While everyone deplores these little romances many must find them enticing, for they persist. But when substantial pressure has been mobilized for change at the margins of education, the results often have been fairly impressive. . . . One implication of my argument is that if we looked for significant instructional innovation in these subregions, rather than looking for it on average, everywhere, we would find more of it. (p. 245)

For these reasons, one must be careful in analyzing the processes of social change, particularly with respect to the incorporation of innovations. The simplest approaches can easily go awry. One fallacy is to assume that an innovation per se causes changes; the converse fallacy is to assume that the operation of an innovation is always subsumed by existing cultural practices and that its details are irrelevant to the issue of social change. One can miss other critical phenomena by failing to consider the distinctive functions and roles of different participants, such as users and developers, or by seeing an innovation as comprising merely fixed, physical artifacts, and not as cultural objects.

In order to study the processes of change involved with the introduction of QUILL into diverse classroom settings, we found it useful to adopt an idealization/realizations model for change. Briefly, the model says that what we see in a case of incorporation of an innovation into a social setting is a *realization* of that innovation. What the developers intend is only an *idealization*. Since realizations are likely to differ greatly from one another and from the idealization, we need to study the various realizations to understand the use of the innovation, its impact on the community, or its meaning for the users.

We see this diversity as a problem for traditional approaches to evaluation, which conceive of an innovation as fixed and well defined and evaluated by a set of uniform measures. These approaches are rightly concerned with precise assessments of performance before and after the use of the innovation and with selection of appropriate treatment and control groups. But attention to methodological details is worth little if we cannot say what the innovation is or whether there is any consistent sense to the notion of the "treatment." Good evaluations of educational innovations need to include a "situated" component, which seeks to understand how that innovation looks in each of its different contexts of use.

The inevitable diversity of use for innovations also presents problems for traditional models of teacher education in which teachers are "trained" in the use of specific methods, approaches, or innovations. Our use of "training" in our early work with QUILL now appears misguided, particularly since it emphasized teachers learning procedures, rather than being supported in their own inquiries into teaching and learning. The training model misses the most salient fact about implementation: that it is a creative process involving critical analysis of the innovation's potential in the light of institutional and sociocultural context, physical resources, student needs, and pedagogical goals. The innovation process doesn't end, but begins, with the teacher.

Implications for curriculum development follow from this view of the teacher's role. Because the innovation doesn't even come into being until it is realized in an actual setting, the goal should not be to establish the endpoint for instruction, but rather, to supply the most useful tools possible for the re-creation process. That is, whereas an innovation may include technologies, activities, assessments, sequencing, and so on, it should be conceived as only a rough guide, to be actively shaped and redefined to fit classroom realities and alternate goals.

When an innovation that calls for significant changes in teacher practices meets an established classroom system, "something has to give." Often, what gives is that the innovation is simply not used. Rarely is an innovation adopted in exactly the way the developers intended. Our study shows that the process of re-creation of the innovation is not only unavoidable, but a vital part of the process of educational change. Critical analysis of re-creations needs to be an important part of any evaluation. We believe that a deeper understanding of this process will highlight the fact that teachers need more support in attempting these re-creations. Their role in the innovation process is as innovators, not as recipients of completed products.

References

Adams, M. J., & Bruce, B. C. (1982). Background knowledge and reading comprehension. In J. Langer and M. T. Smith-Burke (Eds.), *Reader meets author/Bridging the gap: A psycholinguistic and sociolinguistic perspective* (pp. 2–25). Newark, DE: International Reading Association.

Anderson, L. M. (1989). Implementing instructional programs to promote meaningful, self-regulated learning. In J. Brophy (Ed.), *Advances in research on teaching* (Vol. 1, pp. 311–343). New York: JAI Press Inc.

Attneave, F. (1971). Multistability in perception. *Scientific American, 225*, 62–71.

Barnhardt, C. (1984). The QUILL microcomputer writing program in Alaska. In R. V. Dusseldorp (Ed.), *Proceedings of the Third Annual Statewide Conference of Alaska Association for Computers in Education* (pp. 1–10). Anchorage, AK: Alaska Association for Computers in Education.

Barnhardt, C. (1985a, November). *Creating communities with computer communication.* Paper presented at the annual meeting of the American Anthropological Association, Washington, DC.

Barnhardt, C. (1985b). *Historical status of elementary schools in rural Alaskan communities: 1867–1980.* Fairbanks, AK: University of Alaska, Center for Cross-Cultural Studies.

Barnhardt, C. (1991). *The history of education for Alaska Native people.* Unpublished manuscript.

Batson, T. (1988). The ENFI Project: A networked classroom approach to writing instruction. *Academic Computing, 2*(5), 32–33, 55–56.

Beach, R. (1984, April). *The effect of reading ability on seventh graders' narrative writing.* Paper presented at the annual meeting of the American Educational Research Association, New Orleans.

Becker, H. S. (1986). *Writing for social scientists.* Chicago: University of Chicago Press.

Beeman, W. O. (1988). *Intermedia: A case study of innovation in higher education.* Final Report to the Annenberg/CPB Project. Providence, RI: IRIS, Brown University.

Berman, P., & McLaughlin, M. (1975). *Federal programs supporting educational change. Volume IV: The findings in review.* Santa Monica, CA: Rand Corporation.

Bolter, J. D. (1991). *Writing space: The computer, hypertext, and the history of writing.* Hillsdale, NJ: Lawrence Erlbaum Associates.

Borich, G. D. (1990). Decision-oriented evaluation. In H. J. Walberg & G. D. Haertel (Eds.), *The International Encyclopedia of Educational Evaluation* (pp. 31–35). Oxford: Pergamon Press.

Bridwell, L., Sirc, G., & Brooke, R. (1985). Computing and revising: Case studies of student writers. In S. Freeman (Ed.), *The acquisition of written language: Response and revision.* Norwood, NJ: Ablex.

Bridwell, L. S. (1980). Revising strategies in twelfth grade students' transactional writing. *Research in the Teaching of English, 14,* 197–222.

Brienne, D., & Goldman, S. V. (1989, April). Networking: How it has enhanced science classes in New York schools . . . and how it can enhance classes in your school, too. *Classroom Computer Learning,* pp. 44–53.

Britton, B. K., & Glynn, S. M. (1989). *Computer writing environments: Theory, research, and design.* Hillsdale, NJ: Lawrence Erlbaum Associates.

Britton, J., & Great Britain Schools Council (1975). *The development of writing abilities (11–18).* London: Macmillan.

Brown, J. S., Collins, A., & Duguid, P. (1989). Situated cognition and the culture of learning. *Educational Researcher, 18,* 32–42.

Bruce, B. C. (1987). An examination of the role of computers in teaching language and literature. In J. Squire (Ed.), *The dynamics of language learning: Research in reading and English* (pp. 277–293). Urbana, IL: National Conference on Research in English and ERIC Clearinghouse on Reading and Communication Skills.

Bruce, B., Michaels, S., & Watson-Gegeo, K. (1985). How computers can change the writing process. *Language Arts, 62,* 143–149.

Bruce, B., & Rubin, A. (1984). *The utilization of technology in the development of basic skills instruction: Written communication* (Final Report, Contract No. 300-81-00314). Washington, DC: U.S. Department of Education.

Bruce, B., & Peyton, J. K. (1990). A new writing environment and an old culture: A situated evaluation of computer networking to teach writing. *Interactive Learning Environments, 1,* 171–191.

Bruce, B. C., Rubin, A., & Loucks, S. (1984). *QUILL: Teacher's guide.* Lexington, MA: D. C. Heath & Company.

Bruffee, K. A. (1986). Social construction, language, and the authority of knowledge: A bibliographical essay. *College English, 48,* 773–790.

Brunswik, E. (1956). *Perception and the representative design of psychological experiments.* Berkeley: University of California Press.

Caswell, S. (1988). *E-mail.* Boston, MA: Artech.

Cazden, C. (1988). *Classroom discourse: The language of teaching and learning.* Portsmouth, NH: Heinemann.

Clifford, J. (1986). On ethnographic allegory. In J. Clifford & G. E. Marcus (Eds.), *Writing culture: The poetics and politics of ethnography* (pp. 98–121). Berkeley: CA: The University of California Press.

Clifford, J., & Marcus, G. E. (Eds.). (1986). *Writing culture: The poetics and politics of ethnography.* Berkeley, CA: The University of California Press.

Clyne, S. (1990). Adversary evaluation. In H. J. Walberg & G. D. Haertel (Eds.), *The International Encyclopedia of Educational Evaluation* (pp. 77–79). Oxford: Pergamon Press.

Cochran-Smith, M. (1991). Word processing and writing in elementary classrooms: A critical review of the literature. *Review of Educational Research, 61,* 107–155.

Cohen, D. K. (1988). Educational technology and school organization. In R. Nickerson & P. P. Zodhiates (Eds.), *Technology in education: Looking toward 2020* (pp. 231–265). Hillsdale, NJ: Lawrence Erlbaum Associates.

Collins, A. (1983). Teaching reading and writing with personal computers. In J. Orasanu (Ed.), *A decade of reading research: Implications for practice* (pp. 171–187). Hillsdale, NJ: Lawrence Erlbaum Associates.

Collins, A., Brown, J. S., & Newman, S. (1989). Cognitive apprenticeship: Teaching the craft of reading, writing, and mathematics. In L. B. Resnick (Ed.), *Knowing, learning, and instruction: Essays in honor of Robert Glaser* (pp. 453–494). Hillsdale, NJ: Lawrence Erlbaum Associates.

Collins, A., Bruce, B. C., & Rubin, A. D. (1982). Microcomputer-based writing activities for the upper elementary grades. In *Proceedings of the Fourth International Learning Technology Congress and Exposition* (pp. 134–140). Warrenton, VA: Society for Applied Learning Technology.

Collins, J., & Sommers, E. (Eds.). (1985). *Writing on-line: Using computers in the teaching of writing.* Upper Montclair, NJ: Boynton/Cook Publishers, Inc.

Cook-Gumperz, J. (Ed.) (1986). *The social construction of literacy.* New York: Cambridge University Press.

Cuban, L. (1986). *Teachers and machines: The classroom use of technology since 1920.* New York: Teachers College Press.

Daiute, C. (1985). *Writing and computers.* Reading, MA: Addison-Wesley.

Daiute, C. (1986). Physical and cognitive factors in revising: Insights from studies with computers. *Research in the Teaching of English, 20,* 141–159.

Delpit, L. (1988). The silenced dialogue: Power and pedagogy in educating other people's children. *Harvard Educational Review, 58*(3), 280–298.

Dewey, J. (1966/1916). *Democracy and education.* NY: Macmillan Publishing Company, Inc.

Dorr-Bremme, D. W. (1990). Naturalistic evaluation. In H. J. Walberg & G. D. Haertel (Eds.), *The International Encyclopedia of Educational Evaluation* (pp. 66–68). Oxford: Pergamon Press.

Duguid, P. (1988). Institute for Research on Learning. *Technology and Learning, 2,* 5.

Dukes, W. F. (1971). N = 1. In J. A. Steger (Ed.), *Readings in statistics for the behavioral scientist* (pp. 378–387). New York: Holt, Rinehart and Winston, Inc. (Reprinted from *Psychological Bulletin,* 1965, *64,* 74–79)

Edwards, D., & Mercer, N. (1987). *Common knowledge: The development of understanding in the classroom.* London: Methuen.

Elbow, P. (1973). *Writing without teachers.* London: Oxford University Press.

Faigley, L., & Witte, S. P. (1981). Analyzing revision. *College Composition and Communication, 32,* 400–414.

Fetterman, D. M. (1988). Qualitative approaches to evaluating education. *Educational Researcher, 17*(8), 17–23.

Fitzgerald, J., & Markham, L. R. (1987). Teaching children about revision in writing. *Cognition and Instruction, 4*(1), 3–24.

Flower, L. (1981). *Problem-solving strategies for writing.* New York: Harcourt Brace Jovanovich.

Flower, L. S., & Hayes, J. R. (1981). A cognitive process theory of writing. *College Composition and Communication, 32,* 365–387.

Foster, J., Julyan, C. A., & Mokros, J. (1988). The National Geographic Kids Network. *Science and Children, 25*(8), 38–39.

Frase, L. T. (1987). Technology, reading, and writing. In J. Squire (Ed.), *The dynamics of language learning: Research in reading and English* (pp. 294–308). Urbana, IL: National Conference on Research in English and ERIC Clearinghouse on Reading and Communication Skills.

Gee, J. (1990). *Social linguistics and literacy.* Philadelphia: Taylor & Francis.

Goldenberg, E. P., Carter, C. J., Russell, S. J., Stokes, S., & Sylvester, M. J. (1983). *Computers, education, and special needs.* Reading, MA: Addison-Wesley.

Goldenberg, E. P., & Feurzeig, W. (1987). *Exploring language with Logo.* Cambridge, MA: The MIT Press.

Goldman, S. V., & Newman, D. (in press). Electronic interactions: How students and teachers organize schooling over the wires. *Discourse Processes.*

Graves, D., & Hansen, J. (1983). The author's chair. *Language Arts, 60*(2), 176–183.

Graves, D. H. (1978). *Balance the basics: Let them write.* New York: Ford Foundation.

Graves, D. H. (1982). *Writing: Teachers and children at work.* Exeter, NH: Heinemann Educational Books.

Graves, D. H. (1984). *A researcher learns to write.* Exeter, NH: Heinemann Educational Books.

Graves, D. H., & Murray, D. M. (1980). Revision: In the writer's workshop and in the classroom. *Journal of Education, 162,* 38–56.

Griffin, C. W. (1983). Using writing to teach many disciplines. *Improving college and university teaching,* 121–128.

Haas, C. (1989). Does the medium make a difference? Two studies of writing with pen and paper and with computers. *Human-Computer Interaction, 4,* 149-169.

Hamilton, E., & Cairns, H. (1961). *The collected dialogues of Plato including the letters.* New York: Pantheon Books.

Hancock, C. (1985, December). Common ground. *Byte,* pp. 239-246.

Handa, C. (Ed.) (1990). *Computers and community: Teaching composition in the twenty-first century.* Portsmouth, NH: Boynton/Cook, Heineman.

Harman, S., & Edelsky, C. (1989). The risks of whole language literacy: Alienation and connection. *Language Arts, 66,* 392-406.

Hawisher, G. E., & Selfe, C. L. (1989). *Critical perspectives on computers and composition instruction* (p. 231). New York: Teachers College Press.

Hawkins, D. (1980). *The informed vision.* New York: Pantheon.

Heath, S. B. (1983). *Ways with words: Language, life, and work in communities and classrooms.* New York: Cambridge University Press.

Heath, S. B. (1986). The functions and uses of literacy. In S. de Castell, K. Egan, & A. Luke (Eds.), *Literacy, society, and schooling: A reader* (pp. 15-27). Cambridge: Cambridge University Press.

Heath, S. B. (1989). Oral and literate traditions among Black Americans living in poverty. *American Psychologist, 44,* 367-373.

Hymes, D. (1974). *Foundations in sociolinguistics: An ethnographic approach.* Philadelphia: University of Pennsylvania Press.

Ihde, D. (1977). *Experimental phenomenology: An introduction.* New York: Putnam.

Jaeger, R. M. (Ed.) (1988). *Complementary methods for research in education.* Washington, DC: American Educational Research Association.

Katz, M., McSwiney, E., & Stroud, K. (1987). *Facilitating collegial exchange among science teachers: An experiment in computer-based conferencing.* Cambridge, MA: Harvard Graduate School of Education.

Kaufer, D., Geisler, C., & Neuwirth, C. (1989). *Arguing from sources: Exploring issues through reading and writing.* New York: Harcourt Brace Jovanovich, Publishers.

Kinneavy, J. L. (1971). *A theory of discourse.* Englewood Cliffs, NJ: Prentice-Hall.

Kinneavy, J. L. (1980). A pluralistic synthesis of four contemporary models for teaching composition. In A. Freedman & I. Pringle (Eds.), *Reinventing the rhetorical tradition* (pp. 37-52). Conway, AR: L & S Books, University of Central Arkansas.

Kirsch, I., & Jungeblut, A. (1986). *Literacy: Profiles of America's young adults, final report.* (Report No. 16-PL-01). Princeton, NJ: National Assessment of Educational Progress.

Lave, J., & Wenger, E. (1991). *Situated learning: Legitimate peripheral participation.* New York: Cambridge University Press.

Lenk, C. (1989). Doing science through telecommunications. In J. D. Ellis (Ed.), *1988 Association for the Education of Teachers in Science Yearbook* (pp. 25-34). Columbus, Ohio: ERIC Clearinghouse for Science, Mathematics, and Environmental Education.

Levin, J. A., Boruta, M. J., & Vasconcellos, M. T. (1983). Microcomputer-based environments for writing: A writer's assistant. In A. C. Wilkinson (Ed.), *Classroom computers and cognitive science* (pp. 219-232). New York: Academic Press.

Levin, J. A., Kim, H., & Riel, M. M. (1990). Analyzing instructional interactions on electronic message networks. In L. M. Harasim (Ed.), *Online education: Perspectives on a new environment* (pp. 185-213). New York: Prager.

Levin, J. A., & Levin, S. R. (1985). *Writing on the electronic frontier: The San Diego-Alaska connection.* Unpublished paper, University of California, San Diego.

Levin, J. A., Riel, M., Miyake, N., & Cohen, M. (1987). Education on the electronic frontier: Teleapprentices in globally distributed educational contexts. *Contemporary Educational Psychology, 12,* 254-260.

Levin, J. A., Riel, M. M., Rowe, R. D., & Boruta, M. J. (1985). Muktuk meets jacuzzi: Computer networks and elementary school writers. In S. W. Freedman (Eds.), *The acquisition of written language: Revision and response* (pp. 160-171). Hillsdale, NJ: Ablex.

Levin, J. A., Waugh, M., & Kolopanis, G. (1988). Science instruction on global electronic networks. *Spectrum: The Journal of the Illinois Science Teachers Association.*

Liebling, C. (1984). Creating the classroom's communicative context: How teachers and microcomputers can help. *Theory into practice, 23,* 232–238.

Loucks, S., & Crandall, D. (1982). *The practice profile: An all-purpose tool for program communication, staff development, evaluation, and implementation.* Andover, MA: The NETWORK, Inc.

Loucks-Horsley, S., French, L., Rubin, A., & Starr, K. (1985). *The role of teacher incentives and rewards in implementing a technological innovation* (Final Report of NIE Grant No. NIE-G-83-0062). Andover, MA: The NETWORK, Inc.

Loucks-Horsley, S., & Hergert, L. (1985). *An action guide to school improvement.* Alexandria, VA: Association for Supervision and Curriculum Development & The NETWORK, Inc.

Lucas, C. K. (1988a). Toward ecological evaluation. *The Quarterly of the National Writing Project and the Center for the Study of Writing, 10*(1), 1–3, 12–17.

Lucas, C. K. (1988b). Toward ecological evaluation: Part 2. Recontext-ualizing literacy assessment. *The Quarterly of the National Writing Project and the Center for the Study of Writing, 10*(2), 4–10.

McConkie, G. W., & Zola, D. (1985). *Computer aided reading: An environment for developmental research.* Paper presented at the Society for Research on Child Development, Toronto, Canada.

Mehan, H. (1979). *Learning lessons.* Cambridge, MA: Harvard University Press.

Mehan, H. (1979). *Learning lessons: Social organization in the classroom.* Cambridge, MA: Harvard University Press.

Miceli, F. (1969). Education and reality. In N. Postman & C. Weingartner (Eds.), *Teaching as a subversive activity* (pp. 171–181). New York: Dell Publishing Co., Inc.

Michaels, S., & Bruce, B. (1989). *Classroom contexts and literacy development: How writing systems shape the teaching and learning of composition* (Tech. Report No. 476). Urbana, IL: University of Illinois, Center for the Study of Reading.

Miles, M. B., & Huberman, A. M. (1984). *Qualitative data analysis: A sourcebook of new methods.* Beverly Hills, CA: Sage.

Moll, L. C. (1990). *Vygotsky and education. Instructional implications and applications of sociohistorical psychology.* New York: Cambridge University Press.

Morris, W. (Ed.) (1981). *The American Heritage dictionary of the English language.* Boston: Houghton-Mifflin Company.

Mullis, I. V. S. (1980). *Using the primary tract system for evaluating writing* (ETS Report No. 10-W-51). Princeton, NJ: Educational Testing Service.

Nelson, T. H. (1987). *Computer lib—dream machines* (rev. ed.). Redmond, WA: Tempus Books of Microsoft Press.

Neuwirth, C. M. (1989). Intelligent tutoring systems: Exploring issues in learning and teaching writing. *Computers and the Humanities, 23,* 45–57.

Newkirk, T., & Atwell, N. (1988). *Understanding writing: Ways of observing, learning, and teaching* (2nd Ed.). Portsmouth, NH: Heinemann.

Newman, D. (1987). Functional environments for microcomputers in education. In R. Pea & K. Sheingold (Eds.), *Mirrors of mind: Theory, research and development from Bank Street's Center for Children and Technology* (pp. 57–66). Norwood, NJ: Ablex.

Newman, D., Goldman, S. V., Brienne, D., Jackson, I., & Magzamen, S. (1989). Peer collaboration in computer-mediated science investigations. *Journal of Educational Computing Research, 5*(2), 151–166.

Newman, D., Griffin, P., & Cole, M. (1989). *The construction zone: Working for cognitive change in school.* Cambridge: Cambridge University Press.

Nold, E. W. (1981). Revising. In C. H. Frederiksen & J. F. Dominic (Eds.), *Writing: The nature, development, and teaching of written communication. Vol. 2. Writing: Processes, development and communication* (pp. 67–79). Hillsdale, NJ: Lawrence Erlbaum Associates.

Office of Technology Assessment, U.S. Congress (Sept. 1988). *Power on! New tools for teaching and learning* (OTA-SET-379). Washington, DC: US Government Printing Office.

Olds, H. F., Schwartz, J. L., & Willie, N. A. (1980). *People and computers: Who teaches whom?* Newton, MA: Education Development Center, Inc.

Papert, S. (1980). *Mindstorms: Children, computers, and powerful ideas.* New York: Basic Books.

Papert, S. (1987a). *A critique of technocentrism in thinking about the school of the future.* Conference on children in an information age: Opportunities for creativity, innovation & new activities. Sofia, Bulgaria.

Papert, S. (1987b). Computer criticism vs. technocentric thinking. *Educational Researcher, 16,* pp. 22–30.

Parlett, M. R. (1990). Illuminative evaluation. In H. J. Walberg & G. D. Haertel (Eds.), *The International Encyclopedia of Educational Evaluation* (pp. 68–73). Oxford: Pergamon Press.

Pattison, R. (1987, May). On the Finn syndrome and the Shakespeare paradox. *The Nation,* pp. 710–720.

Patton, M. Q. (1980). *Qualitative Evaluation Methods.* Minneapolis, MN: University of Minnesota.

Pea, R. D., & Kurland, D. M. (1986). Cognitive technologies for writing. *Review of Research in Education, 14,* 277–326.

Postman, N., & Weingartner, C. (Eds.). (1969). *Teaching as a subversive activity.* New York: Dell Publishing Co., Inc.

Riel, M. (1987). The intercultural learning network. *The Computing Teacher, 14,* pp. 27–30.

Riel, M. (1989, March). *Cooperative learning across classrooms in electronic learning circles.* Paper presented at the annual meeting of the American Educational Research Association, San Francisco, CA.

Riel, M. M. (1985). The Computer Chronicles Newswire: A functional learning environment for acquiring literacy skills. *Journal of Educational Computing Research, 1,* 317–337.

Romick, M. (1984, April). The Computer Chronicles. In R. V. Dusseldorp (Ed.), *Proceedings of the Third Annual Statewide Conference of Alaska Association for Computers in Education,* Anchorage, Alaska.

Rosebery, A. S., Warren, B., Bruce, B. C., Flower, L., Bowen, B., Kantz, M., & Penrose, N. M. (1989). The problem solving processes of writers and readers. In A. Dyson (Ed.), *Collaboration through writing and reading: Exploring possibilities* (pp. 136–163). Urbana, IL: National Council of Teachers of English.

Rosegrant, T., & Cooper, R. (1983). *Talking screen textwriting program manual: A word processing program for children using a microcomputer and a speech synthesizer.* Glendale, Arizona: Computing Adventures, Ltd.

Rubin, A. D. (1980). Making stories, making sense. *Language Arts, 57*(3), 285–298.

Rubin, A. D. (1983). The computer confronts language arts: Cans and shoulds for education. In A. C. Wilkinson (Ed.), *Classroom computers and cognitive science* (pp. 201–271). New York: Academic Press.

Rubin, A. D., & Bruce, B. C. (1985). QUILL: Reading and writing with a microcomputer. In B. A. Hutson (Ed.), *Advances in reading and language research* (pp. 97–117). Greenwich, CT: JAI Press.

Rubin, A. D., & Bruce, B. C. (1986). Learning with QUILL: Lessons for students, teachers and software designers. In T. E. Raphael (Ed.), *Contexts of school based literacy* (pp. 217–230). New York: Random House.

Rubin, A. D., & Bruce, B. (1990). Alternate realizations of purpose in computer-supported writing. *Theory into Practice, 29,* 256–263.

Rubin, A. D., & Hansen, J. (1983). Reading and writing: How are the first two "R's" related? In J. Orasanu (Ed.), *A decade of reading research: Implications for practice* (pp. 163–170). Hillsdale, NJ: Lawrence Erlbaum Associates.

Scardamalia, M. (1981). How children cope with the cognitive demands of writing. In C. H. Frederiksen, M. F. Whiteman, & J. F. Dominic (Eds.), *Writing: The nature, development and teaching of written communication* (pp. 81–104). Hillsdale, NJ: Lawrence Erlbaum Associates.

Scardamalia, M., & Bereiter, C. (1983). The development of evaluative, diagnostic, and remedial capabilities in children's composing. In M. Martlew (Ed.), *The psychology of written language: A developmental approach* (pp. 67–95). London: Wiley.

Scardamalia, M., & Bereiter, C. (1986). Research on written composition. In M. C. Wittrock (Ed.), *Handbook of research on teaching* (3rd ed., pp. 778-803). New York: Macmillan.

Scollon, R., & Scollon, S. B. K. (1981). *Narrative, literacy and face in interethnic communication.* Norwood, NJ: Ablex Publishing Corp.

Scribner, S., & Cole, M. (1981). *The psychology of literacy.* Cambridge, MA: Harvard University Press.

Sharples, M. (1985). *Phrasebooks and boxes: Microworlds for language.* Paper presented at the World Conference of Computers and Education, Norfolk, Virginia.

Sirc, G. (1988). Learning to write on a LAN. *T.H.E. Journal, 15*(8), 99-104.

Sirc, G. (1989). Response in the electronic medium. In C. Anson (Ed.), *Writing and response* (pp. 187-205). Urbana, IL: National Council of Teachers of English.

Spock, B. (1985). *Baby and child care.* New York: E. P. Dutton.

Stake, R. E. (1990). Responsive evaluation. In H. J. Walberg & G. D. Haertel (Eds.), *The International Encyclopedia of Educational Evaluation* (pp. 75-77). Oxford: Pergamon Press.

Stake, R. E., & Easley, J. (1978). *Case studies in science education.* Urbana, IL: University of Illinois, CIRCE.

Stallard, C. K. (1974). An analysis of the behavior of good student writers. *Research in the Teaching of English, 8,* 206-218.

Stecher, B. (1990). Goal-free evaluation. In H. J. Walberg & G. D. Haertel (Eds.), *The International Encyclopedia of Educational Evaluation* (pp. 41-42). Oxford: Pergamon Press.

Stenhouse, L. (1990). Case study networks. In H. J. Walberg & G. D. Haertel (Eds.), *The International Encyclopedia of Educational Evaluation* (pp. 644-649). Oxford: Pergamon Press.

Taylor, D., & Dorsey-Gaines, C. (1988). *Growing up literate: Learning from inner city families.* Portsmouth, NH: Heinemann.

Thompson, D. (1987). Teaching writing on a local area network. *T.H.E. Journal, 15,* 92-97.

Tierney, R., & Pearson, P. D. (1983). Toward a composing model of reading. *Language Arts, 60,* 568-580.

Tikunoff, W. J., & Ward, B. A. (Eds.). (1977). Exploring qualitative/quantitative research methodologies in education [Special Issue]. *Anthropology and Education Quarterly, 8*(2).

Van Maanen, J. (1983). *Qualitative methodology.* Cambridge, MA: Sloan School of Management, MIT.

Vygotsky, L. S. (1978). *Mind in society: The development of higher psychological processes.* Cambridge: Harvard University Press.

Vygotsky, L. S. (1986). *Thought and language.* Cambridge, MA: MIT Press.

Walberg, H. J., & Haertel, G. D. (Eds.). (1990). *The International Encyclopedia of Educational Evaluation.* Oxford: Pergamon Press.

Wittgenstein, L. (1974). *Philosophical investigations* (rev. ed.) (G. E. M. Anscombe, Trans.). New York: Macmillan. (Original work published 1953)

Wolf, R. L. (1990). Judicial evaluation. In H. J. Walberg & G. D. Haertel (Eds.), *The International Encyclopedia of Educational Evaluation* (pp. 79-81). Oxford: Pergamon Press.

Wolf, R. M. (1990). The nature of educational evaluation. In H. J. Walberg & G. D. Haertel (Eds.), *The International Encyclopedia of Educational Evaluation* (pp. 8-15). Oxford: Pergamon Press.

Wresch, W. (Ed.). (1984). *The computer in composition instruction: A writer's tool.* Urbana, IL: National Council of Teachers of English.

Wresch, W. (1988, April). Six directions for computer analysis of student writing. *Computers and the Language Arts,* 13-16.

Zacchei, D. (1982). The adventures and exploits of the dynamic Story Maker and Textman. *Classroom Computer News, 2,* 28-30, 76, 77.

Author Index

Subject Index

A

Alaska, 55-75
  characteristics of, 56-62
    language and literacy, 58-59
    oil and cultural change, 59-60
    technology, 60-62
  educational system of, 62-75
    bilingual and multicultural education,
      65-66
    classroom organization, 64-65
    school district organization, 63-64
    technology in the schools, 66
Alaska QUILL network, 145-176
  characteristics of use, 156-161
  role in creating community, 145-146,
    149-151, 161-172
    addressing common goals, 168-172
    writing to a friendly audience, 164-168
Alaska QUILL project participants, 67-74
  Ammu, Lynne, 119
  Barnhardt, Carol, 52, 62, 65, 74, 90, 160,
    164-165, 176
  Barnhardt, John, 153
  Baumgartner, Michael, 169
  Bless-Boenish, Bonnie, 84, 85, 119, 157-158,
    160-161, 163, 167, 169, 170
  Bruce, Chip, 161, 163
  Frost-Thompson, Helen, 57, 59, 64, 65,
    74, 99-101, 111, 132, 137-138, 139,
    158-159, 162, 171, 176

Hole, Sydney, 89, 130, 134, 136, 137
Manzie, Ernie, 57, 59, 64, 65, 66, 85, 93,
  101-103, 114-116, 131, 134, 135,
  136, 142, 143, 157, 158, 169-170
McFarlane, Alexander, 86, 117, 126, 132,
  137, 142
Payne, Wilma, 86-87, 97-99, 130, 131,
  132, 134, 143, 159
Ramsaur Goniviecha, Mary, 63, 74, 176
Romick, Marcia, 63
Rubin, Andee, 166
Stand, Don, 91
Tralnes, Sister Judy, 57, 106-109, 136,
  159
Ulroan, Lena, 158
Zecchini, Sandra, 165

C

Collaboration
  as pedagogical goal for QUILL, 19
    addressed in activities, 45-47
    addressed in software, 34, 41, 45
    teacher support for, 51
  idealization of, 20
Community
  connected to communication, education,
    10-11, 14-15
  fostered through telecommunications net-
    work, 145-176

229